JAPANOPHOBIA

JAPANOPHOBIA

The Myth of the
Invincible Japanese

Bill Emmott

TIMES BOOKS
RANDOM HOUSE

This work was originally published in Great Britain by
Century Business, an imprint of Random House UK
Limited, London, in 1992 and in different form as *Japan's
Global Reach*.

Grateful acknowledgment is made to Doubleday, a division
of Bantam Doubleday Dell Publishing Group, Inc., for
permission to reprint thirteen haikus as chapter epigraphs
from *An Introduction to Haiku* by Harold G. Henderson.
Copyright © 1958 by Harold G. Henderson. Reprinted by
permission of Doubleday, a division of Bantam Doubleday
Dell Publishing Group, Inc.

Library of Congress Cataloging-in-Publication Data

Emmott, Bill.
Japanophobia : the myth of the invincible Japanese / Bill
Emmott.
—1st ed.
p.   cm.
Includes bibliographical references and index.
ISBN 0-8129-1907-6
1. Investments, Japanese—United States. 2. Investments,
Japanese—Europe. 3. Corporations, Japanese—United
States.
4. Corporations, Japanese—Europe. I. Title.
HG4910.E53   1993
338.7′0952—dc20   92-50501

Manufactured in the United States of America
9 8 7 6 5 4 3 2
First U.S. Edition

For Carol

Contents

JAPANOPHOBIA

Video Interrogation: Michael Crichton

Case: *Rising Sun* and the *Nakamoto Murder*

Purpose of Interrogation: Clarification of subject role in
distorting American public's opinion of Japanese
multinational investment. Associated enquiry: clarification
of subject role in diverting American public's attention from
true sources of America's economic weakness.

INT: Okay. The tape is running. State your name for the record, please.

SUBJ: Michael Crichton

INT: State your occupation.

SUBJ: I'm a writer of detective novels. My latest one was *Rising Sun*. It came out in February 1992.

INT: Now, we want to talk to you about Japanese investment
in the United States. When did you first become involved in this
issue?

SUBJ: I read a bunch of nonfiction books about Japan's economic behavior. They're listed in the bibliography of *Rising
Sun*. I used them as background for it.

INT: But you said you write detective novels.

SUBJ: Well, as I wrote in the bibliography, although my book was fiction I wanted to question the conventional view that direct foreign investment in American high technology is by definition good. Things are not that simple. I don't think it should be allowed to go on unrestrained, especially when it is by Japanese firms.

INT: And your book was a success?

SUBJ: Yes, it was a bestseller. It has been made into a movie. Americans are mad at the Japanese. They're buying everything. Sooner or later we'll all end up working for them if we don't do something now. Fear about the Japanese sells books, and anyway I'm afraid of them, too. Oh, and the book came out just after George Bush vomited all over the Japanese prime minister's pants.

INT: Did you notice that just at the time your book was coming out, Japanese investment was more or less stopping?

SUBJ: It's fiction, remember.

INT: Did you notice that in a lot of the most famous cases of Japanese investment, like their purchases of Hollywood studios, or of the Firestone tire company, or of big real estate developments, the Japanese ended up losing billions and struggling for years?

SUBJ: No.

INT: Have you ever thought about American foreign investment in other people's countries? Is that bad, too?

SUBJ: That's different. We're proper capitalists. Anyway, when we were investing billions in Europe in the 1960s Europeans got mad at us, too. Servan-Schreiber wrote a book about our multinationals called *The American Challenge*. Those French know how to handle foreigners.

INT: Yes, but did he advocate controls on American investment?

SUBJ: Er . . .

INT: He said that American investment was a symptom of Europe's disease, not a cause of it or a disease in itself. Europe had to cure itself by learning from the Americans and by setting up a proper common market, not by limiting American investment. In fact, he said American investment should be allowed to continue, unrestrained, since if Europe blocked it the investment would simply move somewhere else. The competition would still be there, and so would Europe's disease. Do you know the difference between a symptom and a disease?

SUBJ: Yes.

INT: Do you realize that a lot of people in the media and in Congress spend their time attacking the symptom of Japanese multinational investment? They try to put controls on it and to raise taxes on Japanese firms in America. Bill Clinton even included such tax clauses in his election campaign. Your book contributed to that. It's like winning a football game by making the other side carry lead weights and use fewer players. You might win that game, but it won't make you any better at football, or any better able to beat the next team that shows up. Don't you think those people's time might have been better spent facing up to America's real problems, like inflation, lousy education, and too little investment in infrastructure?

SUBJ: Of course. Everyone on Capitol Hill works full time at avoiding doing that. But you can't blame that on me. Anyway, do you think all Japanese multinationals are wonderful?

INT: I'm asking the questions. But I'll do you a favor by asking one back: do you think all American firms are wonderful?

SUBJ: Of course not. But that's not the point.

INT: Yes it is. Japanese firms are no better than any other firms. There are good ones and bad ones, lawbreakers and law-abiders, creators of technology and stealers of it, successful ones and failures. Same with Americans, same with Europeans. What you have done is to encourage people to see Japanese firms as somehow different, all sharing a common approach and posing a common threat.

SUBJ: But they do try to buy influence in our political system and our communities. Didn't you read Pat Choate's *Agents of Influence*?

INT: Yes, we're interrogating him next. So you think it's worse for a lobbyist to work for Toyota than for Charles Keating or some other S&L fraudster?

SUBJ: Yes, they're foreigners.

INT: We rest our case.

Mr. Crichton, you are charged under section 101 of the Economics Code with a willful attempt to persuade the American public to turn against multinational investment and to cut itself off from the world economy.

Just when most of the Third World is at last realizing that allowing foreign investment and trade helps them become richer in all sorts of ways, you sought to make the world's greatest superpower think and act like those poor countries used to in the seventies. That's a big reason why such countries are still poor now. Yet you conspired to make Americans attack foreign investors just when they should have been thinking about how to prevent themselves from becoming poorer.

INTRODUCTION

We're being disemboweled . . .
MICHAEL CRICHTON

JAPANOPHOBIA is about the arrival of Japanese multinational companies as huge investors in the United States and Europe in the late 1980s. It is not a work of fiction, but rather one of fact and opinion. It is a response to a new and intriguing trend, namely the transformation of Japanese businesses from exporters into truly cross-border companies, owning foreign assets, employing foreign workers, and playing a part in the politics of foreign countries. It is a response to the broad and diverse controversy that those Japanese businesses have provoked. It uses that controversy and the experiences of those businesses to make general observations about all multinationals and to draw wide-ranging conclusions about their future.

And yet, broad as this book's landscape is, the map of America's popular debate on Japanese investment has come to be dominated by one narrow feature. That feature is not even a work of fact, though it is certainly one of opinion. It is Michael Crichton's novel *Rising Sun*. The view put forward in that book, and echoed elsewhere, has been absorbed by more Americans than any piece of business writing about the subject.

The foes of that novel were Japanese multinationals. The argument of this book is that the purported threat posed by such

Japanese firms is a false one. The idea that these companies are foes to every American, rather than simply to their direct competitors, is fiction.

Crichton states in his bibliography that his novel "questions the conventional premise that direct foreign investment in American high technology is by definition good." It is always handy when making an argument to claim that it is going against generally held beliefs. Yet is this really the conventional premise in the United States?

Opinion polls taken among virtually any section of the American population have suggested the opposite for at least the past three years, especially when people are asked about Japan and Japanese investment. Thanks to a stack of nonfiction before him, and now thanks even more strongly to Crichton's fiction, the conventional premise is surely that direct foreign investment (by which is meant Japanese investment) in high technology is by definition a threat to the United States. Not everybody thinks this, of course, and it is true that there are plenty of influential people who think otherwise. But that does not make their view conventional. Popular opinion is highly suspicious of Japanese investment, certainly in high technology but also in other areas as well.

Does this matter, as long as those with "influence" do not all share such a view? It does, because eventually it is the popular view that prevails. Such a view takes a long time to find its way into legislation and administrative controls. But it is now doing so, disguised as efforts to levy "fair" taxes on foreign investors and to "manage" trade. These efforts are directed principally at Japanese businesses.

Words like "fair" and "manage" are nice, positive terms, suggesting that the user's aim is to ensure equity and to replace disorder with order. Never trust any politician or lobbyist who uses these words. They are generally a warning that the real aim is the opposite: in this case to levy unfair taxes and to throttle trade. It is like the common metaphor of the "level playing field." Every time you hear anyone use it, you can be sure that a level field is the last thing they want; they are seeking to tilt it handily in their direction.

This promises to be a tragedy for the United States. To say so is not to argue on behalf of Japan, or to be an "apologist" as the common gibe would have it. Nor is it to treat Japanese (or any other) foreign investors as potential saviors of the American economy. Far from it: Japan sins just as often as it is sinned against, and shows no sign of changing its ways. Moreover, it will take far more than a few Japanese investors to "save" the American economy. For the record, I am not "in favor of" Japan or Japanese investment.

No, the argument is that to treat Japanese investors as a threat that must be fought against is to miss the point. It will do American businesses no long-term good to put restraints or limits on foreign direct investment in the United States. As Jean-Jacques Servan-Schreiber argued in Europe in the 1960s, banning such investment will not make the challenge disappear; the investors will simply compete from a different base and the local weaknesses will remain. Put more brutally, those (like Crichton) who treat Japan and Japanese investors as enemies that must be kept at bay misunderstand three things: business in general, multinationals in particular, and economics as a whole.

———

This book is an attempt to show why these misunderstandings are held, while also showing why they are indeed misunderstandings. As such, it follows the wave of Japanese investment that arrived in America and Europe in 1986–91, as well as tracing its subsequent disappearance in 1991–93 and then making guesses about its future prospects. Most important of all, the book compares Japanese multinational investment with the wave of such investment that emanated from the United States in 1950–75.

The key questions are: Is Japanese investment different? Did American multinationals pose a threat to their host countries? Is there a case for adopting a special attitude to Japanese multinationals as compared with all other businesses in the United States?

It is not giving much away to reveal this book's answers to these questions: no, no, and no. But there will have to be some argument behind those answers. And it is true that there is something special about this surge of Japanese investment; this has not simply been any old period in the history of business. It does have a wider significance. For Japan's new multinationals, as well as for all those affected by them in the West, this has been an extraordinary period of experiment.

Before the 1980s, few Japanese firms felt with any confidence that they could transfer their management methods successfully overseas, especially to Western Europe and North America. Indeed, many Americans and Europeans shared this skepticism, convinced that the Japanese success, especially in the manufacturing industry, depended on that country's particular cultural history, social arrangements, and tradition of docile conformity. But the 1980s have shown that Japanese firms can operate successfully across borders, on a huge scale, and in a variety of different cultures and societies. However, the 1980s have also shown that such firms can operate unsuccessfully as well. The twin myths of Japanese corporate homogeneity and invincibility have both been shattered.

This book offers, in effect, a guided tour of the Japanese overseas experiment and the economic and social laboratory in which it has been conducted. The tour reveals successes and failures, as well as varying strategies and varying degrees of local acceptance. In taking the reader on such a journey, however, it is worth stressing that I do not purport to judge whether Japanese investment is good or bad, whether it should be praised or condemned. Instead, I prefer an agnostic approach.

Like other businesses, Japanese multinationals are neither good nor bad as a group. Each one is merely successful or unsuccessful, a desirable employer or an undesirable one, ethical or unethical, law-abiding or lawbreaking. As always with agnosticism, the reason for this view begins and ends with the poverty or pointlessness of the alternatives. Opposing the presence of Japanese multinationals, *en bloc,* generally relies on a view that they are in some sense malign or that they are responsible for the declining competitiveness of domestically owned industries. Yet this is to have one's eye on the wrong thing. Japanese investment is a symptom, not a disease in itself; it may coincide with poor performance by local companies, or poor macroeconomic policy, but it does not cause such problems.

Indeed, Japanese investment often reflects an effort to exploit such deficiencies, an effort that helps draw attention to the malady in question. If those deficiencies did not exist, the investor would be unlikely to see any advantage in making his investment, in competition with local firms. Yet to stop him making the investment will do nothing to remedy that deficiency. Returning to the medical metaphor, placing controls on the symptom will have no bearing whatsoever on the disease itself.

Similarly, however, there are many misconceptions among the enthusiasts for Japanese direct investment. Its arrival should not, for instance, be expected to "solve" balance-of-payments deficits. Formally, indeed, when it first arrives it is no more than a method of financing such deficits, of paying for an excess of imports over exports. Also, there is no way of telling, in advance, what its effects will be on trade flows. Foreign direct investment will not automatically reduce imports and/or increase exports.

It is even possible for such investment to increase the value of a country's imports. After all, many Japanese companies in the 1980s were investing in America and Europe in order to transfer the output of relatively down-market products out of Japan, where costs had risen too high. That reduced the export of those products, such as family cars, but also released resources in Japan for the production and export of items of a higher value, such as luxury cars. So although the volume of exports to America (i.e., in terms of sheer number of cars) may have fallen, the value rose, since higher-priced autos were being shipped.

Even if direct investment could indeed be shown to have affected the balance of trade for a particular sector, such as the car industry in Britain, this would not guarantee that a host country's overall balance-of-payments position would be affected to the same extent or even in the same way. There are too many other factors at work. A country's balance-of-payments position always reflects its overall macroeconomic position, not merely the arrival or departure of particular companies.

Nor is it correct to argue that foreign direct investment in America is a savior because of its invigorating effect on competition or on the level of technology in the economy. It may well have such an effect (though it does not come with a guarantee of this) and may well be of benefit, but it is too small relative to the whole economy to be given credit for an overall change of trend.

Just as with the critics of Japanese investment, so the enthusiasts risk keeping their eye on the wrong thing. By praising Japanese investment too highly, they too risk ignoring or even subverting the broader tasks of policy. Japanese multinationals cannot be relied upon to set the level of employment in an economy, or of wages, or of capital spending, or of the current account of the balance of payments. These are macroeconomic affairs, set by the market and influenced, in an all-too-imprecise way, by government policy for public spending, taxation, regulation, and monetary control. Nor can Japanese investment be relied upon to change the trend of productivity growth or of any other broad microeconomic indicator.

My agnostic approach does, however, lead to the conclusion that Japanese multinationals should be left to come and go as they please, as long as they abide by the rules set for all businesses. These multinationals are merely an interesting subset of the overall business sector: like other businesses, they should be allowed to compete, to invest, to employ, and, ultimately, to flower or to fade. In deciding that these multinationals are neither good nor bad, I also take the view that as a group they are irrelevant to general government policy.

Multinationals, like other businesses, need to be examined case by case. Except when they break the law, such an examination is not a fitting task for government. Just as it is not the American government's business to vote for or against General Motors or IBM and it is not the British government's business to vote for or against ICI or Amstrad, so it should not be these governments' business to vote for or against Japanese multinationals in general or in particular. Such a case-by-case examination is the task of more expert, discerning, and objective folk: customers, employees, investors, and, dare one say it, business journalists and commentators.

This business journalist has conducted his examination in several ways. The book begins with a general discussion of Japan's new global reach and the issues that it raises, seeking to explain why it has suddenly grown and why it has prompted more interest and controversy than has other countries' foreign direct investment. The book then seeks to place that controversy in the context of the history of multinational firms, showing how and why these firms have raised a fuss over the decades and, in particular, how the fuss has taken a strikingly consistent form. American multinationals in the 1960s faced a similar set of problems to those faced by Japanese multinationals now. That which seems new is in fact pretty old.

These experiences are, however, new to Japanese firms in general and to the big, multinational businesses in particular. And they have taken different forms in different industries. So the book proceeds with four case studies, examining the strategies and experience of the car industry in Britain and America; the takeover by Japan's Bridgestone of the Firestone tire company; the entry into Hollywood by Sony and Matsushita; and the brief and inglorious assault on Wall Street and the City of London by Japan's securities houses and investment banks.

Alongside these case studies is a more general examination of Japanese multinationals, based on a questionnaire sent to about five hundred affiliates of Japanese manufacturing firms in Britain, the United States, and continental Europe. Out of those five hundred, usable replies were received from one hundred fifty companies, a response rate of 30 percent. The full questionnaire is printed as Appendix Two, and the full results as Appendix Three. The aim is to escape from a general problem in business writing that might be called the Fallacy of the Aggregated Anecdote: the tendency to draw conclusions from an arbitrary, or perhaps carefully selected, set of examples. The survey provides a broader base of information on which to judge the state of Japan's manufacturing multinationals and their operating methods, as well as an array of detailed comments from managers at those firms.

The past, present, and future of Japan's multinationals are inextricably linked to two things: the fate of Japan's own economy and the fate of the world economy. No multinational is truly stateless, and certainly not a Japanese one; and no company's strategy can be determined independently from worldwide economic trends. For that reason, the final chapters are devoted to those subjects. They show how financial turmoil in Japan is likely to affect the domestic economy and Japan's international companies, and how changes in the world economy may affect the pattern of multinational investment in the future, regardless of its national origins.

Let the tour commence.

PART ONE

FEAR
AND
LOATHING

I

JAPAN'S NEW GLOBAL REACH

Busy old fool, unruly Sun,
Why dost thou thus,
Through windows and through curtains call on us?
                                    JOHN DONNE

Sleeping, then waking
and giving a great yawn, the cat
goes out love-making.
                                    ISSA

WITH a rush they arrived, in the United States, Britain, continental Europe, and Asia. Suddenly, the Japanese were
building factories, acquiring companies, buying huge, well-known
buildings, consorting with politicians and with royalty, sponsoring
exhibitions, festivals, and charity events, and, most of all, employing millions of people and selling millions of their goods and
services. Japan's new multinational firms had long been exporting
from over there, but having them over here was a new experience.
Their arrival formed part of a worldwide boom in overseas investment by companies from all the rich, industrial countries. And yet
the Japanese arrival caused far and away the most interest and
intrigue.

To some, Japan's new global reach looked sinister, evidence of that country's expanding control over the world economy. A growing share of host countries' banking systems and capital markets, of what were widely considered to be "strategic" manufacturing industries, and of their high-technology production and research appeared to be falling under the ownership of corporate Japan.

To others, these multinationals looked like saviors, bringing their wealth, their management techniques, and their technology to help all of the rest of us achieve more efficient production and a higher standard of living. Their investment brought jobs to depressed regions, was considered to be a vote of confidence in the host economy and its workforce, and was even believed to offer a means to eliminate trade deficits in the United States and Britain.

Why the controversy? Why have Japanese investors caused such a polarized debate when other businesses and other multinationals do not? As is often the case, the best clues can be found in history, and by comparing the Japanese experience with that of the United States itself. Turn your watches back by half a century. Forget, for a moment, about business and about foreign direct investment. When tens of thousands of American soldiers came to Britain in the Second World War, they were not popular with the British, even though Britain and America were on the same side in the war. The GIs were widely resented, and were often treated with suspicion and even some animosity. To anyone young, or someone older who is neither British nor American, this may seem surprising. It will also seem surprising that the explanation for this Anglo-American animosity contains parallels and lessons for the relationship between Japan, America, and Europe in the 1990s. But it does.

Why were the GIs resented? For one thing, the United States had, in British eyes, joined the war somewhat late; while the war in Europe had begun in the autumn of 1939, the United States did not declare war until after December 7, 1941, when Japanese aircraft bombed Pearl Harbor. At first, most of the American troops who came to Britain simply established themselves on their new bases, while British airmen, sailors, and soldiers were away fighting in the air, at sea, and in North Africa. This had a simple but important result. The fresh-faced Americans always seemed to have time on their hands to meet the locals, especially their wives, sisters, and daughters. At least, that was how things were perceived, whether or not the stereotype was true.

In addition, the Americans were wealthier than the British, coming from a country that had not only been at peace for the past two years, but had also been profiting from the war as a major exporter of raw materials, goods, and ships. At long last, America's Great Depression was over. That change in economic fortunes was merely cyclical, part of the ups and downs of all economies. But there was also a more fundamental, structural force at work.

Deep down, the more knowledgable and perceptive among the British knew that a basic change had long been under way: the United States was taking over for Britain as the world's economic and political leader. The British empire was collapsing, an event symbolized by the fall of Singapore to the Japanese in February 1942. For the time being, British dominance, which had been in place for well over a century, was tumbling to Japanese and German rivals. But the long-term trend, which these events were merely confirming, was different: Britain was handing over worldwide hegemony to the American GIs.

With all this in mind, albeit more on the subconscious than the conscious level, the British coined a phrase to sum up their resentment of their American allies. The trouble with Americans, it was said, was that they were "Overpaid, Oversexed, and Over here." In other words, they were too rich, they were too interested in British women, and they were too close for comfort.

It is the same today for Japan and Japanese business. Japanese competition has been around for years. But until the second half of the 1980s it was rather remote, operating from an island archipelago thousands of miles across the Pacific (if you are American) or at the other end of the world, somewhere you could not easily find on a map (if you are European). It exported rather than producing locally, and even if those exports of cameras or cars were welcome, they conveyed little of the Japanese character beyond a low price, a high quality, and a vaguely exotic name (very vaguely: Sharp, National, Pentax).

Asian countries were somewhat more aware of their Japanese neighbor, but it is well to remember that, except for South Korea, Japan is as little a geographic neighbor to other residents of this vast region as San Francisco is a neighbor to New York, or Moscow is to London, or Stockholm is to Cairo. Even to these Asian cousins Japan was no more than a distant relative, more developed industrially, selling in markets of which they could only dream, bothering to do business in Asia only if raw materials were involved.

Now, however, things are different. Suddenly and dramatically, Japan and Japanese business are not somewhere far away. They are in the next town, village, or city, employing local workers, buying (or refusing to buy) local goods and services, contributing to (or influencing, depending on your view) local political funds, charities, museums, and other community groups. They are buying local buildings, golf courses, hotels, and whole companies. They are in the street, in the shop, in the restaurant, in the locker room, on the train, in the school.

They are overpaid, oversexed, and over here. Well, almost. Unlike in the case of the GIs, it is not terribly common to hear Americans or Europeans attack Japanese businessmen for being oversexed. (Though women do, justifiably, criticize them for being sexist. And Michael Crichton's *Rising Sun* did involve an oversexed Japanese called "Fast Eddie" Sakamura.) Nevertheless the Japanese, or more often their companies and their country, do fit the other descriptions: they are seen as overpaid (or, rather, overrich) and worse, for many critics, they are certainly over here.

This matters, most of all, in human terms. Go back, again, to 1941. An important point about the 1941–45 period for America and Britain was that this was the first time that ordinary Britons had seen Americans, at least in large numbers. The elite knew each other well, and even traveled to and fro across the Atlantic, but this was not true of ordinary people. They had seen America in the movies, of course, had heard about it on the radio, and had read about it in their newspapers, novels, and popular magazines. Some of their relatives might have emigrated to the United States, especially in the nineteenth century. But few Britons had ever met an American, unless they worked at one of the handful of American-owned factories that had been set up in the last decade of the nineteenth century and the first few decades of the twentieth. For most, the GIs were a brand-new experience.

It is the same now for Americans and Europeans meeting Japanese. Until the past few years, few ordinary Britons, or Frenchmen, or Germans, or Americans had actually met a Japanese. And, frankly, the reverse was also true: foreigners were unknown to most Japanese, except through television, books, or movies. Of course, Japan, America, and Europe had become increasingly intertwined economically and politically, beginning in a small way with Commodore Perry and the "black ships" with which this American commander forced Japan to open to trade in 1853. Yet those links did not really become well-established until the 1960s and 1970s, and even then they were more apparent than real. At the elite level, contacts were frequent; after all, Japan was America's principal ally and military base in the Pacific. "Internationalization" has been a slogan in Japan many times since the 1860s. But even in the 1960s and 1970s the slogan was no more than that: a slogan. The reason is that there was no human involvement.

Since the mid-1980s, however, all that has changed. For the first time, Japan has entered an era of true internationalization, one that affects ordinary people at home and abroad and involves widespread human involvement. Japan is not "internationalized" in the broad sense that everyone in Japan is affected by it (or even knows what the word means), or that Japan is a cosmopolitan place, or that Japanese feel confident bestriding the world stage: far from it. Japan is never going to be as international as Holland, say, where trade is part of the fabric of the whole country and where the citizens speak such excellent English and have traveled so widely that they make Britons and Americans blush. It is not even going to be as international as Britain, much of the population of which is pretty narrow-minded. Yet in its own internationalization, Japan is already rather like America: intensely parochial, but now ineluctably engaged in the world, affecting it and affected by it. It is that engagement that has changed in the past five years or more; it means that Japanese are now infuriatingly parochial but necessarily international, at one and the same time.

As it develops, Japan's influence on the world is becoming social and cultural as well as directly economic: ideas, practices, preferences, even prejudices are being conveyed through the medium of foreign investment. Japanese are now international employers, international managers, international investors, and international customers. More important still, they are also international teachers, their intense competitiveness and business success forcing Japanese techniques and attitudes into a position high up the agendas of business schools, newspapers and magazines, television, trade union policymakers, and even the strategic brainstorming sessions of companies all around the world.

The numbers make this international engagement undeniable. In late 1990, the Japan External Trade Organization (JETRO) counted a total of 9,560 Japanese-affiliated companies with operations in the United States and Canada. Perhaps a third of those have factories or some sort of full-fledged branch office. In August 1991, a similar count in the European Community found a total of 2,298 Japanese-affiliated firms in the EC. As of November 1989, there were 3,191 such firms in Indonesia, Malaysia, the Philippines, Singapore, and Thailand. That produces a total of a little more than 15,000 firms, which almost certainly is an understatement.

There are no reliable figures for the number of Japanese working abroad for these firms, but the survey conducted for this book suggests that an average of twenty at each one may be reasonable. That produces a figure of more than 300,000 Japanese managers working in these firms around the world. If they are typically accompanied by one family member, the total associated with Japan's global reach becomes at least 600,000 people. This level of overseas employment also means that every year roughly 50,000 Japanese managers return home from an overseas assignment, while roughly 50,000 more depart their homelands to begin one. Many others move from one foreign assignment to another.

Even if these companies employ an average of just 100 locals each, that would produce a total of 1.5 million employed by Japanese firms in the EC, the United States, and Southeast Asia. Nobody knows the correct figure; but it seems reasonable to guess that total employment by Japanese multinationals outside Japan could be at least 2 million people and may even be four times as large as that.

This is not Japan's only source of human influence. In a smaller way, leisure, tourism, and cultural interplay are also making a difference. Once, the only Japanese words that an ordinary American or Briton knew were probably *geisha* and *karate,* and they probably did not know that *karate* was Japanese. Now, they at least know a third: *karaoke,* for bars with these appalling sing-along machines are sprouting up all over Europe and America. Karaoke is more significant than it seems at first blast. It is the first consumer-electronics product with a definite Japanese identity, even though Japanese firms have dominated that business for more than a decade. The Walkman, the compact disk player, the videocassette recorder, none were given Japanese names when exported by Japanese companies. Indeed many were not even given Japanese names when sold at home.

Yet the name *karaoke* has caught on worldwide, not as a brand but as a generic term for the product. Roughly, the word means empty orchestra. It is Japan's first equivalent to Coca-Cola or Big Mac: a name that, worldwide, evokes Japan. Moreover, humble though the product is, it at last evokes something personal and sympathetic rather than inscrutable or menacing or frighteningly efficient: people enjoying themselves, shedding inhibitions, getting pleasantly drunk. Karaoke implies playaholics rather than workaholics, or at least the relaxation that follows a hard day's work.

Though it may have entered Europe and America through the bars and clubs frequented by Japanese businessmen and visitors, karaoke has spread chiefly through local demand. Nevertheless, Japanese visitors are now highly visible, and are also having their own effects. The streets of London, Paris, San Francisco, and Rome are full of identikit Japanese tourists, their bulging wallets a temptation to travel firms, muggers, con men, and overseas branches of Japanese department store chains alike. The yen's strength in recent years and the growing affluence of ordinary Japanese caused a travel boom in 1986–91, with overseas journeys by Japanese rising from less than 5 million a year in 1985 to nearly 15 million by 1991 and 1992. It was not only cheap to travel abroad, whether to play golf or go shopping, but it was also fashionable. The annual deficit on travel spending in the Japanese balance of payments (i.e., the money spent by Japanese abroad minus that spent by foreign visitors in Japan) rose fivefold from $3.7 billion in 1985 to more than $21 billion in 1990.

These days, we take such travel for granted, and forget how new a phenomenon it is and how much difference it has made to our lives. This sudden fashion for international travel in Japan came about ten years after the same fashion had really taken hold in Europe. My family, for instance, was typical in that we never took foreign holidays when I was a child in the 1960s, but to the next generation of Britons, foreign travel, probably to Spain, France, Greece, or Florida, suddenly became normal. All this has been made easier, cheaper, and more convenient by that icon of our times, the Boeing 747 jumbo jet, designed in the late 1960s. Japanese families in the 1970s were rather like British ones in the 1960s: if they took holidays at all, they took them in domestic resorts. That changed in the late 1980s or the early 1990s. Using an updated icon, the Boeing 747-400, which could make nonstop flights from Tokyo to London or New York, Japanese flooded abroad.

So did culture, a fact thanked by many for "increasing mutual understanding." Britain's gigantic Japan Festival of 1991, a long series of exhibitions, sporting events, theater, cinema, and other cultural phenomena, had a particularly strong impact on British awareness of things Japanese. But culture is not an independent factor. The reason is revealing. Just as in the days of the British empire it was said that "trade follows the flag," so today culture follows the Japanese business presence. If British firms and government departments had not wanted to promote Japanese trade and investment, the Japan Festival would not have taken place. It was a British idea, not a cunning Japanese plot to capture the British mind. Yet, also, much of its funding derived from Japanese firms investing in Britain. Culture is a symptom, not a cause. The cause is business.

———

It is business that, most of all, is driving the Japanese to look beyond the confines of their archipelago. And thus it is business that, most of all, is giving Japan a "global reach," a phrase used as the title of a landmark book about multinational corporations (chiefly American ones) by Richard J. Barnet and Ronald E. Mueller, published in 1974. Just as then the power and worldwide networks of American multinationals were assumed to be handing both the United States and American businessmen an actually or potentially awesome control over other countries and their markets, so that is the widespread impression today of Japanese multinational corporations. They have global reach, and it is something to be wary of.

A decade ago, few Japanese companies had much of a presence overseas, beyond the networks of dealers or distributors that handled their exports. Yet between January 1980 and January 1990, Japanese firms made overseas direct investments totaling $280 billion, equivalent to buying or building the entire economy of Australia, India, or Brazil. That was almost ten times Japan's total overseas direct investment in the whole period 1951–79, admittedly in nominal terms (i.e., not adjusted for inflation).

By direct investments is meant sums spent by Japanese-owned firms on things like factories, property, banks, and whole companies. It excludes portfolio investments, the purchases of Treasury bonds, or shares that are generally held for a relatively short time and do not entail any managerial control. Foreign direct investment means, therefore, Bridgestone's purchase of America's Firestone tire company in 1988, or Sony's purchase of Hollywood's Columbia Pictures in 1989, or Fujitsu's purchase of 80 percent of Britain's ICL computer firm in 1990, or the new car factories built in Kentucky and Derbyshire by Toyota, or the controversial purchase in 1989 of a majority interest in Rockefeller Center in New York by Mitsubishi Estate.

Curiously, less attention has been given to Japanese purchases of far more visible entities in shopping streets, travel brochures, and fashion magazines. Daks-Simpson, the parent company of Simpsons of Piccadilly, a rather expensive and quite snobbish department store in the West End of London, is now Japanese-owned. That may (or, indeed may not, given the growing popularity of Japanese food in London) be why Simpsons now has a sushi bar in its basement, frequented it must be admitted by many journalists from *The Economist,* since its offices are just up the street. Aquascutum, a distinctly upmarket British men's clothier, is also Japanese, having been bought by Renown, the biggest Japanese clothing firm, in 1990.

So, for a time, was Hugo Boss, a German fashion house known to most people less for its Japanese ownership than for its magazine advertisements that feature male models so identical in appearance that it is unclear to the cynical eye whether the product being promoted is the hair gel they are all evidently wearing or their sharp double-breasted suits. A 54 percent stake was bought by Leyton House, a Japanese fashion group, for around $300 million in 1989, but Hugo Boss became one of the first Japanese investments to be resold when Leyton House had financial and legal problems in Japan and sold its shares in Hugo Boss to Marzotto, an Italian fashion house. The price of neither deal has been disclosed, and is hard to work out because in both cases the arrangements were complicated. But a fair guess, made by a London-based newsletter, *M&A Japan,* in December 1991, was that the Italian firm paid around $165 million for Leyton House's bundle of shares and options. The Japanese firm had thus lost almost half its original outlay.

More securely in Japanese hands is Bush House, a historic building on the Aldwych in London that houses the BBC World Service radio studios. So is Bracken House, for decades the home of London's *Financial Times* newspaper. Southland Corporation, based in Dallas, Texas, and owner of the 7-Eleven chain of convenience stores, is 70 percent owned by Ito-Yokado, a Japanese store chain that was originally merely the holder of the Japanese franchise of 7-Eleven but stepped into Southland with a $430 million investment when the American firm filed for Chapter 11 bankruptcy reorganization in 1991.

Then there is the Turnberry Hotel in Scotland, one of the world's most famous golfing hotels, and Pebble Beach in California, one of the world's most expensive and expansive golfing resorts, covering 5,300 acres on the Monterey Peninsula. Controversial as they may be at the time, not all such investments are either successful or made with the consummate financial ease now expected of Japanese tycoons. Bought by Minoru Isutani, a Japanese speculator, in September 1990 for an estimated $800 million, Pebble Beach was in effect taken over in February 1992 by two financing affiliates of Sumitomo Bank. Isutani had borrowed most of the money to purchase Pebble Beach from Itoman, a trading company that collapsed in 1991 after losses made on the Tokyo stock market and elsewhere, and had to be bailed out by Sumitomo Bank. Pebble Beach thus remains Japanese-owned, but gone is Isutani's plan to sell club memberships at the resort for Y100 million each ($770,000), an idea crucial to his financing but which caused uproar in California. Even so, the 1992 U.S. Open golf tournament was played on—you guessed it—Japanese-owned Pebble Beach.

The list can go on and on. What is important, however, is that virtually all of the investment is new. In the late 1980s, Japanese foreign direct investment boomed as never before. It did so for several different, though related, reasons.

The straightforward, macroeconomic one is that after 1982–83 Japan suddenly became a big exporter of capital of all sorts, both portfolio investment and direct investment. For almost all of the postwar years, Japan had imported capital, running as it did a deficit on the current account of its balance of payments. But in 1982–83, that deficit swung dramatically into surplus, a surplus that reached $87 billion in 1987, before halving in 1988–91 and then more than doubling in 1991–93. Countries that have big current-account surpluses always export capital in some form because, by definition, they have a surplus of it above what they are spending on imports of goods and services and interest payments. They do not, however, necessarily export it in the form of direct investment: the surplus might show up in an increase in their central bank's holdings of foreign currencies and securities, for instance, or in portfolio investments overseas by domestic institutional investors and banks.

At first, the bulk of Japan's capital surplus was exported in the form of portfolio investments. In 1980, Japan abolished its exchange controls, which were longstanding restrictions on investment overseas by Japanese residents. In the early 1980s, regulations were also eased governing the proportion of their investment holdings that Japanese pension funds and insurance firms could devote to foreign securities. These measures gave Japanese institutions their first chance ever to diversify their assets internationally, to spread their holdings beyond Japan.

In 1985, Japan's net exports of long-term capital totaled $65 billion; in 1987, the annual total peaked at $137 billion. More than two thirds of both of those sums were accounted for by pension funds, insurance companies, and other institutional investors, diversifying their portfolios by filling their trunks with American

Treasury bonds. This was the period when Japan could legitimately be described as the chief financier of America's federal budget deficit, for Japanese entities were buying up to 40 percent of the bonds issued to finance the deficit.

During this time, direct investment was gradually increasing. New overseas direct investment by Japan in 1980 had been $4.7 billion; in 1983, it was $8.2 billion; in 1985, it was $12.2 billion. It was also changing in the sorts of destinations chosen: in the 1970s, most Japanese foreign direct investment was made in search of natural resources and so was focused on places like Indonesia and Canada; in the early 1980s, it was increasingly being made in search of markets rather than supplies and so gravitated toward the richer economies of the United States and Europe. Even so, as a proportion of total Japanese exports of capital, direct investment was still peanuts.

But that began to change in 1985, thanks to the next macroeconomic influence on Japanese investment: the rise of the yen. The first half of the 1980s had been dominated by the strong dollar, treated with "benign neglect" by the Reagan administration but given strength on the world currency markets by high American interest rates. The dollar rose and rose, climbing from its 1978 low of Y175 to Y250 and above. Thanks to this strong dollar and the weak yen, Japanese exports became more price-competitive every year in America and other markets, producing Japan's big current-account surplus and America's huge deficit. It was therefore commercially sensible for many Japanese firms simply to build their products in cheap-yen Japan and export them, rather than building their factories in the United States or Europe.

In February 1985, however, this began to change as the dollar hit a peak against the yen and started to drift downward. In September 1985, the finance ministers of Japan, the United States, West Germany, France, and Britain met at the Plaza Hotel in New York and agreed to try concerted action to encourage a further fall in the dollar. Since the markets were headed in that direction anyway, it worked, and the dollar fell from around Y250 to almost Y120 by the autumn of 1988. This altered the calculations of Japanese businesses in two ways. It suddenly made it far more costly to produce goods at home for export compared with producing them abroad; and it suddenly made foreign assets (such as Columbia Pictures, Firestone, or Bush House) look far cheaper in yen terms.

Then came a third change for businessmen's calculations. Japan's economic policymakers became worried that the strengthening yen might cause a recession in Japan, so the Bank of Japan pushed interest rates down in order to expand the money supply and make capital cheaper. These low Japanese interest rates sparked a vast speculative boom on Tokyo's stock and property markets, increasing the value of the collateral against which Japanese firms could borrow and making it seem costless to issue new equity and equity-linked bonds. Capital appeared to be virtually free. For anyone who was holding it, the world therefore appeared to be his oyster.

Thus was born the boom in overseas direct investment by Japanese multinationals. By 1989, Japan's total net export of long-term capital had fallen to $89.3 billion; by 1990, it had fallen further, to $43.6 billion. But within the declining totals, direct investment was taking up a bigger and bigger proportion. Net outflows of direct investment in 1989 were $45.2 billion, or half the total; in 1990, they were $46.2 billion, or more than 100 percent of the total.

In other words, Japan's overseas portfolio investment had ceased. Japan was no longer financing America's federal budget deficit, nor anybody else's. In net terms, portfolio inflows to Japan exceeded outflows: that is, money was being repatriated by Japanese investors or being sent there by foreigners. But Japanese direct investment rolled on. Japanese multinationals were establishing Japan's new global reach by buying assets, building factories, opening offices, and recruiting workers all around the world. They paused in 1991, 1992, and 1993, as recession hit their markets in the United States and Europe. Total foreign direct investment into the United States fell to $22.2 billion in 1991 compared with $70.6 billion in the peak year of 1989; of 1991's total, Japanese investors accounted for $4.3 billion, still 25 percent of America's inflow but way down from the annual average in 1988–90 of $17.3 billion.

These Japanese investors had another reason to pause: the speculative boom in Japanese stocks and property had, since January 1990, turned into a spectacular bust. That bust meant that capital was no longer cheap for Japanese firms. Indeed, speculative ventures inside Japan or outside had become very expensive indeed. In 1991, Japan had record levels of bankruptcies, many of them related to property and stock speculation: the liabilities of bust firms quadrupled from the previous year, passing Y8.2 trillion ($63 billion).

Those bankruptcies mean that the more marginal and speculative overseas investors are either being forced to retrench or have been wiped out altogether. They also mean that Japanese banks are swamped by bad debts and are themselves withdrawing from their own overseas activities. Most of all, they even mean that the big, solid, well-known Japanese manufacturers, such as Sony, Matsushita, Honda, Nissan, Komatsu, Bridgestone, and many others, are more strapped for cash than they have been for at least five years and, in some cases, for more than a decade.

Many of those Japanese manufacturers are now suffering from what might be called "investment overstretch." The hubris of their 1980s success and the temptations of apparently abundant, cheap capital made them overambitious, spending billions on overseas acquisitions. The jump in their cost of capital, the slide in their share prices, the decline in their profitability: all these represent Nemesis, the Greek goddess of retribution who, in Greek tragedies, invariably followed hubris. Japanese multinationals are now having to consolidate rather than expand further, establishing themselves in their new homes while repairing their balance sheets back in Japan. But they will not go away. Once established, global reach does not disappear overnight. That was true of American multinationals, whose international strength was probably peaking just as Barnet and Mueller put the finishing touches to their book and yet, nearly twenty years later, still play a leading role in many economies around the world.

It will be the same for the Japanese multinationals. Their expansionist strength has peaked. But they will now consolidate their position and, in many cases, will resume their growth in the 1990s using local resources rather than Japanese ones. The frantic growth of 1985–90 has provided many different experiments from which Japanese multinationals can and will learn. And in the 1990s, there will be new targets for foreign direct investment by multinationals of all nationalities, including Japanese ones: Latin America, India,

China, and eventually Eastern Europe and the countries of the former Soviet Union. The global reach of Japan's multinational corporations has only just begun.

———

So, like it or not, the new global reach of Japanese multinational corporations is a fact of life. The first step to understanding it lies in answering a simple question. Why are they here? But the answer is that there is no simple answer. Japanese multinationals are not investing abroad in a single way, for a single motive, or as part of a single strategy. The macroeconomic background offers a general explanation for Japanese investment. But a macroeconomic explanation is really a description of what has happened rather than a clue about the strategies and reasoning of individual businesses. Here, therefore, are six different reasons why Japanese firms have rushed to invest offshore in America, Europe, and Asia.

1. *Managerial advantages:* some Japanese firms think they can work profitable magic combining cheap(ish) foreign labor with Japanese capital, techniques, and products. Although that has been made possible by the rise of the yen, this type of investment can also be seen as a sort of arbitrage opportunity.

If, say, British or American workers are skilled and fairly well-educated but mainly employed by inefficient local firms, then the market wage will be set by the productivity achieved by local managers and the machinery that they use. If a firm can bring in superior managerial techniques from outside (in this case, Japan), then higher productivity may be achieved while the market wage remains determined by inferior local productivity levels.

The profit for Japanese companies from building a car factory in Tennessee or Tyneside, say, then becomes larger than the return to a local producer from making a similar investment. Such higher profit margins make an overseas investment worthwhile, but also enable the foreign firm to undercut local competitors if it wishes to increase market share.

2. *Business obstacles:* trade barriers, or the threat of them, sometimes force Japanese firms to set up factories inside their foreign markets rather than shipping the goods across the oceans.

In the 1980s, such obstacles included voluntary restraint arrangements for Japanese car exports to America and Britain, as well as compulsory restraints on exports to France, Italy, and Spain, and import controls on products such as videocassette recorders and computer printers in the European Community. These business obstacles need not always be actual barriers. Sometimes firms invest in anticipation of probable future barriers to trade.

3. ***Seductive dealing opportunities:*** to some Japanese firms, foreign assets, including property, companies, or simply creative people, look cheap. All that is needed is the power of Japanese capital and one day, young Yoshio, all this could be yours.

This is less true now than in 1987–90 when yen interest rates were low and Japanese financial markets were soaring. But it remains a factor. If a Japanese investor has a dollop of money that he could use to buy or build a hotel in Japan or a hotel in France, the fact that the choice of France would be cheaper might well sway the decision.

4. ***Mature markets, or intensifying competition, or both:*** in some businesses, local production can offer the advantage of greater flexibility in responding to local market requirements and indeed greater awareness of what those requirements are. If competition is fierce and products become less differentiated from one another, it may make sense to produce locally to steal a march on competitors and to tailor products intelligently to differentiate them from others.

Although this can also be done by establishing local "intelligence" networks and using them simply to educate your global exporting, this may be more difficult with a complex product (for example, a car). When products require a large number of component parts, the task of coordinating information about local requirements across a group of outside suppliers becomes harder. It may be easier if the whole production system, including parts suppliers, is implanted into the local market. Then the parts suppliers, too, are likelier to become more attuned to local needs.

5. ***Local technology:*** in some businesses, a Japanese firm might possess an advantage in manufacturing hardware, for instance, but be less good at other essential processes, such as computer software. In that case, rather than spending billions trying to get better at it at home, it may make sense to purchase overseas expertise, or to develop it in an overseas center of excellence, and then combine it with Japanese hardware. Many computer firms are following this course.

6. ***The pursuit of Japanese customers overseas:*** if a Japanese firm has clients at home in Japan that suddenly move their business overseas, it may well make sense for that firm to try to follow them.

When Japanese portfolio investment overseas boomed in 1983–89, for instance, those firms that had traditionally handled the domestic investment of Japanese pension funds and insurance companies—Japan's big four securities firms—rushed overseas to try to handle the same business over there. The same is true of suppliers to manufacturing firms: when the manufacturers' factories move offshore, so do the suppliers, if they can get the business. And it is true of travel firms: Japanese hotel chains and travel agencies that have a strong brand name at home naturally seek to exploit that reputation abroad among the rising numbers of Japanese tourists. Just as Sheraton and Hilton exploited Americans' propensity to travel in the 1970s, so Japanese hotel chains are seeking to do so now.

————

Six reasons why Japanese businesses invest abroad; this list is not exclusive, nor are these motives entirely separate from each other. Many Japanese multinationals have invested abroad for a mixture of these reasons. Carmakers such as Nissan, Toyota, and Honda, for instance, have done so because of managerial advantages, business obstacles, and the effect of mature markets. None of these is the sole explanation. Across the whole range of multinationals, the whole range of motivations can be found.

That is why it is futile to search for a stereotype of the Japanese multinational. So far, two stereotypes have become commonly believed: a positive view of a sleek, meritocratic enterprise, staffed by well-respected and well-treated workers wearing matching tracksuits and eating together with the chief executive in the same canteen; and a negative view of a sprawling, megarich Japanese conglomerate, using profits from its protected Japanese sales to subsidize its investments overseas, refusing to buy from American or European suppliers unless it can steal their technology at the same time. Doubtless both sorts of firm exist. But neither stereotype accurately reflects either the average firm or the variety that can be found.

This variety of purpose and performance can be illustrated most clearly if some of the humbler Japanese multinationals are examined, rather than the headline grabbers such as Toyota, Sony, or Honda.

There are two heartlands of Japanese manufacturing investment, both in economies of more or less the same size: California and Britain. Roughly a fifth of the Americans employed by Japanese firms are in California; roughly half of the Europeans thus employed are in Britain. Both California and Britain have plenty of headline grabbers, full of uniform-wearing industrial paragons who jabber constantly about managerial techniques such as *kanban* (just-in-time stock delivery), *kaizen* (continuous improvement), or quality circles (informal teams of workers set up ad hoc to solve quality problems). But both also have the humbler sort of investor.

The Californian variety of humble Japanese was depicted most vividly in a study published in early 1992 by Ruth Milkman, a sociology professor at the University of California at Los Angeles. She visited fifty Japanese-owned factories, each with more than one hundred employees, that made products ranging from medical products, plastics, and car parts to metal goods. She asked the American managers at these plants whether they employed the various Japanese techniques such as kanban, quality circles, flexible work teams, and the like. Most of them did not know what she was talking about. Out of twenty firms that she looked at more closely, only four had just-in-time systems, and only two used quality circles.

By and large, these firms were sweatshops. And far from avoiding hiring "minorities," an accusation often made about Japanese firms, cheap minority labor, often women from Latin America and Asia, was precisely the reason many of these sweatshops were there. They sought a cost advantage; often they had built their factories in the United States to avoid some sort of a trade barrier. They were neither paragons nor dastardly enemies plotting the downfall of America. They were neither better nor worse than American firms seeking the same cheap labor.

Now come to Britain. The Japanese are investing in a lot of places, but it is notable that, in Europe, Britain is far and away the favorite: Japanese direct investment in Britain in recent years has been more than four times Japanese investment in Germany, five times that in France, and ten times that in Spain. Put in more refined statistical terms, at the end of March 1990, Britain accounted for 37.6 percent of Japan's $42 billion stock of foreign direct investment in the European Community, ahead of Holland's 24 percent, Germany's 8.2 percent, and France's 6.9 percent.

Why Britain? It is not because of language; the Japanese are barely more proficient at English than at any other language and do not base business decisions on such flimsy grounds. Nor do they base it on the fact that Japanese and Britons both drink tea and live on islands. Nor is there much personal affinity. The response of the *Sun* (a British tabloid) and other popular newspapers to Emperor Hirohito's death in January 1988 suggests, if anything, the opposite. Wartime memories run deep. Despite this, there may be some political reasons: Britain has opened a welcoming door to foreign investment of whatever nationality. But it is not unique in that; so have many other European countries.

Japanese firms' preference for Britain has aroused fierce controversy in the European Community among those (mainly French) who think Britain has been traitorous in luring in too many Japanese investors. Jacques Calvet, the boss of Peugeot-Citroën, a French carmaker, has claimed that Britain is becoming an offshore aircraft carrier from which Japanese firms can launch their attack on Europe. Calvet does not to choose to mention, however, that Britain is also a pretty handy offshore aircraft carrier for his own company, since his Peugeot-Talbot subsidiary in Coventry (the former Rootes/Chrysler) is a spectacular and extremely profitable success, producing the Peugeot 405 both for the domestic British market and for overseas. The real oddity, though, is that if Britain really is an aircraft carrier, it must be one for American firms, too, for American multinationals show an even greater preference for investing in Britain: 41 percent of the $164 billion that American firms had invested in the EC by the end of 1990 was in Britain.

Note, first, that the American total in Europe is four times as big as Japan's $42 billion. But note, also, the point already made, that Americans, too, prefer Britain. Why?

The likeliest reason is not entirely complimentary, either in the American or the Japanese case. Britain offers the best combination of low labor costs (the lowest in Europe except Spain) and relevant skills inside the trade barriers that surround the European Community. Spanish or Portuguese workers, for instance, are thought to be less skilled and less predictable than British ones. Even that is not much of a compliment: by and large British skills are "relevant" because the country's workforce is less well-educated and less well-trained than that in France or Germany, for instance. In other words, at present wage levels, British workers are better suited to fairly humdrum tasks—like assembling Japanese televisions, computer printers, silicon chips, earthmoving equipment, or batteries.

Take, for instance, Oki Electric's factory in the Scottish town of Cumbernauld, near Glasgow. In 1987, this Japanese firm took over a big factory left vacant by Burroughs, an American computer firm, and equipped it swiftly to employ four hundred twenty people making dot-matrix computer printers. In Japan, Oki uses robots to do that. At Cumbernauld, working admittedly with smaller volumes of production, it uses mostly eighteen- to twenty-three-year-olds who, according to the (Scottish) personnel manager, need a great deal of training. But, with unemployment in the Cumbernauld area at more than 10 percent for most of the 1980s, there are plenty of people around to train.

That is not meant to be rude, just realistic. Oki came to the EC because its market is rich but protected, so business obstacles demanded local production. Having decided to invest in Europe it did not go to what Scotland calls its "silicon glen" in search of state-of-the-art technology, but rather it looked for nimble fingers and willingness to do assembly line jobs. Despite an array of electronics firms in Scotland, components supply was not an attraction either. Oki's printers contain only about 40–50 percent local components; newer models only about 30 percent. Oki does fit some of the Japanese stereotypes: everyone wears company jackets and offices are open plan. Teams of workers get daily briefings rather than simply orders from above. Oki is no sweatshop; but neither is its use of Japanese methods the key reason why it is where it is.

It is the same story in South Wales, Britain's other center of Japanese electronics investment. There, Professor Sig Prais of the National Institute of Economic and Social Research has surveyed Japanese factories. At one television plant he was told by a frank Japanese manager that Welsh workers are better than Japanese ones because they are more willing to do boring work. But the machines run for less of the time than in Japan because it is harder to keep them maintained. Unskilled female labor is easy and cheap to find. Maintenance engineers are thinner on the ground. Whether it is good or bad for such Japanese firms to come to Britain in these circumstances is irrelevant: the important point is that not all Japanese multinationals come in order to place a stirring vote of confidence in the local economy, or to set up an industrial paradise, or to set up a beachhead for their carefully planned assault on Europe. The truth is much grimier and more complicated than that.

———

If the truth is grimy and complicated, so have been the reactions to Japanese multinationals all over the world. As always in such matters, those criticizing Japan's global reach are noisier than those praising it, just as letters to the editors of newspapers tend to be from Outraged of Oklahoma, not Satisfied of Saratoga. Take Michael Crichton's novel. The flap jacket hype of *Rising Sun* states that the book offers a "headlong chase through a twisting maze of industrial intrigue . . . a no-holds-barred conflict in which control of a vital American technology is the fiercely coveted prize—and the Japanese saying 'Business is War' takes on a terrifying reality." Japan's global reach, in other words, has become the stuff of thrillers.

A more mundane but nevertheless typical sort of complaint about Japanese multinationals appeared on the letters page of *Business Week* on September 30, 1991, from John A. Grubb of Savoy, Illinois:

Like a lamprey eel on a Lake Michigan brown trout, Japan Inc's growing Midwest automobile-manufacturing and parts *keiretsu* [industrial group] is methodically sucking the life out of our American automobile industry.

It's too bad that Japan can't grow up as a nation and earn the respect that it craves. The country could start by rejecting its repulsive business practices, which are tantamount to cheating on an exam, or winning a race but failing the steroid test afterwards.

Japan chooses to run a $350 million public relations blitz in this country rather than open its markets and embrace acceptable business practices at home and abroad.

In Europe, the most florid language has come from France. For example, there was Calvet and his comment, mentioned earlier, about Britain as Japan's offshore aircraft carrier. The cover of *L'Express* magazine of June 20, 1991, announced, in effect, that the planes had already been launched: *"Comment le Japan nous envahit,"* ("How Japan Is Invading Us"), it said. The previous December, one of *L'Express*'s magazine rivals, *Le Nouvel Economiste,* had entitled its cover story in even more dramatic fashion: *"Les Japonais sont des Tueurs"* ("The Japanese Are Killers, or Butchers"). The subtitle was *"Comment les Nippons ont organisé patientment et impitoyablement l'encerclement de l'économie Française et Européenne"* ("How the Japanese Have Patiently and Pitilessly Organized the Encirclement of the French and European Economies").

Of course, these sentiments are pretty similar to those directed at Japanese competition in general; they are merely fiercer versions of phrases bandied about for decades about Japanese firms. Yet they have gathered intensity as Japan's global reach has grown, and the local investments of Japanese multinationals have become new targets for attack. This has involved a new and especially irritating conflict of interest and emotion for critics of Japan. Below the inflammatory title cited above in *Le Nouvel Economiste* was a photograph of Akio Morita, the chairman of Sony. The caption read: *"Akio Morita (Sony). Stratégie favorite pour s'implanter: séduire les élus locaux, via la carotte de la création d'emplois"* ("Favorite strategy for establishing himself: seduce local politicians via the carrot of job-creation"). There lies the conflict: every job that Sony creates turns somebody in favor of Japanese investment. They are employing our people and paying them wages. The cunning devils.

Perhaps seduced by job-creation, the British have been pretty enthusiastic about Japanese multinationals. Rarely a month seems to pass without another conference set up by a regional development agency or some other proinvestment body to endorse the relationship between Japan and Britain, or Japan and the New Europe, or Japan and the northeast of England, or whatever. But even in Britain, not all the natives are friendly. At the 1991 annual conference of the Trades Union Congress (TUC), Britain's union federation, a resolution was debated and passed condemning Japanese firms for bringing to Britain "alien" approaches toward industrial relations. The motion, which was proposed by the Manufacturing, Science and Finance Trade Union of managerial and technical staff, was supported by the Trade Union Congress's general council, even though the TUC general secretary, Norman Willis, read out a long list of reservations about it. Ken Gill, general secretary of the MSF, made a comment that would not have sounded out of place in the United States: "The intention of the motion was that there should be a higher level of British investment in British industry and an end to dependence on foreign capital. That is not racist; it is looking after British interests. When foreign companies invest in Britain they should be prepared to observe the practices of the country."

Is he right? Yes, in a sense he is: many Japanese employers coming to Britain have indeed brought with them an alien approach to industrial relations. They have sought to identify a single union to organize workers in their factory, have picked that union themselves, and have negotiated contracts with that union, contracts which stipulate the procedures that must be followed before a strike can be called. This is alien in the sense that single-union deals were not typical in British industrial relations before the 1980s. It is also undemocratic: the Japanese company chooses the union rather than (as in the United States, for instance) leaving it up to the workers to choose the union they wish to join as well as whether they wish to join it.

Yet it is a bit rich of Gill or others to condemn Japanese firms for this: the "typically British" practice is even less democratic than the Japanese alternative. Until the Thatcher reforms of the 1980s, many unions operated closed shops. If somebody wanted a job at a unionized factory, he or she had no choice but to join the union. Compared with closed shops, single-union deals are positively benign. Workers do not have to join the union, and they retain the right to strike.

In any case, Japanese firms are not the first to seek to circumvent old British union practices. IBM, which employs around twenty thousand people in Britain and has been making computers there since the 1950s, has never had any union at all. Nor has it had any industrial-relations problems. If any firm's methods are alien to Gill's union it is IBM's: and it is his union that would, in principle, be the most appropriate to organize the American firm's workers. This is the oddest but also the most notable point about the reaction to Japanese multinationals: it is far more hostile than the reaction to firms of other nationalities, or to multinationals in general. Japanese firms are not the only, or even the main, ones that have been investing abroad.

In the 1980s there was a boom in cross-border investment in the richest industrial economies, with British firms buying American ones, American firms buying British ones, and German, French, and Dutch firms buying both. Bass, a British brewer, now owns Holiday Inn, that quintessentially American hotel chain. Häagen-Dazs ice cream? It may have originally been made in America, but it is now owned and sold the world over by Grand Metropolitan, a British food and drink firm that also owns Burger King and for a time owned Inter-continental Hotels before selling it to Seibu of Japan. Sony may have bought Columbia Pictures but MGM-Pathé, Samuel Goldwyn's old firm, fell to Giancarlo Parretti, an Italian businessman chiefly financed by Crédit Lyonnais, a state-owned French bank that later took the studio over from Parretti.

Japan is not even the biggest multinational investor in America and certainly not in Europe. In 1990, British direct investment holdings in the United States accounted for 2 percent of U.S. gross domestic product; Japanese holdings accounted for only 1.5 percent. Neither of these figures is large compared with the American presence in overseas economies: according to the 1992 *Economic Report of the President,* American holdings of direct investment accounted for 6.7 percent of Britain's GDP, 8.2 percent of Holland's, 11.9 percent of Canada's, 1.9 percent of Germany's, and 0.7 percent of Japan's. Compared with that, Japan's presence in the United States (or anywhere else) is a pinprick. And, as stated earlier, the stock of America's direct investment in the European Community at the end of 1990 was $164 billion; Japan's in the same year was just $42 billion.

Why all the fuss? To understand the reason, think again about the arrival of American GIs in Britain during the Second World War. Like the Japanese now, there were not many GIs in wartime Britain, relative to the population. But they were new, and visible well beyond their numbers. Objectively, the only thing distinctive about Japanese multinational firms now is that they are the newest kids on the block. But there are also plenty of subjective factors that make them visible well beyond their numbers. Chief among these is that, especially to Americans but also to some Europeans, they symbolize a long-term, rather fundamental change: the apparent seizing of business leadership by Japanese firms.

Many Japanese feel that to single them out for attack must be racist. Sometimes, it may be, but more generally it is a sign of Japan's overall economic success. The Japanese either appear to represent a defeat that has already taken place—Japanese supremacy in the car industry, say, or in consumer electronics—or one that is about to happen. Put generously, the battle is for world leadership; put more aggressively (as by Edith Cresson, France's then prime minister, in 1991) it is a battle for world conquest. Either way, Japanese multinationals are seen as the country's forward troops, setting up beachheads, pouring out of Trojan horses, acting like termites—all depending on your chosen metaphor. None of those metaphors would be used for Renault or Bass or Grand Metropolitan, or even for Ford, even though in 1989 it bought the maker of that proudly British car, the Jaguar.

Japanese multinationals have global reach, just as other multinationals do. Like the others, they are over here. But they are thought of as different. According to this view, they compete unfairly, they are out to conquer our markets and to colonize our vital industries, they only buy from one another rather than from us, they only give decisionmaking power to their own Japanese expatriates. Those are the conventional wisdoms now held in the pubs and presidiums of Europe, America, and even Asia. Given how rapidly Japan has established its global reach, where will it all end? Are we all to become, one way or another, subjects of corporate Japan's new worldwide empire?

2

FROM HUDSON BAY
TO GLOBALONEY

Lightning play—
that yesterday was in the east,
is in the west today.

KIKAKU

To Americans, experiencing their first big wave of inward investment for more than a century, the debate over multinationals in general and Japanese ones in particular feels like a new phenomenon. But it is not. Hostility to multinational companies is nothing new. Americans should know this better than anyone. For in the past, American multinationals have generally been the world's favorite targets for loathing. Which raises an important question: have American multinationals been loathed for the same reasons as Japanese ones are now loathed?

First, a general observation. Business, it often seems, was not made to be liked. Even though companies are the vehicles through which most wealth is created and even though they enable people to earn a better living than they could through the solitary use of their own skills, they are more often vilified than praised, more often feared than trusted. Many critics forget that the essence of the corporate form is the suppression or harnessing of individual aims and interests into a cooperative endeavor. Even though most of the technological advances that have improved both the quality and the duration of human life have come from businesses rather than any other organizational form, corporations are commonly viewed with suspicion and distaste. This is more true of managerial corporations than entrepreneurial ones. And it is truest of all for the multinational corporation.

One reason, of course, for the general suspicion of business is that companies do harm as well as good, and plenty of it besides. But so do individuals; companies are no more likely, or unlikely, to commit crimes, whether against legal or ethical codes, than individuals are. It is just that when they do, it is done on a larger scale and affects more people. It is rather like the remark attributed to F. Scott Fitzgerald: Fitzgerald said that the very rich are different from you and me; to which, according to Ernest Hemingway, someone replied, "Yes, they have more money."

That is the difference with companies, too, but with an important twist. Although companies are nothing more than collections of people earning and using large amounts of money, they appear peculiarly inhuman. All have some sort of character, which lives on as employees leave and join. Yet it is hard to anthropomorphize a company, to think of it as akin to a person, or even to liken it to an animal, except in cases where the image is a frightening one: a giant, a mammoth, or a leviathan. The millions that modern firms spend on designing logos and corporate images attempting to depict their firms as birds (doves, usually, rather than vultures) or animals (cuddly, not cruel) or positive human images (pied pipers, trumpeteers, heavenly messengers) are doomed to failure. The kindest image that anyone ever applies to companies is the dinosaur.

With all this in mind, it is not surprising that business becomes even less liked the bigger it gets. Small, entrepreneurial businesses are felt to be on a human scale. The success of their founders invites empathy more often than envy; if only I had thought of that, appears to be the common response. Big, faceless corporations invite distrust, however, and not a little fear. Yet it was not always like this; the distinction between corporations and entrepreneurs is a twentieth-century phenomenon. The capitalism against which Marx inveighed was the entrepreneurial sort, in which a small band of owners and investors risked their capital and were assumed to obtain their rewards through the exploitation and increasing impoverishment of their workers. That was also the capitalism that concerned Charles Dickens in Victorian London, and it was what inspired fears of America's "robber barons" such as Andrew Carnegie or Cornelius Vanderbilt.

Yet nowadays entrepreneurial capitalism gets a much friendlier reception, even when the companies are huge. A firm headed by Bill Gates, Donald Trump, or, indeed, Ross Perot seems far easier to accept and understand than an IBM, a British Telecom, a Matsushita, or a Deutsche Bank. An entrepreneurial company has a human form, a form that is an object of admiration, like a movie star. The reason for the firm's existence and its actions seem clear: the enrichment and self-aggrandizement of its founder. At least we know where we stand.

That is not the case with an ordinary corporation: its motives are not clear, its loyalties are hard to discern, its ultimate ownership impossible to pin down. The modern managerial corporation, an invention of the twentieth century, has arguably had more effect on more people's lives than any other single development in the rich capitalist world. Moreover, almost universally in Britain and America, and to a large extent in other industrialized countries, the ultimate ownership of managerial corporations is now in the hands of millions of people, through their pension funds and insurance policies. We now have what Peter Drucker, in a perceptive 1976 book called *The Unseen Revolution,* termed pension-fund socialism. Yet these managerial corporations, whose incomes flow to millions of present and future pensioners, are still unpopular at best, hated at worst.

Take that suspicion and multiply it by ten: you now have a reasonable estimate of the widespread view of multinational firms. There is nothing new about this. It was true most plainly in the 1960s and 1970s when the principal multinational objects of loathing were American-owned companies, and Raymond Vernon, a professor at Harvard University, wrote in his 1977 book, *Storm over the Multinationals,* that "the multinational enterprise has come to be seen as the embodiment of almost anything disconcerting about modern industrial society."

The basic reason for this suspicion of multinationals is the same as that of domestic managerial firms: that they seem inhuman and alienating, and that their true motives and loyalties are obscure. But this suspicion takes an aggravated form for international businesses, because whatever their loyalties actually are, by definition they must be loyalties to foreigners. Multinationals, in other words, appear like agents of a foreign power, whose interests are surely different from those of the host country. Quite how that foreign power exerts its influence over the multinational is at all times obscure. Indeed, for multinationals of all stripes, the occasions when they are resented as foreign agents are matched by roughly as many occasions when, in their home country, they are resented as unpatriotic for investing abroad and employing foreigners. The scariest notion of all is what bridges this apparent contradiction: that multinationals are stateless entities, loyal to no one but themselves.

At least until recent developments in transportation and communications enabled even small firms to build global organizations, "multinational" has always been a synonym for "big." That adds to its apparent menace, despite the fact that the arrival of multinational firms commonly implies an increase in competition, a decrease in prices to consumers, and an attack on domestic monopolies. If America's Procter & Gamble had not invested in Britain to sell its Daz and Ariel, for instance, the local soap and detergent firm, Lever Brothers (part of Unilever), might have a virtual monopoly with its Persil. The arrival of Japanese and European car firms in the American market since the 1970s, for instance, has broken the dominant position previously held by General Motors and the oligopoly formed by GM together with Ford and Chrysler.

The size of global firms is far more of a problem, however, for poor countries than for rich ones. Their fear, especially common in the 1970s, is that they will find themselves trapped in a weak negotiating position with powerful multinationals, for whom withdrawal from the country would matter little. But the company's presence matters a great deal for the country since it will employ tens of thousands of people and will have a big impact on wages and wealth. The proportion of multinational investment devoted to the Third World has always been small; but to many small Third World countries, multinationals can account for a large proportion of GDP, employment, or investment. The risk is that this enables multinationals to subvert the power of the host state to their own ends, forcing laws on pollution, say, or monopolies to be bent in their favor. Such worries explain why many poor countries closed their borders to foreign direct investment in the 1960s and 1970s, preferring to import foreign capital in the form of debt rather than equity—leading directly to the debt crisis of the 1980s.

Yet today's Japanese multinationals, along with multinationals of other origins, are again being welcomed and even solicited by the Third World. Poor countries are shedding their old worries and seeking to open their borders to trade and investment. Paradoxically, it is in the world's two most powerful entities, against which no company however large can stand comparison, that the biggest fuss is being made about sovereignty and loss of control, and the mixed loyalties of Japanese multinational corporations. Those two entities are the United States and the European Community.

———

Listen to a citizen of the United States, and you might think that foreign investment and worldwide competition had just been invented. This is true even if the speaker is a businessman. These days, every American chief executive worth his salt announces portentously that his industry is now "globalizing," and that this is his newest and most powerful challenge.

The following mantra is chanted, whether by advocates or critics of the whole process: around the world, tastes are converging; time and space have suddenly been shrunk by the jet aircraft, the satellite, and the desktop computer; businesses must focus on the "triad" of Europe, America, and Japan; markets are changing faster than ever before, amid intensifying competition; globalization is unavoidable; soon my business will be dominated by ten (or six, or three) major firms; we either have to be one of them or a niche player, for there will be nothing in between.

Sometimes, this globalizing trend is bemoaned, as in a cover story in *The Atlantic* of March 1992 entitled "Jihad versus McWorld," written by Professor Benjamin Barber of Rutgers University. Using

47

the Big Mac hamburger as his symbol of "the onrush of economic and ecological forces that demand integration and uniformity. . . . pressing nations into one commercially homogeneous global network," Professor Barber worried that this trend is forming a "centripetal black hole" for citizens wishing to govern themselves democratically.

Others praise the force of globalization, urging both companies and governments to accept it and to embrace it wholeheartedly. One of the foremost evangelists in the global pulpit is Kenichi Ohmae, a Japanese management writer who runs the Tokyo consultancy of McKinsey & Company and is probably the only Japanese economist or management guru who is well-known in the rest of the world. His 1990 book, *The Borderless World,* ended with a heartfelt "Declaration of Interdependence Toward the World— 2005" in which he urged governments and politicians to say that "we avow that the security of humankind's social and economic institutions lies no longer in superpower deterrence but is rather to be found in the weave of economic and intellectual interdependence of nations."

Stirring stuff. All of this may be true; or none of it. But whichever it is, one thing is certain: none of it is original. The arrival of the global business, or the global market, has been predicted and perceived for at least the past thirty years. There is something about futurologists that makes them always pick dates for their predictions that are fifteen years ahead. Perhaps this is near enough to be both credible and alarming (or exciting, depending on your purpose), but far enough ahead to be irrefutable. Note that Kenichi Ohmae's declaration was dated 2005, fifteen years after his book's publication. And so it was that in his 1967 call to arms against the menace of American multinationals Jean-Jacques Servan-Schreiber, a French publisher and pundit, wrote that "Fifteen years from now, it is quite possible that the world's third greatest industrial power, just after the United States and Russia, will not be Europe but American industry in Europe." That was supposed to happen by 1982, remember, by which time in fact the challenge of American multinationals had faded, Russia was collapsing (though nobody realized it even then), and the real candidate for pole position was Japan.

Shortly after Servan-Schreiber was worrying away in Europe, an eminent economist at the Massachusetts Institute of Technology, Charles Kindleberger, wrote in 1969 in his book *American Business Abroad* that the global firm was about to kill the nation state: "The international corporation has no country to which it owes more loyalty than any other, nor any country where it feels completely at home. . . . The nation state is just about through as an economic unit. . . . The world is too small."

The strongest and most striking announcement of the arrival of a new, global commercial world was a book published in 1974 by Richard Barnet and Ronald Mueller. Called *Global Reach: The Power of the Multinational Corporations,* it announced the arrival of the planetary enterprise, a global corporation that for the first time had the organization, technology, money, and ideology to make a credible try at managing the world as an integrated unit. This new entity was "transforming the world political economy through its increasing control over three fundamental resources of economic life: the technology of production, finance capital and marketing. . . . the production process increasingly ignores national frontiers."

This was all true: the trend was moving in this direction. But what is surely notable, almost two decades later, is not how much the global company has transformed the world economy but rather how little it has, given the trumpet blasts with which its arrival was announced. All the forces that lay behind its arrival have continued, or even accelerated, since Barnet and Mueller were writing: jumbo jets make short trips from London to New York or even Tokyo both possible and affordable; transport costs for goods have fallen considerably; cheap, powerful computers and communications make the transmission and reception of information ever easier, month by month. If these were, as was thought in the 1970s, powerful forces in favor of the global company, then by now huge global companies might be expected to dominate the world economy. Yet, significant though they certainly are, they do not dominate it.

Many companies are large but few are genuinely global, if by that is meant that they treat the world as one market and have no loyalties to any particular nation. Nor has big business taken over:

it is not the case that two hundred to three hundred global corporations control 80 percent of all productive assets in the non-Communist world. Yet in the early 1970s, Professor Howard Perlmutter of the Wharton School predicted that exactly this would happen by 1985 (fifteen years, again).

There are two reasons for the surprising absence of a global market dominated by global companies. One is that although markets have indeed globalized quite rapidly, with both trade and foreign direct investment outpacing world economic growth, this has not had as its main effect the wholesale transfer of sovereign national power to a few global corporations. National governments do now realize that their economies are interdependent with one another and that their policies cannot pretend to be independent, but in this they have yielded power to the neutral forces of world markets, world demand and supply, and world currency movements, not to the apparently sinister forces of global companies. Indeed, global companies feel vulnerable to world market forces in the same way as countries do. The second reason, moreover, is that the technological forces pressing toward globalism are not the only forces pressing on international companies.

Global companies ebb and flow for a wider variety of reasons than merely technological ones. Technology has certainly been an enabling force in the past few decades, but it is not the only factor, nor does it operate exclusively in the interests of huge multinational corporations. The rise of one group of multinationals has often been mirrored by the decline of another; and the integration of the world economy has helped many small firms as well as big ones. In any case, the world economy is not yet even as integrated as it was in the two decades before 1914.

The idea of an international company goes back centuries. The Hudson's Bay Company that in 1670 began to trade on the edges of colonial America is one of the earliest, but then before it there were medieval international banks, and after it came other British colonial traders in India and elsewhere. The first real spurt of globalization, however, came in the second half of the nineteenth century.

Britain was then the world's dominant international power, so it will not be surprising that some of the new global firms were

British. Sir Marcus Samuel's Shell oil company took its first tanker through the Suez Canal in 1892, and shortly afterward bought half the Texan oil supply for the next twenty-one years. In the 1880s, London merchant banks were financing the building of railways not only in the United States but also in Latin America; it was over Argentine bonds that Barings, then the most powerful London bank, collapsed in 1890. Lever Brothers, founded in Britain in 1884 to make soap, was soon also manufacturing it in Switzerland, Australia, Canada, Belgium, France, Holland, the United States, and Germany. In those years, however, most of the overseas investment by Britain and, to a lesser extent, by France and Germany was made through portfolio investment in stocks and bonds. Every year for decades, Britain exported capital equivalent to 5–10 percent of its GNP. By 1890, for instance, Britain's investments in America accounted for almost 20 percent of American GNP.

That makes it all the more remarkable that, despite Britain's industrial and political strength, the most striking trend of the period was in fact the internationalization of American business. While Britain invested chiefly through purchases of stocks and bonds, America invested abroad chiefly through what were, with hindsight, multinational corporations. The first direct American investment in manufacturing in Britain came as early as 1856 when five Americans from a New Brunswick firm called J. Ford and Company set up a rubber factory in Edinburgh. It did not last long, at least under American ownership. But it was followed in 1867 by a more notable and durable investor, the Singer sewing machine company.

By the 1880s, a whole series of American industries were arriving, especially in electric lighting, electric traction, and telecommunications: the Edison-Swan Electric Company, British Thomson-Houston, and, in 1899, Westinghouse. Manufacturers of matches, tobacco, shoes, and food arrived, including H. J. Heinz. In 1900, there were seventy-five American subsidiaries in Britain; between 1901 and 1914, a further seventy manufacturing subsidiaries of American firms were set up. And, sure enough, there was a backlash: in 1902, a book was published called *The American Invaders,* by F. A. McKenzie. Perhaps this was mere revenge: in the 1880s, British investment in America had been the target of a series of published attacks, alleging that having failed to conquer America by force in the war of independence, Britain was now trying to buy it.

According to a 1958 book on American investment in Britain by Professor John Dunning of Reading University in Britain, now one of the world's leading academic experts on foreign investment, one thing that many of these American investors had in common was that they were bringing with them manufacturing techniques and machinery that had been invented with the large and rapidly expanding American market in mind, and which were superior to those in use in Europe. They were, in other words, in a similar situation to that of many of the Japanese multinationals in the 1980s: investing abroad to exploit the superiority of their manufacturing techniques compared with local rivals.

Just as Toyota and Honda have recently gone to the United States to build cars in competition with the big-but-backward local firms, so American car companies came to Europe in the early 1900s, where the car had, after all, been invented. Ford arrived at Trafford Park in Manchester in 1908, assembling its cars from imported components. Its local content was thus exceedingly low, but its methods of manufacture, already using mass-production techniques rather than the craft-based methods of the European firms, more than made up for the cost of shipping those parts. Five years later, Ford was already Britain's biggest car producer, making 6,000 cars in 1913 out of the country's total output of 25,000.

Interrupted by the First World War, the trend resumed in the 1920s and 1930s, although it was fueled by a new phenomenon: protectionism. New laws in 1915, 1921, and 1927 imposed tariffs on a wide range of American goods entering Britain, forcing American firms to manufacture locally if they wished to retain their presence in the market. Since by now America had become the world's biggest exporter of capital, the funds were abundantly available for such direct investment. As in Japan's multinational growth in the 1980s, although most of the early movers built their own companies and factories, eventually American investors switched to takeovers of existing British firms. In 1922, an American drug firm called Liggett bought the

Boots Pure Drug Company, a firm still famous in Britain and one that returned to British ownership in 1933.

Most notable of all was the purchase in 1925 of the Vauxhall car company in Britain by America's General Motors, swiftly followed by investments in tire manufacturing in Britain by the two top American firms, Goodyear and Firestone. The decisionmaking that lay behind the Vauxhall acquisition shows how little the basic questions and options change for such business ventures. Alfred Sloan, the man who built GM up from 1918 until his retirement in 1957 when it was by far the world's biggest car company, wrote in his memoir, *My Years with General Motors,* that "We had to decide whether, and to what extent, there was a market abroad for the American car. . . . We had to determine whether we wanted to be exporters or overseas producers. When it became clear that we had to engage in some production abroad, the next question was whether to build up our own companies or to buy and develop existing ones. We had to devise some methods of living with restrictive regulations and duties. We had to work out a special form of organization that would be suitable overseas."

GM's first thought, in 1919, was to buy 50 percent of the Citroën car company in France. After long negotiations, Sloan and his colleagues decided against it. One reason was that "the French government did not like the idea of American interests taking over an enterprise that had contributed importantly to the war effort." Sloan then tried to take over Austin, the largest British producer. But, among other problems, the price demanded was felt to be too high. So in late 1925, GM bought a smaller firm, Vauxhall, for $2,575,291. Vauxhall is still one of GM's main European assets, along with Opel, a German carmaker in which the firm first bought an 80 percent stake for $26 million in 1928. In 1991, GM Europe (i.e., Opel and Vauxhall) made net profits of more than $1 billion, while the parent firm lost almost $5 billion in the United States.

Overseas investments, followed swiftly by compatriot parts suppliers: it is the same pattern that appeared when Japanese carmakers invested overseas in the 1980s. This is what happens when an industry chooses to shift production abroad because it feels it has managerial advantages over rivals in the countries in which it invests. Such advantages tend to be shared with suppliers, since those suppliers have evolved alongside the manufacturer at home and have become accustomed to meeting its requirements. This gives the suppliers, who follow on their customer's coattails, an advantage over rivals abroad.

During the 1920s and 1930s, world trade was contracting, thanks to economic depression and to protectionism. Overseas investment continued, albeit chiefly in order to circumvent high tariff barriers. It was not until the 1950s and 1960s that trade began to expand swiftly again, and alongside it foreign direct investment accelerated too. Some of that foreign investment was motivated by the search for natural resources, especially oil and metals. That search was primarily in developing countries, a fact that brought multinational oil and mineral giants face to face with Third World governments. At times, the companies appeared to be engaged in more diplomatic negotiations than even their home governments were involved in, most notably in the Middle East. But of the foreign investment that was devoted to manufacturing and services businesses, one source and one destination dominated: America was the source, Europe the destination.

IBM, Ford, Kelloggs, Heinz, Procter & Gamble, Bendix, ITT, Sperry: all these firms and many more established themselves as dominant players in the European markets for their products. At the same time, the way in which such international firms operated began to change. While previously they could be stereotyped as having been organized as country-by-country clones of the parent company, with all reporting lines leading back to the head office, during the 1950s and 1960s American firms developed such large international networks that they began to organize on a more genuinely worldwide basis. At least in the main markets, companies organized themselves chiefly by products rather than countries, with global or regional coordinators for those products. Managers reported through a matrix, with lines heading both to their country managers and to the product specialist at the head office. Now, for the first time, people began to speak of the global company, planning and coordinating its operations on a global scale.

Still, these global companies had just one nationality: American. The one-way flow out of America and into Europe was what stimulated Servan-Schreiber's critique in 1967. His key observation was not only that American companies were now a powerful presence in Europe but also that their principal advantage was organizational. It was, in his view, their superior ability to administer large corporations and to coordinate activities over a wide geographic area that made it so hard for European companies, used to operating in their single national markets, to compete with them. The flow of multinational investment in the 1960s was so dominated by American business that, quite naturally, analysts sought explanations in the American market itself.

Raymond Vernon, in a 1971 book, *Sovereignty at Bay,* saw the multinational as a peculiarly American phenomenon, arising from special American circumstances:

> According to my argument, the special conditions of the American market—high per capita income, scarce artisan labor, costly labor in general, large internal markets including military purchases—generated innovations that later would be wanted abroad. The special conditions of the European market, on the other hand, encouraged innovations with a less certain international future. Whereas a global secular growth in the demand for high-income and labor-saving products was reasonably sure, one could not be nearly so sanguine about the growth in demand for material-saving and capital-conserving products.

This was a perfectly reasonable generalization at the time. As Vernon himself observed, it was just beginning to be contradicted by an increase in European investment in the United States, with British Petroleum buying Sohio in 1969, for example, though at the time this did not appear to refute the general proposition.

Two major events were, however, about to produce a sudden change in the determinants of international investment: the abandonment of fixed exchange rates in 1971 and the consequent devaluation of the dollar, which made foreign assets look more costly to American firms and American ones cheaper to foreigners; and the oil price hike of 1973–74 that, together with an associated boom in the prices of other commodities, suddenly boosted the demand for just the material-saving and capital-conserving products in which Vernon saw a European advantage. More portentously, such an advantage was also held by companies in another country: Japan.

Dominated by American money, controversial in Europe and the Third World: that was the global company of the early 1970s. Inflation and recurrent recessions in the 1970s halted the growth in foreign investment, especially by American firms. Many even began to repatriate their capital. It was in the 1980s that foreign direct investment really began to take off. By then, however, things were very different indeed. American money no longer dominated; Europe no longer worried so much about multinationals; and the Third World had already by and large turned its back on them. And even more different than these factors was the sheer scale of multinational investment.

In the 1960s, foreign direct investment (FDI) grew at twice the rate of world GNP. Between 1983 and 1989, worldwide FDI grew at a compound annual rate of 28.9 percent; in the same period, world exports were growing by just 9.4 percent at a compound annual rate, and world GDP by 7.8 percent. In other words, FDI was now growing almost four times as fast as output and three times as fast as trade. Most FDI arises from the rich, developed countries; in the 1980s, a growing share also *went* to those same rich countries. Japan, the United States, and the European Community played host to 65 percent of all inward flows of FDI in the 1980s, a figure not far short of their 77 percent share in outward flows. In other words, most of their outward flows were to each other.

The table shows the shift in where the money was coming from. In 1985, Britain was the biggest source, followed by the United States. But by the end of the 1980s, Japan had pulled well clear of the United States and even overtook Britain in 1989. It fell back again, behind Britain, in 1990–91. It is worth noting, however, that America remained a large source of outward FDI, even though it was also playing host to plenty as well. The same two-way flow was true of Britain.

Why did FDI boom during the 1980s? There are no clear

Outflows of FDI from Five Major Source Countries, 1985–89
(in billions)

Country	1985	1986	1987	1988	1989
France	$ 2.2	$ 5.4	$ 9.2	$ 14.5	$ 19.4
Germany	5.0	10.1	9.2	11.2	13.5
Japan	6.4	14.5	19.5	34.2	44.2
Britain	11.1	16.5	31.1	37.0	32.0
USA	8.9	13.8	28.0	13.3	26.5
Total G5	$ 33.7	$ 60.2	$ 97.1	$ 110.2	$ 135.6

Source: United Nations Center on Transnational Corporations

answers, but there are plenty of plausible ones. One was the widespread release of controls on the movement of capital by countries all around the world. Britain abolished exchange controls in 1979, Japan did so in 1980. The last set of capital controls inside the EC disappeared in 1990–91. Controls on the export of capital do not thwart FDI altogether, since investments can be made using capital from a variety of sources, not just the home market: local borrowing, for instance, or debt raised on international capital markets such as the Eurodollar market in London. But the relaxation of exchange controls nevertheless made it easier to shift capital across borders, and encouraged domestic institutional investors to diversify their portfolios internationally. One way to do that is to buy foreign stocks and bonds; another is to provide money to the companies whose shares you own domestically to enable them to buy other companies abroad. Yet another is to buy foreign real estate—a purchase that is generally included in measures of direct investment rather than the portfolio sort.

At the same time, two of the countries concerned—Britain and the United States—were passing through a considerable restructuring of their domestic economies. Companies that had succeeded in one shape or form in the 1960s and early 1970s were now in trouble, and began a radical program of divestment of unwanted assets. Conglomerates built in the late 1960s were being broken up. In other words, there emerged an active market in companies and their divisions, stirred up all the while by corporate raiders making hostile takeover bids using junk bonds or bank loans. In such a turbulent market, it was not surprising that many of the bidders for companies and divisions were foreign.

Most notably in the United States, but also in Europe, a further factor was protectionism. In the late 1970s and early 1980s, America imposed restraints on imports such as machine tools, semiconductors, steel, cars, motorcycles, and textiles. The European Community raised its barriers to electronic products such as videocassette recorders, computer printers, and compact disk players. Both used antidumping levies to provide extra protection for domestic producers, especially in electronics. Such trade protection forced foreign firms to invest locally if they were to exploit their managerial and technical advantages for local sales, just as American companies had been forced to do in Britain between the wars.

A further important change was linked to the growing role played in all the rich economies by service businesses. In all rich countries, manufacturing was gradually declining as a proportion of output and services were taking a rising share of economic activity. Many services cannot easily be traded internationally: hotels or restaurants, or accounting or consultancy, for instance. This means that the main way to grow internationally in services is by foreign direct investment. At the same time, the rapid improvements in computer and telecommunications technology had more impact on services than on manufacturing; information is the raw material of most services, and technology lowered the cost of moving, obtaining, and organizing it. And, at the same time, cheaper travel and growing affluence were causing a worldwide boom in another service business: tourism. The result was that while services made up around 25 percent of the world stock of foreign direct investment in the early 1970s, by the late 1980s the share of services in FDI was almost 50 percent, and growing.

It is small wonder, given such growth in multinational investment during the 1980s, that the idea of the global company has returned. Just around the corner, we are again being told, is the company managed with a genuine disregard for national borders, with its top managers recruited from all around the world, and with its headquarters positioned equidistantly, at least in mental terms, from all its main markets. Kenichi Ohmae is again the chief evangelist for such a view. A more sophisticated notion is advocated by Christopher Bartlett of Harvard Business School and Sumantra Ghoshal of the European Institute for Business Administration (INSEAD, by its French initials) in France in their 1989 book, *Managing Across Borders: The Transnational Solution*. Bartlett and Ghoshal say that companies are (or should be) ceasing to worry so much about the structure of their worldwide operations and are paying more attention to the decision process and psychology of their firms. Their aim is to build a "transnational" firm that not only is global, but thinks as if it is. Previous multinationals, apparently, have really been collections of local firms, sent orders by a head office whose main attention is devoted to the home market.

One thing is clear: such a firm is the exception and not the rule. That is certainly so in terms of the outward appearances of companies. Few have foreign board directors; a survey by Korn/Ferry, an American headhunter, in March 1990, showed that of billion-dollar American industrial and service firms only 19 percent had a non-American executive on the board, a figure that had declined from 21 percent in 1980. Few have the headquarters of a major product division located outside their home base. IBM's announcement in 1991 that it was to move its worldwide telecommunications-services division to Britain aroused a great deal of attention precisely because this is so unusual.

Moreover, despite the widespread notion that global companies are now stateless, the number that do not have a strong national identity, which includes a dominant national market, can be counted on the fingers of one hand. Asea Brown Boveri, a Swiss-Swedish engineering multinational, always pops up in studies of globaloney precisely because it is so unusually stateless. Others are always from small countries: Philips of Holland, for instance, or Nestlé from Switzerland. Yet even these are, respectively, extremely Dutch or Swiss in the ownership of their shares and in their management structures. Despite being as international as they come, neither has yet had a foreign chairman or chief executive, nor is there any prospect of this changing.

Ah, but the trend is in this direction, is it not? Perhaps, but then Raymond Vernon also thought it was in 1971 when he wrote *Sovereignty at Bay*. He admitted that few American multinationals were structured as properly global firms, and that few employed foreigners in top executive positions, but he felt that the trend was in that direction. It probably was, and still is. But it is extremely slow.

———

One reason it may be slow is that the cast list of multinationals seems to change so much and so rapidly. While in the early 1970s it would have seemed reasonable to track the development of American firms and then extrapolate into the future, American firms are no longer at the top of the global list: their place has been taken by French firms, British firms, German firms, and, yes, Japanese firms.

These new entrants compete fiercely with one another, with the older American multinationals, and with local firms, always thwarting the development of a stable, global business. More important even than this, the past decade has enabled small firms to become global, both as a way to grow rapidly and as a way simply to spread more widely. Most notably in the computer business, firms like Compaq and Dell became global almost before they had become big players in their domestic market. Small, flexible, vibrant: that has been the new business mantra, especially in America. Firms like GM or IBM have had to concentrate on getting smaller and nimbler, simply to survive. They've had little time to worry about their transnational psychology.

Whatever the cast list and whatever the typical size, shape, or nationality of the multinational firm, the problems posed by and for these companies are remarkably consistent. A few problems have been added to the list since American firms set up in Britain a hundred years ago, but the list is essentially unchanged since American firms were at the center of critical attention in the 1960s and 1970s. Some critics may think that Japanese multinationals pose special problems and threats, but there really is nothing new under the sun.

The basic issue with all multinationals concerns national autonomy. Do these disloyal giants limit a country's control over its own economy or, more specifically, over its technological capabilities?

Do they in some sense narrow a country's choices? That was the view of Servan-Schreiber in France in the late 1960s, and it was the worry expressed by a book published in the United States in early 1992 by Robert Kearns, a member of a think tank in Washington called the Economic Strategy Institute. His book is called *Zaibatsu America: How Japanese Firms Are Colonizing Vital U.S. Industries.* That subtitle, with the word "colonizing," provides a powerful hint of Kearns's view. Although Japanese investment has provided a temporary boon to local and state economies, Kearns said that "we are rapidly losing control of the vital parts of our economy."

Associated with this is a worry about innovation. Multinationals may be investing in advanced industries such as computers, semiconductors, artificial intelligence, drugs, and cars. They may even be setting up technical facilities abroad. But, compared with local firms in the same industries, the worry is that multinationals perform their high-level research and development at home. This, it is feared, deprives the host country of jobs for top scientists and designers, and keeps the really valuable jobs back home. Kearns quotes John Stern, head of the Tokyo office of the U.S. Electronics Association, as saying that "Japanese investment is used as a vacuum cleaner for acquiring technology and exporting it home. If America intends to win the race based on innovation, it must stop selling its running shoes to the competitors."

This view is widely held about Japanese firms buying American technological specialists, and it is extended to firms like Sony, Matsushita, and Toyota that build electronics products and cars in America or Europe. It will be a familiar complaint to Vernon, for he reported similar grumbles and fears about American multinationals in the 1960s and 1970s when he observed that "multinational enterprises tend to place the innovation process itself close to headquarters."

The reason is eternal, and is more or less the same whether the multinational is American, European, or Japanese. Advanced research is risky and costly, even if the potential rewards are high. That means that firms' top executives want to retain a tight control over it. They also want to ensure that there is close cooperation between those developing new products and those likely to be introducing them to the market. If the main marketing men are at the head office, and especially if the home market is the multinational company's most important one, then the biggest R&D projects will stay at home. To repeat: this is true of all multinationals. Foreign direct investment is not the way for an industrial country to ensure that, within its borders, top-level research and development takes place. That does not mean that opposing FDI is the right policy either. Just that it is not the solution to a lack of R&D.

Both autonomy and innovation also reflect a third worry: about the location of decisionmaking. This is, in a way, two worries in one: that decisions made at the head office might give a low priority to local interests abroad, making investments unstable and liable to be withdrawn abruptly; and that local managers will be low-level types, frozen out of the main executive ranks. The first of these worries was common in Europe in the 1960s and 1970s. Branch plants of American multinationals were lured to depressed regions, often by grants and low-interest loans, but then were prone to withdraw at the first sign of difficulty back home, or when the grants ran out. Probably wrongly, few Americans or Europeans now have this worry about Japanese firms: they assume that the Japanese invest for the long term, unlike their own myopic companies. Although this is true of many Japanese firms, it is not true of all of them. And even the long-term investors will find it easier to fire employees or close factories abroad than at home.

As we shall see in later chapters, the worry that local managers have no real say is more widespread for Japanese firms than for others. It is an odd worry: if these locals do not like their jobs, presumably they can leave. If local managers are as good as they think they are, such staff turnover will prove a problem for Japanese multinationals, not a strength, and if the presence of those Japanese firms is itself a problem, then it evidently contains part of its own solution. In any case, to put the whole issue into perspective, try this passage from *Liar's Poker,* Michael Lewis's best-selling account of life at the London office of Salomon Brothers, an American investment bank: "For all his worldly ambition, [John] Gutfreund remained remarkably parochial and introverted. That's why, for example, that it never occurred to him that anyone would manage his London office but Americans."

Outrageous. Clearly the British government should have excluded Salomon for that reason alone. Well, no. Like much of Lewis's book this was anyway a bit unfair, since at the time Lewis was writing, Salomon Brothers' Tokyo office was being run by a Briton, Deryck Maughan. It had evidently occurred to Gutfreund that a non–American might be able to run a Salomon office somewhere. After Gutfreund, the long-time chairman of Salomon, resigned in 1991 because of a bond-trading scandal, Deryck Maughan became chief operating officer of the whole investment bank. Nevertheless, unfair or not, the passage helps to remind us that Japanese firms are by no means alone in sending expatriate managers to run their overseas branches, and even in not promoting locals to the parent board. American firms are just as bad, or good, depending on your view.

Labor unions have a more interesting worry about multinationals. Remember that Britain's Trade Union Congress complained in 1991 that Japanese multinationals were importing "alien" management practices for industrial relations? This sort of complaint also appeared in the 1960s and 1970s about American firms. In both cases, the definition of "alien" is not, generally, that multinationals are harming the interests of the workers; more often, it is that they are harming the interests of the unions by adopting somewhat benign policies toward their workers. In Belgium in the 1960s, for instance, unions felt that, as Vernon wrote, the "human relations" practices of some foreign-owned subsidiaries were alienating the workers from their union organizations. In this they were like the Japanese today: by treating employees like human beings, they seemed to be removing the need for a trade union.

Clearly, multinationals in poor countries were rather less likely to be accused of being too benign. But in rich countries, as in poor ones, there have long been worries about lawbreaking and unethical activities by multinationals that are again being raised about Japanese multinationals. One sort of complaint is that they import too much; if their investment is simply made to circumvent a trade barrier then the local content of whatever they are assembling may be pretty low. In some cases, there is room to accuse the multinational of cooking the books to make local content appear higher than it really is. Similar book-fiddling accusations are also made over taxation: that multinationals distort the prices they pay for imports from sister firms abroad in order to shift their profits from high tax jurisdictions into lower tax areas, or simply to home, where their political contacts are stronger and thus where they prefer to pay their tax. Such distorted transfer pricing was a common accusation in the 1960s and 1970s, by both poor countries and rich ones. It is no surprise to find it being repeated now against Japanese investors.

National autonomy; loss of technology and innovative capacity; the stability of investment; the location of decisionmaking and the power given to or withheld from local managers; the alienation of workers from labor organizations; devious behavior concerning local content and transfer pricing: all these and doubtless more form the unchanging litany of grievances against multinationals, whether they are American firms in the 1960s or Japanese ones in the 1980s and 1990s. Multinationals were certainly not made to be liked.

PART TWO

SUCCESS
AND
FAILURE

3

CARMAKERS ON
CRUISE CONTROL

Snail, my little man,
slowly, oh, very slowly,
climb up Fujisan!

ISSA

MICHAEL Crichton, it will be recalled, set as his target in *Rising Sun* the issue of foreign investment in American high technology. What sort of technology is "high"? The answer depends on your point of view. The layman would think of microchips, advanced computers, genes, and aerospace. Talk to a maker of machine tools, however, or even of cars, and they will certainly think their industries qualify. If a car man cannot describe the automobile (which, it is true, was pretty advanced as recently as the 1890s) as high technology and still keep a straight face, he calls it "strategic." It comes to the same thing: in the lobbyists' lingo, both are synonyms for "please give generously."

The car industry is indeed an important one, most notably because of its size: it is one of the biggest employers, directly and indirectly, in any of the top industrial economies; it is one of the top spenders on research and development; and it is generally a rich-country consumer's second biggest individual purchase, after his house. It is also one of the most multinational of industries.

From the early 1980s to today, the output of vehicles produced by Japanese firms in factories in America has risen from 50,000 to a little over 1.5 million a year.

Those figures show how prominent the car industry has become in the debate over foreign direct investment. They also suggest how important the industry is to Japanese firms as a case study in the whys, wherefores, and hows of overseas investment. The basic strategy of all the Japanese car firms has been to build their own factories in foreign markets rather than to enter joint ventures with local firms or to expand through takeovers. The main problems that poses, and therefore the subject of this chapter, are: is such organic expansion too slow, and how quickly should the Japanese firms localize their employment, parts procurement, and R&D?

―――――

One of the worst mistakes made by Michael Dukakis during his campaign for America's presidency in 1988 was a speech attacking foreign investment. He made it while "on the stump" at a car-parts manufacturer called Moog Automotive, near St. Louis, Missouri. He had chosen foreign investment as a desperate, populist issue, yet the audience was cooler even than the Democrat had become used to. Unknown to him, the stump on which he was standing happened to be owned by Italians.

Tell that story to one of America's many grumblers about Japanese investment and the response usually is that Dukakis would never have made that mistake at a Japanese firm: he would have been able to tell the difference. Japanese firms do not blend into their surroundings. They are run by Japanese, the real decisions are made at the head office, foreign managers have no chance of promotion, and all the fancy design work is done at home, leaving the overseas factory as just an assembly plant for imported components.

This is why Japanese car factories are known rudely as "transplants": unnatural organs vulnerable to rejection by their new body. The word is an absurdity, for if the Japanese car factories are "transplants," the term should also be applied to any General Motors factory outside the company's home state of Michigan, and certainly any GM factory in Britain or Germany. The fact that the word is not usually applied in those cases shows that it is intended to be an insult.

The word is used far less often in Britain, and it would be hard to find a Briton who would have sympathized with Dukakis. Nissan is extremely popular in the northeast of England: it became even more so in January 1992 when, in the midst of Britain's gloomy, wintry recession, it announced plans to expand output there by a third (to 300,000 cars a year), to invest £200 million, and to hire 600 new workers, bringing its total to 4,600.

There is also a general reason why Britons would not emulate Dukakis: Britons are far more accustomed to foreign investment than Americans are, especially in the car industry. Ford made its first investment in Britain in the early 1900s, and since 1950, car making in Britain has been dominated by American "transplants." Vauxhall, owned by GM since 1925, and Ford, which established its own factories, have long been the biggest American presences in Britain, but Chrysler also entered the market by purchasing the Rootes car company in 1967, with factories in Coventry and Glasgow.

Until it sold the loss-making Rootes to France's Peugeot for just one dollar (yes, one dollar) in 1979, Chrysler also provided the extreme example of the "American style" of management. Although the former Rootes was nominally run by British managers, in fact the bigger decisions were all made at the head office in America. In particular, whenever there was a strike at Rootes, American managers would first seek to handle the negotiations by telephone from the United States, and then fly in to sort it out. So Britons are used to the idea that in multinationals, decisionmaking often stays at the head office, for good or for ill.

For that reason, the arrival of Nissan in northeast England in 1986, of Toyota in Derbyshire in the Midlands in 1989–93, and the gradual buildup in operations by Honda at Swindon, to the west of London, raised few sensitivities about Japanese methods. The only area of concern lay in industrial relations. Where British car plants (including American transplants) had traditionally been fully unionized, with their factory workers represented by dozens of different unions competing with one another, Nissan proposed simply to have one union, which would not even be able to insist that all factory workers join it. This caused a bit of a flap among trade unionists, but none at all in the media or in public opinion. By 1986, the conventional wisdom in Britain was that one of the car industry's biggest weaknesses was that it had a union closed shop, with representation divided between several unions. So Nissan was not only seen as providing jobs, but was also seen as offering a better way of managing industrial relations.

This calm reaction would not be true of France or Italy, which is one reason why there are no Japanese car factories in those countries. However, America still offers the most extreme case of sensitivity about Japanese investment.

About thirty miles south of Nashville, in the small town of Smyrna, Tennessee, stands an attempt to fight such rejection. Nissan's ten-year-old car and truck plant is a huge complex of white, impersonal, low-rise buildings. But outside the main entrance stands a tall flagpole, at the top of which flies as large a sample of the Stars and Stripes as any patriot could hope for. This firm wears its Americanness like a badge.

The Japanese presence at Nissan in Tennessee has been pared to a minimum: just twenty-five expatriate Japanese managers and only a few cultural references. There are no morning exercises, and there is scarcely an *ikebana* (Japanese flower arrangement) to be seen. By the production line stand such American paraphernalia as basketball nets and Ping-Pong tables for use during breaks. The boss, Jerry Benefield, is as American as they come. Small wonder: he spent eighteen years working for Ford, ending up as manager of its Dearborn assembly plant. Most of his senior colleagues and his predecessor, Marvin Runyon, came from the same stable.

Nissan is the extreme case among the six Japanese carmakers settling into America. Honda has many more Japanese managers at its Ohio plant—three hundred expatriates out of total employment of around ten thousand. Toyota in Georgetown, Kentucky, lies in between with about seventy Japanese. But all face an awkward balancing act. The more Japanese they are, the more criticism and, perhaps, aggravation they attract, both locally and nationally. Stay Japanese or become local? The solution sounds obvious: become American, run by Americans, as quick as you can.

Yet it is not that simple. After all, these car multinationals are in the business of making money and building their market shares. The quicker the carmakers become "local," the greater the risk of degrading themselves to the style and practice of local rivals, losing the advantage of their superior methods. After all, the reason these firms are able to expand by investing overseas is that, currently, they are more successful than their American rivals, and they do things in a different, Japanese, way. So they must not become too American, too quickly. That is a common (if unprovable) criticism at Smyrna and, to a lesser extent, at its British plant: has Nissan merely imported Ford managers, with all their faults?

Ford faced the same problem after 1911 when it shipped its mass-production methods across to old-fashioned Europe, where the automobile had been invented and was still handmade by teams of craftsmen. At first, it managed to overcome resistance to this switch from highly skilled work to a more mundane, but more efficient, form of production. But after 1915, Ford lost control. In the bitter atmosphere of the First World War, Henry Ford's opposition to American entry to the war rebounded against him in Britain, where he was considered a German sympathizer. This hit Ford's sales, damaged morale at its plant, and weakened its control over its British managers. The result was that, despite Ford's intentions, in practice Ford's British plants had to compromise with European methods, and thus lost some of their mass-production advantages. Even now, Ford's factory at Dagenham, to the east of London, remains less efficient than its American factories. Such are the perils of becoming too "local."

In the Japanese case, this balance between being local and being Japanese is largely a question of timing. Ultimately, the Japanese carmakers do have to become local to succeed. But they must do so in their own way, at their own pace, not just in a fast, superficial manner. The reason they have to become local is not because they should adopt British or American ways, but rather that their preferred methods of lean, waste-free production and close relations with just-in-time suppliers cannot work across oceans. Japanese manufacturing systems have to be set up, in full, locally, with imported parts and remote decisions cut to a minimum. At the same time,

Toyota, Nissan, and the others will find it hard to expand their market share if they do not design their cars, and many of the thousands of parts contained in them, to meet local tastes.

The result is that in the short term, the more local the Japanese carmaker becomes, the worse it will fare. But in the long term—over a decade or more—the test of success will be localness. The Nissan and Toyota production systems, different though they are in details, do have one thing in common: both work best when the supply, design, and manufacturing chain is operating over a short distance. Those carmakers that succeed in building a more or less complete manufacturing, supply, and design organization in America and Europe will be likeliest to survive and prosper. In other words, it will be those carmakers that do just what the grumblers demand—cut imports, use local suppliers, and do R&D on the spot—that will become truly threatening to General Motors, Ford, Volkswagen, and Fiat.

———

One area in which localness is unavoidable is employment: factory workers more or less have to be Tennesseans or from the north of England, dealt with in their own way. Yet handling and recruiting people is a task at which the Japanese are famously different from their American or British counterparts. So how do the car companies work, as Japanese or locals?

In some ways, a comparison between Nissan and Toyota in America and the same firms' factories in Britain reveals as much about those two countries as it does about the firms. They are tuned in to local characteristics, moods, and interests. Walk around the plants: though the machinery is similar, the atmosphere is not. Nissan's British plant at Sunderland, in northeast England just south of Newcastle, may be slick by local standards, but it is grubbier and more human than its older Tennessean cousin or Toyota's newer Kentucky factory. There is more litter, and piped pop music blares out of the loudspeakers. Rules seem less strictly enforced. In the American plants, discipline is tighter, the atmosphere far more clinical. They are noisy, but the sound is of production machinery, not of music. Transistor radios can be heard in Nissan's American plant, but not many.

One big difference that is especially striking to a British observer is that in the American factories many of the welders and fitters are women. At Toyota's Kentucky plant, 25 percent of the 3,400 factory workers employed there in 1990 were women, doing jobs on the production line itself. That would not happen in a British car factory, and sure enough there are none to be seen on Nissan's production line in Britain. In that respect, Britain is more like Japan than America.

The trappings of Japaneseness are worn differently on either side of the Atlantic. British workers felt uncomfortable with the slogans common in Japanese factories, so there are none at Nissan in Britain's northeast, but the American plants are full of them: "Let's talk quality"; "Quality today, success tomorrow"; "Professional Results In Daily Efforts" (spot the acronym?); "Best die-change team, 1988"; "Be alert, don't get hurt." Company uniforms are voluntary in all three plants, but seem less widespread among British workers (though almost universal among the managers).

While Nissan uses its flag at Smyrna to underline its American-ness, the British plant has no such patriotic symbol, but neither does it have many Japanese decorations. Toyota in Kentucky seems less ashamed of its origins, with Japanese carp streamers and a huge red daruma (papier-mâché Buddhist monk) for luck. Morning exercises are broadcast on a television network called TNN (Toyota News Network) that has monitors throughout the factory and offices, but doing the exercises is purely voluntary.

Some other superficial appearances seem more Japanese—but are often more "Japanese" than Japan really is. Toyota in Kentucky and Nissan in Britain emphasize their managers' open plan, egalitarian offices. Yet in Nagoya and Tokyo many top managers have private offices (as do Nissan's American managers). Indeed Nissan's original Japanese boss in Britain had his own office, so he could spend the day in it reading his paper; it was Ian Gibson, his British successor, who came from Ford, whose idea it was to move into the open. Similarly the absence of parking privileges and separate dining rooms, celebrated features of the Japanese firm abroad, exaggerate the absence of hierarchy at home. Top bosses have their own privileges in Japan, such as use of a fleet of chauffeur-driven limousines. But exaggeration is the point: the aim is to make things appear strikingly different from American or British equivalents.

Negotiating arrangements differ markedly across the Atlantic. Of the three plants, only the British one has a recognized trade union, the Amalgamated Union of Engineering Workers. It is not a closed shop, and membership is low—about 35 percent of total employment and 50 percent of shop-floor workers—though managers claim to have encouraged people to join. And the main group talking shop with workers is not the union but a quarterly "company council," with delegates elected by all employees.

At Smyrna, Nissan discouraged union membership, fighting off an effort in 1989 by the United Auto Workers to organize the plant. The UAW has tried a little recruitment at Toyota's Kentucky plant but with scant response. At both plants managers suspect that the UAW plans to wait until the next phases of expansion and hiring are complete before it attempts another recruitment and representation drive.

This pragmatic response to local conditions is reflected in wages. To reduce the desire for formal negotiating sessions but to remove suspicions that Southern workers are being treated as low-cost, both of the American plants tie wages to national industry levels, taking an average of pay at American and other car firms in the United States. So workers are paid market rates, which generally places their pay above that in other local factory jobs in Kentucky and Tennessee. Nissan in Britain, however, gives its union a role by holding pay negotiation sessions every two years for which there are no formal industry benchmarks.

Both American firms use annual or semi-annual bonuses, and are searching for ways to link more of managers' pay to performance. But Peter Wickens, Nissan's British personnel director, rejects the idea of productivity pay or bonuses for workers or managers. It encourages "short-term thinking," he says. He is also puzzled by the fact that the Smyrna and Georgetown plants both have a pool of job applicants selected for them by their state governments, from which they make the final choice. Such a practice would puzzle any Briton, accustomed as all are to the idea of America as the home of rampant free-market capitalism and a minimum of government involvement. Yet the state governments are interfering in company recruitment procedures. Wickens would not dream of handing selection or filtering to anyone else, whether the union or a local government. That is his job.

———

But how good are these companies at actually doing their job: making cars? While employment mixes local and Japanese flavors, manufacturing is firmly Japanese. That, after all, is what Nissan and Toyota are skilled at. The methods of quality control they use are Japanese, and can be drilled, they find, into British and American workers and managers just as well as into Japanese employees. Much of the machinery is imported and differences in layout occur only because the American and British plants have more space and are newer than their Japanese counterparts.

Productivity, measured by cars per man-hour, is just as good as in Japan. But that comparison is not a very illuminating one, albeit for a most revealing reason. A car factory is not an independent unit: it is part of a much wider network of manufacturers, deliverers, designers, and, ultimately, salesmen. Once parts and ideas come to the assembly line, the overseas factories are virtually as good or bad as their Japanese counterparts at turning them into cars, which they send out of the factory doors. But the whole carmaking process is still not as efficient overseas as it is in Japan.

The trouble is that none of the overseas car firms is nearly as Japanese as the owners would like it to be. Critics think this means that Japanese firms prefer to import more parts and to retain control in Japan. But it is just the opposite. In the long run the key to being more Japanese is to import fewer parts and to transfer more control.

The essence of Japanese manufacturing cannot simply be wrapped up and shipped overseas. Two things are crucial: the elimination of waste in production and stocks by "just-in-time" delivery of parts; and close cooperation with parts suppliers over production quality as well as R&D. One cannot be achieved without the other. Neither is possible across oceans. This whole process has been called "lean production" by two professors at the Massachusetts Institute of Technology, James Womack and Daniel Roos, and a British professor at Cardiff Business School, Daniel

Jones, in their excellent book *The Machine That Changed the World*, published in 1990. They argue that lean production is taking over from the old "mass production" method pioneered by Ford and General Motors, because lean methods are more flexible and involve far less waste.

Production cannot be "just-in-time" and "lean" when parts are imported from thousands of miles away in Japan. These words are frequently used at the overseas plants, along with the other famous buzzwords of Japanese car production: *kanban, andon, kaizen*. But none of these words has yet been fully turned into action.

Toyota keeps three days' worth of stocks of imported parts in Kentucky, compared with one and a half days' worth of American parts. But it holds an average of just four hours' worth of stocks at its Japanese plants. It is not simply a question of distance: hundreds of miles in America can be crossed faster than thirty miles in crowded Japan. What matters is the certainty of supply schedules. To improve that, Toyota uses a transport firm, Ryder, to collect parts from American suppliers rather than relying on them to deliver. Some "just-in-time" delivery is possible: all three plants visited in both America and Britain boast that their car seats (which are too bulky to store) are made by local firms to synchronize with the car assembly line. But none can manage synchronous delivery for any other parts.

For some parts, the problem is scale. Engines and transmissions are usually made by car firms themselves, but with larger production runs than for cars since the same engine can be used in many different models. The small scale of overseas car output, therefore, makes it still sensible to import most engines from Japan. Nissan now assembles engines at Smyrna and Washington from imported kits; Toyota plans to make them at Georgetown when it doubles annual car output from 200,000 to 400,000 in the next few years. Honda already makes engines abroad.

But with most parts the problems are quality, reliability, and development. Until the Japanese arrived in the 1980s, American and British suppliers had to meet lower standards than are now demanded by the Japanese. They also had little experience either designing parts together with the customer or having the customer vet (and interfere with) the suppliers' own factories. Most European and American carmakers either make their parts themselves or draw up a specification and ask suppliers to tender for the right to build the part.

That is not the way the Japanese firms work. In Japan, they ask suppliers to do some of the design and development work for parts, and work closely with them to ensure that the quality is as good as the carmakers achieve on their own production lines. To do that, they not only need to find suppliers willing to work their way, but also they have to build a commercial relationship in which each is dependent on the other. That takes time, but also requires scale: as long as the carmakers' output—and thus demand for parts—is small, it is hard to force suppliers to change their ways.

All three factories prefer to have one supplier for each part. Ideally they would prefer that that supplier only work with them. In Britain, Nissan sends "supplier development teams" to parts firms to advise on the suppliers' own factories and to start designing new parts. Other firms are trying similar tactics. From the supplier's point of view, this can either be seen as irritating interference or as the helpful arrival of a free team of management consultants. Those who think the former is true tend to lose the Japanese business; those who believe the latter, get it and keep it. They do not always enjoy it, but they keep it.

What this means is that the logic of Japanese carmakers' own methods is pushing them to buy more parts locally—regardless of political rules about local content. Their "lean" production is impossible without it. All three claim local content of 60–80 percent, depending on the car. But they will not match Japanese efficiency until they hit 100 percent. Ultimately, that will require them to replicate the close-knit *keiretsu* (industrial groups linked by cross-shareholdings) they have in Japan. The members of the groups need not be owned by Japanese, though they often will be. (Toyota says that 35 percent of its 175 or so suppliers in America are wholly or partly Japanese-owned.) What matters is that they are local, and plugged in to the carmakers' own design, development, and production schedules.

———

If these local partner-suppliers are chiefly Japanese-owned, it will cause a great deal of annoyance in the host country, especially in America. This was foreshadowed during then president Bush's visit to Japan in early 1992, when he campaigned on behalf of the American car industry. Bush tried to persuade Japanese consumers to buy more American cars and for Japanese producers to buy more American car parts. He did not just mean imports to Japan: he also meant car parts made in America and used in America.

In 1991–92, Honda found itself at the center of quarrels in both America and Europe over the local content of its cars manufactured in America. Customs officials in America accused it of falsifying the figures for the local content of its cars made in Ontario, Canada, in order to qualify them for export to the United States under the U.S.-Canada Auto Pact. Under that pact, Honda can ship the cars across the border duty-free only if local content exceeds 50 percent. The disagreement extended also to cars made in Ohio, which Honda claims have a domestic American content of 75 percent, by which it means that 75 percent of the American price of the car is accounted for by local labor, parts, and other expenditures. Nonsense, said an under secretary at the Department of Commerce, Michael Farren, basing his comments on work by his department and by academic studies. Such figures are a sham, he said.

What an irony it was that almost at the same time colleagues of Farren in the U.S. government were saying exactly the opposite in meetings with officials from France and the European Commission: of course Honda Accords exported from Ohio to Europe are American cars; they have 75 percent local content. You cannot possibly count them as Japanese and thus exclude them.

This whole issue is nonsense. It is nonsense for two different sorts of reasons, however. The first is that local-content claims and counterclaims merely represent the efforts of businesses to get around bad laws. American and European firms do exactly the same thing as Japanese firms in similar circumstances, with similar bad laws. The law is at fault, not the local-content claim. The second reason is that arguments about local content are in fact only surrogate arguments against Japanese investment itself, regardless of the content. Generally, what critics dislike is that a company is

Japanese-owned. Where its content "really" came from is beside the point.

The first of these reasons is well-illustrated by the crazy juxtaposition of local-content rules linked to import quotas for Japanese cars with other local-content rules in the United States laid down by the Corporate Average Fuel Economy law of 1975. These separate fuel-economy targets for domestic and imported cars; a "domestic" car is defined as one with 75 percent or more American-made content. Fuel-economy targets are set for a manufacturer's whole model range, so carmakers establish a mixture of domestic and imported models to comply with the overall, average target.

Ford, for instance, deliberately raised the import content of its American-made Crown Victoria car in order to put this gas-guzzler in its foreign fleet, so that it could be balanced by its more economical Festiva car, which it imports from South Korea. Nissan similarly classifies the Sentra model that it makes at Smyrna as foreign, to balance its less economical imports, though it excludes it from its count of imports under the U.S.-Japan voluntary restraint deal for car imports. And on their joint venture production line at Fremont, California, Toyota and General Motors make two virtually identical cars, the Toyota Corolla and the Geo Prizm. Toyota calls the Corolla an import for fuel-economy purpose while GM calls the Prizm domestic. Does this make any sense?

Local-content worries would not exist if there were not restrictive laws such as those on fuel economy. More importantly, they would not be there if countries did not seek to restrict imports of completed products. Those barriers incite local-content frauds; it is the barriers themselves that are to blame.

The second reason—general opposition to Japanese investment—often appears almost subconsciously. In November 1991, for example, *Business Week* carried a long article headlined "Honda, Is It an American Car?" It sought, in an apparently careful and learned way, to dissect Honda cars to find the true origin of their content. Now, it is true that such content can be ambiguous; there is no doubt that there is plenty of room for the massaging of figures. Car companies employ auditors from the big accounting firms to certify the local content of their production at the same time as they are certifying that the company's financial accounts are true and fair. Accounting firms are famous for their "flexibility" in accounting, so they can certainly be persuaded to be flexible in certifying local content.

It is also true that such content audits are difficult, because the trail must be followed through suppliers' own factories. Just because a component in a Honda car happens to come from a factory in America does not necessarily mean that it should be counted as 100 percent American; it, in fact, might have been assembled from a combination of imported parts and locally made ones.

Yet *Business Week* did not recognize this genuine ambiguity. Instead it pursued a false one: the mere ownership of companies selling parts to Honda. It had an impressive chart called "The Riddle of a Crankshaft," in which it traced the crankshaft back to the steelmaker that produced the original steel bar: Copperweld Steel Company, which is 63.4 percent Japanese-owned. Next, the bar went to TFO Tech Company, a 100 percent Japanese-owned plant in Jeffersonville, Ohio, to be forged; then on to a 100 percent American firm, Metallurgical Services Company in Dayton, for heat treatment; back to TFO for more processing; and then to Honda. "Honda says the crankshaft . . . is 100 percent American because it is fabricated entirely in the U.S.," wrote *Business Week*. "But many of the suppliers are owned by Japanese companies. Thus it's hard to determine the true 'domestic content.'"

No, it is not in the least bit hard, based on the information given: the crankshaft is quite definitely 100 percent domestic. The only possible circumstance in which it would not be 100 percent domestic would be if the fabricators, regardless of their ownership, were importing part of its content. That could be true of a Japanese-owned firm, and it could also be true of an American-owned firm. One hopes that *Business Week* would also count parts from Italian-, British-, or German-owned suppliers as nondomestic, but one suspects not. The aim of the author is to oppose Japanese investment in general by ranking it as in some way alien, not to address the question of local content versus the imported sort.

Thus the Honda Civic is often described (by *Business Week* and others) as only 36 percent American, since 38 percent of its content (in 1989) was imported by Honda and 26 percent came from U.S.-based Japanese suppliers. At least some of that 26 percent ought to count as domestic to someone really interested in content; but it does not count as domestic to someone solely interested in opposing one sort of ownership.

A more interesting observation than the *Business Week* article has been made by the Economic Strategy Institute, a Washington-based think tank run by Clyde Prestowitz, a former Japan negotiator in the Department of Commerce. In a 1992 report called "The Future of the Auto Industry: It Can Compete, Can It Survive?" the institute pointed out that Japanese transplants appear to be choosing to import their parts from Japan even though local parts made by American firms are cheaper. For a small car and with a yen-dollar exchange rate of Y130, the institute reckoned American-brand parts would cost $3,389 while Japanese-brand parts cost $4,124. So Japanese transplants have been deliberately raising their own costs by $735 per car, or by even more at stronger yen exchange rates.

A comparison of this sort is inevitably too simplistic. The institute's estimate is unable to take account of such issues as quality, design suitability, long-term relationships, and so on. The institute cites the figure as part of an argument that the transplants have not, yet, lived up to expectation in terms of their contribution to the American economy, since, perversely, they are not buying parts even from competitive local suppliers. From the point of view of Ford, General Motors, and Chrysler, however, this should be pretty good news, since it shows that at least in one respect their Japanese rivals are not competing very hard. From the Japanese point of view, however, what it may well suggest is this: that the commercial pressures for using local sources are getting more and more powerful.

Another reason why many Americans, especially those in Washington or in American car parts firms, do not like the notion that Japanese carmakers prefer to buy their parts from Japanese-owned firms is that they suspect not uncompetitive behavior but rather anticompetitive behavior. These purchases are used to show that Japanese are thus reproducing their *keiretsu* industrial groups abroad, and *keiretsu* is a word generally thought of as a synonym for unfair. The keiretsu involve preferential purchasing from firms tied together by cross-shareholdings.

Yet this criticism will not get very far. Keiretsu are not illegal in America, even though the Federal Trade Commission has been ordered to investigate whether they might be defined as illegal under American antitrust laws. Nor are they unfair, unless all commercial competition is deemed unfair: Nissan, Toyota, and the other firms use them because to do so is commercially advantageous in the long term. Reliable quality, a close relationship over design, dependable delivery: these are all commercial factors. Contrary to what Americans often say and think, price is not the only commercial factor.

———

So far, no Japanese carmaker has managed to reproduce its native strengths abroad. For the time being, however, the weaknesses resulting from long supply lines and independent parts producers are being outweighted by other strengths, relative to their American and European rivals.

In Britain and America, Toyota and Nissan remain more efficient manufacturers than local rivals: their costs are lower thanks to their newer plants and younger workforces, and they produce cars that customers want. But not always: Nissan has fared badly in selling its luxury car, Infiniti, in America, and its British market share suffered in 1991 from a fight with its distributor. Nissan admits that its British plant is not yet making money, but says it is not losing much either. It expects the plant to move into profit in 1993 or 1994, once the scale of its production has increased. In 1992–93, Honda's American sales took a tumble. Nevertheless, the Japanese carmakers get things right often enough that their combined market share is still rising, and they can remain confident that they will soon be making good profits from car production abroad.

For how long? There is no guarantee that the good times will last. Many American and European firms are closing the gap in manufacturing productivity and quality. They are beginning to practice lean production. Some are even making cars that customers want. If there is one thing that Japanese managers respond to it is commercial pressure such as this. Toyota, Nissan, and the others will, therefore, seek to eliminate the weaknesses in their overseas production. In other words, they will become more local.

To achieve that, their most important task has already been outlined: to reproduce their parts networks in America and Europe. But there are also two other tasks. One is to shift more research and development from Japan to the overseas subsidiaries. The other is to find a way fully to exploit their foreign managers.

In a world instantly connected by a finger on a facsimile machine, it might seem unnecessary to decentralize research and development. One lab, one set of engineers, and a worldwide sales force would seem to be all that is needed if it is true that companies and markets are becoming more global. Yet markets are not global: tastes differ, even in cars. And as it becomes easier and cheaper to span the globe, knowledge of local wrinkles is becoming more important in beating off global rivals, not less.

This need not apply to basic research and design. Toyota needs only have one team inventing electric cars or ceramic engines—and sure enough, that is what it has. Some important components can be more or less standard, worldwide, notably the engine. But other sorts of research need to be done on the spot. This can involve the whole car, where a market has a special taste for a certain type (such as four-wheel drives in America). Or, more often, it involves particular parts and features. Moreover, closer links with parts suppliers require that the carmaker has designers and researchers nearby.

This is why all the big Japanese firms are setting up research centers in America and Europe. This often seems to be just a sop to political pressure to bring in higher-paid jobs; but in fact it is a commercial necessity. What all of these firms are evolving toward is a worldwide structure that resembles something like this: a strong Japanese parent with two full-range subsidiaries, one in Europe and one in America, both surrounded by a full range of suppliers. Each of the three will design cars and components to match local tastes. Ultimately, no components will be shipped across oceans, though some designs will be. But each will export cars to one another. A "European" car, for instance, would be designed and built in Britain for the local mass market, but also exported as a niche product to Japan and America. Such niche exports to Japan will be a rarity, but they will happen.

None of the Japanese firms is anywhere near this point; their range of one or two vehicles at each plant is too small. Honda in Ohio may be the closest, with its wider range and higher output, though its progress in Europe is slow. In mid-1991, Honda announced exactly this sort of intention, to shift from having worldwide models to having regional models. Six months previously, it had launched its Accord station wagon (or "estate car," as Britons would call it) in America, the first Japanese car to be both designed and built in the United States. By the end of the decade, all the Japanese carmakers wish to be doing this.

———

To manage that properly, however, all need to address the other task: how do they accommodate, keep, and fully exploit non-Japanese managers? This is a different problem from the one that is commonly alleged. The American and British managers of the Nissan and Toyota overseas manufacturing plants do not worry about their never becoming chairmen of the parent companies. Their chances of being chairmen of Ford or General Motors would be pretty slim too, even if they worked for Ford or GM. Moreover, the chances of becoming the parent firm's chairman would also be nonexistent (based on past experience) if they were a British manager at an American "transplant" in Britain. They might run Ford of Europe, or Vauxhall, but they stand no chance of taking over the top job in Detroit.

Nor is interference a big issue. There are few Japanese managers at Smyrna, Georgetown, and Washington, and those that exist are seen as teachers rather than meddlers, despite their slightly sinister-sounding names, such as "advisers," "coordinators," or "shadow managers." A few locals may resent them, but this resentment is not a major problem. Most decisions a plant manager must make could not be made in Tokyo anyway, so the need for head-office approval hardly matters to such people.

The problem the Japanese must address is, rather, an opportunity that could be grabbed—or missed. Apart from lean production and quality control, one of the other big domestic advantages of the best Japanese manufacturers has been the way they garner information within their own firm and how they use it to make decisions. Compared with the stereotyped Western firm, they operate from the bottom up rather than from the top down: information flows freely up the organization and decisions are made, or at least initiated, at relatively low levels. Some people call this "middle-up-and-down," because, in fact, the main center of initiative is in middle management. But whatever is the right description, the effect is the same: there is no team of generals that sends the orders to the troops.

In principle, that ought to make Japanese firms the ideal global companies. Information should flow up the overseas subsidiaries and to the parent; decisions would be heavily decentralized. But for that to happen, the foreign managers have to be treated the same way as domestic managers. They have to want to pass on information, have to trust that it will be taken seriously, and have to be given appropriate decisionmaking powers.

American and British managers are not about to leave in a huff, at least not in numbers sufficient to worry their employers. But this will become more of an issue as more design and development work is shifted overseas. Language, culture, and distance are all potential barriers. If Nissan, Toyota, and the others can overcome them, they have the chance to grow on such a worldwide scale that they would certainly overtake both General Motors and Ford in a decade or more. If not, they will have found the limits to their corporate power. The inability to reproduce their organizational and motivational strength will limit their ability to expand around the globe.

———

Have the Japanese carmakers expanded too slowly or too fast? Have they localized to a sufficient extent? These are the main questions posed by the massive investments made abroad by Toyota, Nissan, Honda, and the smaller Japanese car firms.

Japanese carmakers have taken the most cautious approach to investing abroad of the big industries being studied in this book: all have chosen organic growth rather than sudden, dramatic growth through acquisition. Yet, partly because they began the process early in the 1980s, the carmakers are also further down the road than other Japanese multinationals, and they have been more successful.

The organic method of growth is the first reason for that success. It has meant that, more often than not, the companies remain in control of their problems rather than being swamped by them. It has not all been smooth sailing: Mazda's factory at Flat Rock, Michigan, for example, has been beset by labor troubles, a high accident rate, and local controversy. It is always tempting to blame such problems on exaggeration by muckraking media folk. But a well-balanced and convincing 1991 book on the plant, *Working for the Japanese: Inside Mazda's American Auto Plant,* by Joseph and Suzy Fucini, shows that these problems were genuine, and that they came about mainly because of hasty, ill-conceived management.

Those American Mazda managers at Flat Rock appear to have shared a weakness common in British factories: they sought to exploit their newfound freedom from local ways of doing things and old restraints by becoming more dictatorial, not more consensual. These were, in other words, mistakes made by giving too much power early on to local American managers.

At present, the Japanese carmakers that have fared best have been those that maintained fairly tight Japanese control. Nissan in Britain is an exception to that rule: it is quite autonomous, yet seems to have performed well. In most cases, however, Japanese control must be maintained until the plant is more mature and until local managers have been fully schooled in Japanese ways. Nissan's British plant may have fared better because its British managers are relatively young. The mistake elsewhere may be to appoint seasoned old hands from the local car companies.

In the longer term, however, all the car companies will have to set up stand-alone local subsidiaries with a full range of local suppliers, partners, and designers. Honda's claim that its cars will be regional as opposed to global is probably an exaggeration; tastes do not differ that much. But the emphasis will have to be regional, and the companies will have to use their regional centers as genuine sources of information and expertise for the whole worldwide company, treating Americans and British as they would middle and senior managers in Japan. Those car firms that do achieve this can look forward to a period of dominance in the car business as long as that which GM enjoyed after 1950. Those that do not achieve it will find that their business has peaked, as GM's did after 1975.

4

MUGGED IN HOLLYWOOD

The New Year's gifts:
even the baby at the breast
puts out her little hands.
ISSA

Coming to see cherry bloom
he had his money stolen—
the country bumpkin.
SHIKI

THE story had everything. An American cultural icon falling to a foreign power. The glamor and personality of Akio Morita, just about the only Japanese businessman that more than a tiny number of Americans has heard of. The thought that Columbia Pictures' new Japanese owner might censor any references the studio's movies might make to Japan or to the Second World War, or, more sinister still, that it might deliberately seek to manipulate the minds of Americans. The prospect of a tussle between America's show business elite and the superefficient Japanese, to whom egomania is virtually a swear word. How would the Japanese manipulate their software businesses to support sales of their hardware? How long would they tolerate vastly expensive projects like the $70 million that Columbia spent on Steven Spielberg's film

Hook, an update of Peter Pan that was released in December 1991?

The selling of America was now clear for all to see. It is small wonder that Sony's purchase of Columbia Pictures (which, confusingly, owns two studios, Columbia and Tri Star) for $3.4 billion in 1989 caused an outcry. That outcry had barely died down when, in late 1990, Sony's much bigger archrival, Matsushita, went even further by spending $6.1 billion on MCA, owner of Universal Studios.

No one yet knows the ending. The Japanese adventure in Hollywood is barely into its second reel. Yet what we do know is that all expectations have been confounded. Right after the titles rolled, Hollywood started its usual tricks: it was mugging the rich guests. Hollywood put its hands into these fat Japanese wallets and took out billions and billions of dollars. This has also happened to an array of smaller Japanese investors, dabbling in film finance chiefly for tax reasons. But it has happened most spectacularly at Columbia Pictures, recently renamed Sony Pictures, and at MCA. Neither Sony nor MCA is likely to earn their money back from Hollywood in less than a decade. And in 1992–93, both firms were looking groggier than they had in living memory, hit by a combination of the slump in Tokyo share prices and a sharp economic slowdown in their home market, Japan. The entertainment investments have been profitable at the operating level, but have made too little money to cover the debts incurred for their purchase.

How could this happen? That is the simplest, but also the most important, question posed by the Japanese firms' investments in the American entertainment business. Beyond that, these investments raise two main questions: why have Sony and Matsushita felt obliged to handle their entertainment software businesses in a completely different way from their conventional electronic hardware businesses? And might these investments actually pay off in the long run (a run that Japanese firms are famous for) because of a synergy between software and hardware that has not yet been imagined?

———

The Great Hollywood Mugging is a surprise because Japan's big electronics companies are not tourists on their first trip away from home. Far from it; they are among Japan's most experienced overseas investors. Sony, the best known of all the electronics firms abroad, has had factories in Taiwan since 1967, in San Diego, California, since 1972, in Spain since 1973, and in Wales since 1974. It employs some thirty thousand people at its manufacturing plants in Europe, the United States, and Asia (excluding Japan), and that does not count the thousands more employed in sales and distribution. Matsushita Electric Industrial, the world's biggest consumer-electronics firm, seller of the National, Panasonic, Technics, and Quasar brands, and far bigger than Sony, began manufacturing overseas even earlier, opening its first radio assembly plant in North America (Puerto Rico) in 1965 and buying Motorola's consumer-products division in 1974. These firms have operated across borders for many years. You would expect these multinationals to make all their moves with assurance, expertise, and grace.

You might expect that, but you would be wrong. Since 1988, Sony and Matsushita have both been conducting an ambitious and costly experiment, one that has not proceeded at all smoothly. It is an experiment first within the field of consumer electronics: they are seeking to merge their long-held supremacy in electronic hardware for consumers with a business at which they are novices, namely entertainment "software," by which is meant films, television programs, video games, and music. Sony began Japan's drive into software with its $2 billion purchase of CBS Records in 1988; Columbia and MCA then represented an even bigger leap.

If that were not ambitious enough, this is also an experiment in global management: by moving into Hollywood, Sony and Matsushita have become Japan's first genuinely global firms, letting some of their main worldwide businesses be controlled from overseas. This is an extraordinary development, almost certainly the most daring move being made by any big Japanese company. Allowing Americans to run one of their most important, and expensive, activities is not only daring but extremely risky. Kenichi Ohmae of McKinsey, and Sumantra Ghoshal and Christopher Bartlett (from INSEAD and Harvard Business School) will be delighted by the fact that Sony and Matsushita have now established the worldwide headquarters of their software divisions in the United States. Such a move exemplifies these management writers' efforts to convince international firms that to become truly and successfully global they need to break the dominance of their domestic headquarters. Yet the consequent loss of control is proving less than invigorating.

Plenty of Japanese firms talk about sharing control between three headquarters—in Japan, America, and Europe. But it is only talk. Control remains in Japan. Until now that has been true at Matsushita and Sony. When Japan's two biggest consumer-electronics firms built factories abroad to make their hardware, they gave some say to local managers over design details, production levels, and marketing. But the big decisions were still being made in Osaka and Tokyo. In entertainment, however, things are different. Those businesses are headquartered in America, not just in name but in reality. Control over a 7 percent slice of Matsushita's worldwide sales has been delegated to Los Angeles, and control of more than 20 percent of Sony's sales is divided between New York and California. The Japanese owners have an influence, but only at the margin. So not only have the Japanese spent money, they have also ceded influence. The explanation is the same for both these events, even though one was accidental and the other deliberate.

Clues that a mugging might be taking place ought to have been there right from the start, if anyone had cared to look. By the way in which they handled the acquisitions, both Sony and Matsushita showed that they doubted their own abilities to deal with the entertainment business. During the negotiations both ceded surprising amounts of responsibility and initiative to local American advisers, people who were not even directly employed by the Japanese. The most important of these advisers in both cases was Michael Ovitz, the chairman and founder of Creative Artists Agency (CAA), the most powerful of Hollywood's talent agencies. Ovitz's position as an intermediary between the studios and the stars gave him exactly the blend of independence, expertise, and personal relationships that the purchasers needed. He was also an impressive character, impressive in ways that appealed to Japanese businessmen: a shrewd and hard negotiator who manipulated people and their image of him not through flashiness or charisma but rather through a carefully understated aggression.

Ovitz took virtual sole control of Matsushita's venture into Hollywood. For several months, he and some assistants from CAA apparently lectured a team of managers from Matsushita on the basics of the entertainment industry. He was instrumental in Matsushita's choice of MCA over other possible acquisitions, and he personally selected the lawyers, investment bankers, and public relations advisers who represented the Japanese firm during the transaction. Normally, an acquirer chooses its own advisers.

Ovitz made himself the sole channel through which those advisers contacted Matsushita, as well, more remarkably, as the sole channel through which communication flowed between the Japanese firm and MCA. In fact, according to Connie Bruck, writing in the September 9, 1991, issue of *The New Yorker,* it was only at the final stage in the negotiations that top executives from Matsushita and MCA actually met, at a dinner at New York's Plaza Athenee hotel. (Ovitz does not confirm or deny stories of this sort.) This might have been understandable if Matsushita had been planning all along to boot out MCA's management: in that case, why bother to meet them? But it was not; virtually from the start, Matsushita had intended to keep MCA's bosses in place, including Lew Wasserman, who had run the firm since 1946, and Sidney Sheinberg, who took over as president in 1973.

Part of this can be put down simply to the influence and personality of Michael Ovitz. But most of it has another explanation: a blend of the dazzling effect that Hollywood has on most outsiders, with the fact that, as Japanese manufacturers of electronics hardware, Sony and Matsushita felt culturally a million miles away from the entertainment business. They needed someone to hold their hands; and Hollywood, that factory of fantasies, has long succeeded in creating the myth that its business can only be understood and dealt with successfully by insiders.

Sony's first thought when it paid its $3.4 billion for Columbia was, indeed, that it would hire Michael Ovitz to run the firm. Perhaps because he knew what a mess it was in, he declined. At least that is the account he has allowed to become conventional wisdom; Mr. Ovitz is always careful to deliver his views "off the record" and through friends, but in such a systematic way that the idea becomes firmly established. My interview with Ovitz was firmly off the record. Bruck has an alternative version: that Ovitz wanted to run CBS Records as well as Columbia, a proposal that Sony rejected. Whichever version is true (and both are equally plausible), this sent Sony hunting elsewhere for new outside managers. The offer prospectus issued by the Blackstone Group, Sony's investment bankers, for the Columbia deal says that Sony "began the process of interviewing entertainment industry executives who were known in the industry for their managerial expertise."

Well, it just goes to confirm that you should never believe things that are written in financial prospectuses. At any rate, Sony did not hire anybody known for "managerial expertise": it actually hired two film producers, who thus had plenty of experience in making a movie but none at all in running a big company. Columbia Pictures is not just a pair of studios, but also includes a cinema chain (Loews), a television production company, and what was then a joint venture with General Electric, RCA-Columbia Home Video (Sony has since bought GE's half share). The producers brought in to run this entertainment conglomerate were Peter Guber and Jon Peters, whose most recent claims to fame had been *Rain Man,* starring Dustin Hoffman and Tom Cruise, and *Batman,* financially one of the most successful films ever made. Jon Peters had earlier become a Hollywood legend by graduating from being Barbra Streisand's hairdresser to being her lover and her film producer.

With the recruitment of Guber and Peters, Sony quickly found that what is needed above all in Hollywood is an open checkbook. To gain their services, Sony had to buy their small production firm, Guber-Peters Entertainment, for $200 million. It transpired that the pair had a contract with Warner Bros., part of Time-Warner, another media giant, which stipulated that they could work only for that film studio. So Sony bought Warners' contract out with cash and asset swaps that Warners reckons were, altogether, worth more than $500 million. Sony says the figure was lower, but has failed to offer an alternative value.

Sony then gave Guber and Peters a deal that was generous even by Hollywood's lavish standards, with annual salaries of $2.75 million, to be raised to $2.9 million after three years, with both figures adjusted for inflation. They and five underlings were promised a $50 million bonus pool, plus 8 percent of any rise in Columbia's notional value over five years. Not content with that, Columbia's new managers also reached for Hollywood's favorite strategic tools: new corporate jets and a list of party caterers.

In all, including its assumption of Columbia's debts and the cost of renovating studio facilities, Sony shelled out at least $5 billion in 1989–91, possibly as much as $6 billion. That compares with annual profits for the whole of Sony during that period of, at best, $830 million. Nobody in Hollywood thinks the Japanese firm will ever get value for that money. With splendid understatement, Michael Schulhof, the New York–based head of Sony's software businesses, admitted to me that "when you rebuild, you always overdo it a bit." He said it will take three years (from the purchase) to tell whether the firm is working. Sony is now "tightening up the running of the studio," he added.

The oddest part of this whole affair is that Schulhof, Sony's most senior American employee, is about as tailor-made for the Japanese firm as any foreigner could be. Unlike the case of Jon Peters or of Peter Guber, it is easy to see why Schulhof fits in and is trusted. Like Akio Morita, the chairman, and many of the other top Japanese in the firm, Schulhof is a physicist by training and early career, one who boasts of having published thirty papers on physics and having patents in eight Sony products.

Morita is the sort of person who, when sitting at a conference, will suddenly jump up and go to try to fix the sound system if he thinks it is not working properly. One can imagine Schulhof doing the same thing. Though clearly a determined and businesslike character, he is more understated than the typical American executive (a little like Ovitz, if with less obvious hustle). In his case, Sony showed it can pick like-minded people—so why not in Hollywood? Almost certainly it is because of the Hollywood myth that only creative types with fancy hairdos can handle the business.

Peters, whom most critics blame for the overspending, left abruptly in May 1991, his departure eased by a generous severance deal. Nevertheless, Hollywood insiders still think Sony Pictures is top-heavy. It is the only large Hollywood firm to have a big central corporate team, a team of American bosses whose skills and functions appear to duplicate those of the managers actually running the two studios, Columbia and Tri Star. Not only that, Sony Pictures is the only Hollywood firm that has its ultimate head office in New York. Others are controlled by New York firms, including Time-Warner. But at Sony Pictures, Schulhof is directly in control. And the doors continue to revolve: in October 1991, the chairman of the Columbia Pictures studio, Frank Price, was pushed out even though he had only joined the firm a year and a half previously. It takes far longer than that to turn a slate of movies from mere ideas into actual celluloid and then cash flow. His place was taken in late 1991 by Mark Canton, previously at Warners.

CBS Records, Sony's earlier foray into entertainment, has also had some ups and downs. Walter Yetnikoff, the flamboyant character who ran the firm profitably after Sony bought it, left suddenly in September 1990. Three months earlier he had signed a new three-year contract to run the renamed Sony Music Entertainment, a deal reportedly worth $25 million. Yetnikoff had, however, been instrumental in Sony's hiring of Guber and Peters for Columbia. And in 1991, Sony signed a lavish contract with Michael Jackson to make his next six records for Sony and to act in films for Columbia. The deal has been estimated to be worth from $40 million to $60 million for Jackson and includes the highest royalty rate of any recording star. But it is quite a gamble for Sony. If Jackson's new records sell anywhere near as well as his 1983 *Thriller* album, which sold 40 million copies worldwide, then the deal will pay off handsomely. But his popularity has been declining.

Are the changes at the top at Sony Pictures and Sony Music a sign that the Japanese are moving in at last? No: Sony has only one Japanese manager at Columbia, observing the firm's Culver City studio. The tightening will be done by Schulhof in New York, if it is done by anyone, and the companies will continue to be run by Hollywood types. It is the same story at MCA, albeit without so many jets and parties. The big difference between the two acquisitions was that, while Columbia's management was turbulent, MCA's was stable. Matsushita left Lew Wasserman and his team in place. Its few Japanese staff are not even at the studio.

Matsushita has long been more conservative than the brassier Sony. In MCA, it chose a firm with a similar spirit; under Wasserman it has long kept a far lower profile than is typical for Hollywood. Still, the two Japanese firms' policies toward the entertainment business is being driven by the same simple point: the parent company's obvious ignorance. When Japanese firms operate factories abroad, they act as teachers, bringing in their superior manufacturing methods. In the entertainment business it is different. The Americans are the teachers and the Japanese are the students.

Although the Japanese can learn about the entertainment business, they cannot take it over unless American culture ceases to dominate the world music and film markets. The vital ingredient, in other words, is in America. This will be true as long as English-speaking popular culture (i.e., American culture) dominates world markets for film, television, and music, which looks like it will be a very long time indeed. And in both music and film, much of the profit goes to those who add the value—the stars and the producers—regardless of who owns the firms. Hence the mugging. Aware of this, Sony and Matsushita have concluded that, if they are to stay in entertainment, they have do things the American way. That means no penny-pinching, and it entails giving the American managers a free hand. Logical as this may sound, it is an uncomfortable formula for Japanese bosses accustomed to being in control.

Of course, Japanese firms are celebrated for taking the long-term view, so perhaps they can endure this discomfort. MCA is making profits, albeit smaller than in previous years, and it is too soon to say whether, despite their autonomy, the top managers will lose interest now that Matsushita owns the firm. Sony's music business also remains profitable, with CBS Records (renamed Sony Music) providing $450 million in operating profits on sales of $3.4 billion in the year to March 31, 1991.

Life is getting tougher for these Japanese firms because of financial frolics back in Japan. Neither Sony nor Matsushita can rely on cheap capital any longer. Already, Sony has found it harder than it expected to raise new equity to repay the debt taken on with Columbia. In November 1991, for example, its Japanese parent sought to float off up to a third of Sony Music Entertainment in Tokyo. But the issue bombed, with no takers at all for the shares on the first day of trading. The issue was underwritten, so Sony got its $915 million, but at the cost of its reputation and that of Nomura Securities, the chief underwriter, as well as of slumping share prices.

To get even a modest return on the billions of dollars that the Japanese have put in will require big and steady profits from the studios, something that no studio has ever been noted for. Sony Pictures is successful at the box office; together with the music business, it is expected to provide around $800–900 million in operating profits to the parent in 1993. But that is before accounting for depreciation and debt servicing; since the investments totalled around $8 billion, even a modest 10 percent charge would wipe out those profits. Alternatively, future returns could be boosted by something magic and, currently, unimagined: a big impact from the software businesses on sales of hardware. Synergy, in other words. Currently, the hardware and software businesses are far apart—not least in the manner in which the businesses are managed.

———

A visit to Matsushita's headquarters in Osaka, or Sony's in Shinagawa in Tokyo, could not be more different from one to these companies' offices in Hollywood. Despite a generous dose of fancy bits of electronic equipment, the Osaka and Shinagawa headquarters are workmanlike, roll-your-sleeves-up kinds of places. The same is true of Matsushita's American headquarters in Secaucus, New Jersey, or even Sony's flashier building in Manhattan. And it is certainly true of a visit to Sony's main British factories in Bridgend in South Wales.

The way in which Sony and Matsushita manage their overseas manufacturing operations is much more typically Japanese than are their adventures in Hollywood: foreign managers, foreign employees, but well "shadowed" by Japanese expatriate staff. Here the Japanese see themselves as the teachers. This was well illustrated by a letter published in the *Financial Times* on November 22, 1991, written by Tony Parr, a former Sony employee. He wrote:

> Sir, Re Christopher Lorenz's article, "Japan should give locals a chance" (November 15), I worked for Sony at its Bridgend CRT plant as the utilities engineer for several years during the 1980s and can therefore comment, at least on Sony's practices, with some authority.
> Sony had a shadowing policy then, and it has one now. Its

policy (and probably shadowing policies in general) had several effects:

> Japanese process engineers and managers were able to influence buying decisions in favour of Japanese products;
> The cost of these people was included in factory budgets as consultancy, at consultancy rates. The general effect was that profits were transferred back to Japan;
> Frustration was felt by "local" staff because of the feeling of constantly having their shoulders looked over and having to justify their actions to their shadows.

> The differences in attitudes towards work [between Japanese and British] are cultural and will not be changed by "locals" taking Japanese language lessons and having beers with Aki after work. If the Japanese are happy to lead a way of life that to us is insane, then good luck to them.
> However, it does not follow that we should emulate them. By "us" I mean most of the local engineers and staff employed by Sony.

There is nothing unusual about Sony's shadowing policy; most Japanese firms put expatriate Japanese into such positions, calling them advisers or consultants or associates or some such euphemism. They are used to maintain control and to act as the conduits for the transfer of technology and management techniques. But Tony Parr's letter is worth quoting because it puts into perspective a different claim often made about Sony and Matsushita: that, having been overseas manufacturers for almost twenty years, in their factories they have become more "local" than most Japanese multinationals.

In some respects, they have been innovators, it is true: Sony, the second Japanese manufacturer to set up shop in Wales when it arrived in Bridgend in 1974, was the first in Britain to negotiate a single-union agreement. It handed the Amalgamated Engineering Union the sole rights to organize its workers, and did so with a broad set of conditions stipulating, for instance, that there could not be strike action until a set procedure for settling disputes had been exhausted. Matsushita followed Sony into Wales, setting up a single-union deal with the General and Municipal Workers

Union. To an American or Japanese this may not seem strange, but to a Briton it was new. At the nearby Hirwaun television plant, jointly owned by Hitachi and Britain's GEC, there were seven different unions.

Moreover, Sony's chairman, Akio Morita, frequently makes speeches about his policy of "global localization"; similar sentiments are echoed by top people at Matsushita. And most of the top jobs in the overseas operations are indeed taken by locals. At Sony, the heads of Sony America and Sony Europe, Michael Schulhof and Jakob Schmuckli, respectively, are even on the parent company's main board.

Yet this is where the truth begins to separate from the rhetoric. To have foreigners on the board is indeed unusual among Japanese companies, but it is not as significant as it looks. Unlike in America or Britain, a Japanese board of directors is largely a ceremonial institution, with far too many members to have any effective executive role. At Sony, Schulhof and Schmuckli share board meetings with thirty-three others. The real management decisions are made outside the main board, by the top Japanese executives, led by Morita and his president, Norio Ohga. That is what makes the entertainment business so exceptional; it is the only case where the big decisions are made by foreigners, and outside Japan.

Nevertheless, Sony's multinational management structure has evolved over time in an interesting way. In the 1970s, when it began to spread manufacturing overseas, it set up separate subsidiaries country by country, headed up by what Ken Iwaki, Sony's deputy president, calls "country kings." Each of these locals reported directly to Tokyo. For many products, Japan was the main manufacturing base, but sales and marketing decisions (including price) were devolved to the country kings. This produced a bad botch-up in the early 1980s when a downturn in the world economy coincided with poor sales for Sony's videorecorder standard, the Betamax. Since the factories felt no responsibility for overseas sales, they just shipped lots of the product, regardless; thanks to that, in 1981, Sony had record profits and of course paid Japanese tax on it. But the profits had not really been made, for what was happening was that stocks of unsold videorecorders were piling up overseas.

That bad experience forced a change. Since 1983, Sony has given each business group in Tokyo overall responsibility for overseas sales, marketing, and stock levels. Then, there were six such groups; now the firm has twenty-three. Schulhof plays down the business groups' role, saying that it is something of a fiction: just coordination, really. There may be something to that, since coordination is bound to be the main reason for the group's existence. Nevertheless, it still means that the basic power has returned to Japan—probably rightly.

One reason for this is cited by Iwaki. In the mid-1980s, once the yen began to strengthen against the dollar and the Deutschmark, like other Japanese manufacturers Sony accelerated its expansion of production capacity abroad. Soon, local factories accounted for a sufficiently large proportion of sales that the Japan-based managers felt that decisions involving production quantities had to be shifted to local managers, to be made in connection with those involving sales and marketing. At the same time, new factories were regional producers rather than being set up country by country, so Sony also set up a regional headquarters structure for America, Europe, and Asia. But there was also another factor pulling in the opposite direction. In the 1970s, many of Sony's products were quite different country by country, depending on local tastes and circumstances. But in the 1980s, the firm's major products were essentially global ones, such as the Walkman personal stereo, the compact disk player, and the 8mm video camera. So decisions about such products had to be made globally—i.e., in Tokyo.

Now, therefore, things happen like this: the big, strategic decisions on major products are made centrally in Tokyo, helped by meetings twice a year between the top managers of all various regional headquarters. Of those two meetings, one takes place in Tokyo, one outside Japan. Once those strategic decisions have been made, other decisions—about prices and production quantities, for example—are devolved to regional management. Advertising campaigns are run separately, but Tokyo is trying to coordinate them. Country managers have the authority to make spending decisions only up to about Y1 billion ($8 million), while regional chairmen have double that spending power. Above those sums (not large by the standards of multinationals), spending requires permission from an investment committee in Tokyo.

Basically, research and development is centralized. However, as at Matsushita, local R&D centers concentrate on adapting technology to local requirements (e.g., different voltages or broadcasting systems). They also do some work on production technology, now that more factories are located abroad. Occasionally, basic development does take place abroad; according to Iwaki, the digital video-tape recorder was developed in Britain, at which point similar work in Tokyo was stopped. But most R&D is done in Japan.

Personnel has gradually become a more international affair, with transfers of foreign staff between countries, although this remains rare. In 1991, for example, the number two man at Sony's Bridgend television factory, a Briton, moved to Pittsburgh in America to run the TV factory there. Currently about seven hundred Japanese staff are working at factories overseas, and about three hundred are working in sales. All this means that more and more of Sony's Japanese staff have international experience: about 25 percent of administrative staff have served abroad and, reckons Iwaki, about 5–10 percent of the engineering staff. More than half of the board of directors have worked abroad.

The whole picture was summed up nicely by Iwaki in a speech in November 1990:

> Decentralization is often cited as an effective tool to motivate people. There is always an irresistible temptation to delegate responsibility as the company grows in size. In retrospect, Sony's localization in the initial stages was not decentralization in the true sense. It was simply a state of little control and coordination. . . . Decentralization with the absence of a common thread that ties the corporation together will only lead to disintegration or degeneration. Without doubt, decentralization and delegation will continue at Sony as operations spread out over the globe, but it will always be coordinated from a global perspective.

In other words, a global firm cannot afford to delegate too much power to locals. The risk is that it will fragment.

It is a similar story at Matsushita, although the manner in which it is told is somewhat different. There, the facts are smothered by the firm's cultural trait of wishing to place everything in the context of a syrupy philosophy, a trait inherited from the founder, the late Konosuke Matsushita, who died in 1989.

In the lobby in Secaucus, New Jersey, there is a bust of Matsushita, underneath which it says, "His philosophies are the compass we use to guide ourselves around the world." Even in this office building, there are slogans: "It takes all of us to be the best"; "Panasonic: where the customer comes first." The first few words of the corporate brochure of Matsushita Electric Corporation of America, the main American subsidiary, are written by the parent firm's current chairman, Masaharu Matsushita, son of the founder. He states the firm's corporate principle as: "Through our industrial activities, we strive to foster progress, to promote the general welfare of society and to devote ourselves to furthering the development of world culture."

This is the firm, remember, that pioneered the Japanese habit of having a stirring company song and of early morning exercises. Most Japanese firms do not have a song, but in the early days of reporting about Japan's export effort, Matsushita featured so prominently that it must have seemed to many that it was a typical company. It is not. No other hugely rich Japanese entrepreneurs have followed Konosuke Matsushita's example and set up a foundation with a name like the PHP Institute: the letters stand for peace, happiness, and prosperity.

One should not be too cynical about Matsushita's feel-good philosophy. But this characteristic has to be borne in mind when interviewing the firm's top executives, because so much of what they say is imbued with it. In other words, they cannot give a straight answer. Ask Koju Suzuki, who is the managing director in charge of the overseas projects division at Matsushita's Osaka headquarters, how his firm chooses between local production and export, or local decisionmaking and the central sort, and his answer is full of philosophy. His firm's aim is to contribute to the community, to serve local society; the profits it makes are the fruit of its contribution to society.

Try a similar question to Richard Kraft, chief operating officer and thus the most senior American at Matsushita Electronic Corporation of America (MECA), and you get a similar answer, albeit laced with some economic terms. His firm must strive for balance between the economies of the United States and Japan. A big bilateral trade deficit causes aggravation that is bad for both sides; MECA must seek to produce locally roughly 50 percent of what it sells locally in order to ensure mutual prosperity between Japan and the United States.

This is all worthy stuff, even if it is economic and commercial nonsense. Political attitudes in America to Japanese exports make Kraft's words a forgivable nod in the direction of the hotheads; in Britain, where virtually nobody worries about the trade balance with Japan, these words would not be heard. What is really odd about all this is that these philosophical words bear precious little relation to Matsushita's actions, which have been based on admirably hardheaded commercial reasoning.

Compared with Sony and with many other Japanese electronics firms, Matsushita has been slow to shift production abroad, let alone decisionmaking. In 1985, Matsushita's overseas production accounted for only about 12 percent of its worldwide sales (levels of 20–30 percent were typical among foreign competitors). Then came the rapid rise of the yen against the dollar and other currencies. And then, perfectly sensibly, Matsushita changed its policy, announcing a plan to shift a total of 25 percent of its output overseas, beginning with relatively low-tech, low value-added items such as radios and electric fans. At MECA the targets look higher, partly because of political sensitivities, but probably mainly because of a desire to snuggle closer to the rich local market: Kraft says his target is for American production to make up 50 percent of American sales in dollar terms by 1995, against roughly 20 percent at the start of 1991 and 30 percent at the start of 1992.

The point is that if Matsushita's philosophy had actually been followed in practice, the firm would already have transferred a far higher proportion of its production to America, Europe, and elsewhere by 1985. It did not do so for perfectly good commercial reasons—it found it more efficient to manufacture in Japan for export—and because of its own conservatism. Although the firm does own factories all over the world (it even has one in Tierra del

Fuego, at the southern tip of South America), it is not a terribly international, cosmopolitan place. The staff members are very Japanese, relatively few speak foreign languages, and some probably even see Tokyo as a foreign country.

The company recognizes that parochialism, and is making quite an ambitious effort to change it. Foreign managers have long been flown to Japan to learn the ropes—how to organize factories, exchange business cards, get drunk with their colleagues. Currently, the firm brings in about 700 of such trainees each year, albeit for short periods. In 1991, however, Matsushita took a bolder step. It launched a program to import 100 foreign managers a year from overseas subsidiaries into its Japanese offices and factories. Naturally, they will learn a lot while they are there. But the real aim is to shock Matsushita's Japanese managers into learning how to deal with foreign colleagues and issues.

Advocates of this therapy at Matsushita's Osaka headquarters wanted to be even more ambitious, bringing in 1,000 foreign employees a year. The firm is acutely aware that it is years behind Sony in developing an international corps of managers, whether Japanese or foreign. Its bosses fear that its stay-at-home managers could hold it back, now that it is at last pushing more manufacturing overseas and that it has become a Hollywood media mogul.

Yet some shocks are too great: the 1,000-a-year plan was scaled down because it would have put a huge strain on overseas units. After all, there will be no extra Japanese managers going abroad to balance numbers. The idea is that the foreigners work alongside Japanese equivalents, but not just as assistants: they will have their own responsibilities. They will not all be top managers, though some will be; the rest will include engineers and younger employees. In any case, they will add to the headcount in Japan and have to be replaced back home. The "100" project was launched in April 1991, and the first foreigners arrived in August of that year. The visitors are from all around the world, which is why those who need it are given language training—not in Japanese, but in English. Neither they nor their Japanese colleagues are allowed to use interpreters: they are supposed to communicate in English.

Even 100 a year will strain the foreign operations. Many of those sent to Japan are supposed to be senior managers and will stay for one or two years. Richard Kraft points out that although his firm employs 12,500 people in the United States, the team of senior managers is pretty small. Sending 20 people to Japan each year, as is planned, will be tough. So will finding jobs for them back in America two years later. But at least parochial old Osaka will never be the same again.

This has been slow to happen, but mainly because it was not necessary in the past. Kraft joined Matsushita in 1974 when, in what was for those days an unusual move, the Japanese firm bought a set of existing American factories. This was the consumer products division of Motorola (now known chiefly for its chips and its portable telephones), making televisions, car radios, and the like. Kraft was in Motorola's sales division, and stayed on with his new Japanese masters. It took from 1974 until March 1991—seventeen years—before Matsushita introduced its first locally designed television receiver, now manufactured at the former Motorola factory at Franklin Park, Illinois. According to Kraft, when the Motorola division was taken over, the Japanese firm's manufacturing and design abilities were far ahead of those at the American factory. The previous owner had not invested much in the plant, so the first three years of Japanese ownership consisted mainly of the wholesale replacement of machines, production lines, and other manufacturing systems.

That brings us to 1977 or so. But it was another decade before very much local design and decisionmaking would take place. Why? Chiefly, because Matsushita did not have to, and did not want to. Although American tastes differ from Japanese ones, the Japanese firm felt comfortable with studying those tastes and requirements from a distance. Its cost advantage over western rivals was sufficiently great that it cannot have worried too much about being beaten in the marketplace. Since 1985, that cost advantage has narrowed. More important, perhaps, there is now more competition in all Matsushita's consumer-electronics products. Some of it is from Western factories and even Western companies; much of it is from cheaper producers in Asia. So at long last Matsushita has a commercial incentive to transfer a much larger proportion of the total manufacturing system—design, R&D, components supply, as well as assembly—in order to get an extra edge from being closer to customers and their tastes.

It is not transferring as much of its manufacturing system as are the Japanese carmakers, for example. Just-in-time manufacture is less a feature of electronics assembly than it is of cars, which are far more complex and bulky products. Some of its bulkier products, such as compressors for refrigerators, do need local supply. But televisions and computers can rely on worldwide sources for parts, since printed circuit boards, for instance, are easy and cheap to transport. Local supply can offer a small advantage. But if it is not there, Matsushita will shed few tears. However, what about the product for which there is now an admirable local source, 100 percent owned by the Japanese company: entertainment software?

——

Richard Kraft is on the main board of MCA, so he flies off pretty regularly to Hollywood. An engineer by training (he also has some patents, like Schulhof), he must find Hollywood a novel experience, to put it mildly. The question is: will Matsushita's ownership of MCA help Kraft sell more videorecorders?

When the Japanese "invasion" of Hollywood began in 1989, the air was thick with talk of synergy. Part of the reason was that it was widely assumed that the cunning Japanese must have some sort of hidden agenda, and they do, after all, sell millions of the things on which films and records are made and played. In the early 1980s, when Sony and Matsushita shot it out in the video market with rival tape standards, Betamax and VHS, many commentators felt that victory was substantially determined by the availability of software. If video rental shops stocked more titles in VHS than in Betamax, then more consumers would buy VHS machines, sending Betamax's market share spiraling downward. Next time, therefore, Sony would not make the same mistake: by owning a software house it could (or so the reasoning went) ensure that there would be an ample supply of titles available on its standard for the next video or audio gizmo.

What is now clear, however, is that ideas of synergy between the software and hardware businesses—Spielberg videos helping to sell

Sony videorecorders, or snazzy high-definition-television equipment helping to make better films—are being played down. No
one claims that these will offer more than a small bonus in the
immediate future. Kraft says that his firm and MCA are indeed
trying to find some synergy, but it was not the main reason for the
acquisition. If any synergy pops up, it will be cream on the cake.
Schulhof makes similar remarks. Echoing an extremely tired industry cliché, he says that software and hardware are different wheels
on the same car, and that he is the driver (the president of Matsushita in Japan, Akio Tanii, has been quoted as making an almost
identical remark). Synergies will grow over time. But they are not
a big factor right now.

In fact, the idea of synergy falls down on a basic point: software
and hardware businesses alike depend on selling to all comers, not
just to their corporate cousins. If Columbia can get Sony's HDTV
gadgets, so can Warner's. Sid Gannis, one of Peter Guber's top
team at Sony Pictures, talks of the need "to introduce the talent to
the technology," which is probably true. Film producers are a
cautious lot, despite their Armani suits and flashy special effects.
Basic techniques of editing film, for instance, have not changed
since the 1930s. Movies have been shot on 35 millimeter film for
decades. Sony is probably in a slightly better position to encourage
its own producers to play with its new video toys, most notably
high-definition television, which is currently chiefly used only in
postproduction work in movies. Steven Spielberg experimented
with some high-definition gadgetry when making *Hook*. But any
progress made in the technology of filmmaking is likely to spread
quickly across the other studios. Films are not, in any case, driven
by technology; they are driven by ideas about how to entertain.

What about synergy in the other direction, from software to
hardware? This also falls down on a basic point: that whether shops
stock music on a particular new sort of medium is a decision for
the shops, not the record company. And even the record company
is unlikely to want to endanger its sales by pushing artists on to a
new sort of disk or tape. The case of digital audio tape (DAT) is
a fine example. Sony makes DAT machines and promoted the new
technology eagerly; but its ownership of CBS Records (called
CBS/Sony in Japan) did not help the format become established.

Indeed DAT is virtually dead; what was touted as the next new mass market product is likely to end up trapped in the professional market.

It is more likely that synergies will come in forms of entertainment that are outside the current categories. In video games, for instance, Nintendo's dominance has had much to do with its encouragement of software producers. This might, in principle, be repeated in other new areas, such as the publication of reference books on CD-ROM (compact disk, read-only memory) or in so-called "multimedia," in which users are able to play with a combination of video, audio, and computer to create their own somewhat participative entertainment. Both Sony and Matsushita have set up multimedia divisions in America for this purpose. Yet all these things look like just what Kraft and Schulhof now admit they are: a bonus, the cream on the cake.

So why bother to own software businesses? It remains an open question. The Japanese firms are taking big risks for an improbable reward. At least there are more synergies between Sony and Columbia than there were with the studio's previous 49 percent main shareholder, Coca-Cola, but that is not saying much. For the time being, Japan's future in Hollywood will depend on how well its American managers run the firms—nothing more. In effect, Sony and Matsushita are bankers to an industry not known for paying its debts.

For the longer term, this awkward experiment in globalization is nevertheless a sort of insurance policy. Sony and Matsushita know that the consumer-electronics business is mature. They know that they have failed to make much of an inroad into their natural neighbor in hardware, computers. So software is the alternative route. They wonder whether, at some point in the future, technology will again change the way in which people are entertained, perhaps to provide synergies between hardware and software in some unknown way. By definition, skeptics like myself cannot spot what this magic innovation will be, but that does not prove that it will never exist. Meanwhile, Sony and Matsushita are tying up billions to own entertainment businesses—just in case.

Still, essential questions nag. How could such savvy folk as Sony and Matsushita get mugged in Hollywood? Why do they manage their software and hardware businesses so differently, one localized virtually to the extent of ceding control, the other tightly in Japanese hands? And is there a magic synergy between software and hardware that will, in time, bring the big payoff from these Hollywood investments and disadvantage competitors who are not in both industries?

The answer to how the mugging happened is that the Japanese had no choice but to make themselves vulnerable. That did not oblige them to spend billions, but it did make them a potential target. They had no choice, that is, once they had determined to gain a strong position in the market for English-language entertainment software. They could only achieve this by acquisition. Once they had made those acquisitions, they had no real choice but to hand over control to local (American) managers, since this business is alien to them.

Such a transfer has never been necessary for these firms when manufacturing. In that area, they are teachers, not students. But in software the roles are reversed, and always will be as long as the United States continues to dominate the world entertainment market.

The case for a hardware manufacturer to get into entertainment software is a poor one. Sony and Matsushita are brilliant in the consumer-electronics hardware business, and are among the most successful Japanese overseas manufacturers. The reason for this success overseas is that both firms have had a clear idea about what their advantage is over foreign competitors, and how to exploit that advantage through local manufacture. One advantage lies in product innovation in Japan; for that reason neither firm has needed to build ambitious and costly R&D facilities overseas. The other advantage has been in manufacturing technology and organization. Both firms have exploited this abroad by maintaining tight control of their overseas affiliates and sending large numbers of Japanese managers and engineers to supervise manufacture.

So far, so successful. But if the same tests are applied to software—what is your advantage and how can you exploit it?—the answer is much less clear. Neither Sony nor Matsushita have any advantage in the creation of entertainment software. There is no evidence of any real advantage for a software vendor in being owned by a leading hardware firm. The only thing these firms bring to the picnic is money.

It is too soon to say whether that financial advantage has been exploited effectively. But the likelihood is that it has not, and that, in any case, it is not a very valuable advantage. Plenty of people have money available for entertainment. There is no cash shortage; what is short is creativity and distribution power.

Both Sony and Matsushita paid way too much for their studios. Probably, the reason was hubris first and synergy only a distant second. Will Nemesis follow? In Matsushita's case, the firm can afford it. But in Sony's case, it cannot. Morita's firm is financially weak. The funneling of more than $6 billion away from the hardware parent and into Hollywood is likely to put a real obstacle in the path of Sony's business development. If the industrial world's recession, and that of Japan, lasts a great deal longer, it could even place Sony's future independent survival in doubt. Put bluntly, by acquiring Columbia, Morita may well have bet his company. Even in Japan's protective financial system, that could prove to have been a bad mistake.

5

THE CASE OF FIRESTONE

The bridge is down
and people stand upon the bank,
The summer moon . . .
                                        TAIGI

DRIVE from Chicago down the freeway to Akron, Ohio, and you are unmistakably in the old industrial heartland of America. Only a few minutes off the freeway, cruising down Main Street, not far past Syl's Furniture and the Ton Yee laundry, a huge light brown brick building looms into view. On the roof stand big red letters that spell out the word "F-I-R-E-S-T-O-N-E." Next to them is a familiar (at least to Americans and Britons) logo of a red shield containing the letter "F" in old-fashioned writing.

It is not until you turn into the parking lot that it becomes clear that the name of the firm founded in 1900 by a thirty-one-year-old man called Harvey S. Firestone has changed. It is now Bridgestone/Firestone, for since May 1988 it has been owned by Japan's biggest tiremaker. At the time, the purchase was the biggest ever made by a Japanese company overseas, at a cost of $2.6 billion. (Subsequently, the purchase was overtaken by Sony's takeover of Columbia Pictures and then by Matsushita's acquisition of MCA.)

Yet when it took place, Bridgestone's takeover was a headline grabber, and not only in America. It boldly violated one of the then conventional wisdoms about Japanese multinationals: that they prefer to grow by building their own factories rather than by acquiring others. And, by doing so, it set up one of the toughest experiments of all in the internationalization of Japanese business: Bridgestone had not only to turn an American multinational from loss into profit, but had also to find ways to make Japanese management methods fit not merely with American ways but also with methods used by Firestone all over the world. The new Bridgestone/Firestone company now manufactures tires on six continents, operating in thirty countries.

Parking one's car back at the huge brick building in Akron, it takes a little time to find the clues as to how much things have changed. At street level there is a sign saying "Bridgestone/Firestone," and there is a Bridgestone tire dealership on the building's forecourt. But few Americans know that Bridgestone is a Japanese firm, and that the name is a reversed translation of the name of the Japanese founder, Ishibashi. Bridgestone sounds so American, and very like Firestone, which is, after all, why Ishibashi adopted the name in the first place. Next to the tire dealership and by the parking lot is an old building with a sign on it: CLOUSER'S RESTAURANT. On the sign it says, in English, that it also sells newspapers, racing forms, smokers' supplies, work gloves, and sundries. Underneath, at last, is the first clue that the old Akron firm is now Japanese. In the Japanese *kana* script, words say: *"Kurousar no restoran."* It means "Clouser's Restaurant."

Even in the reception area, it still seems as if this is the old Firestone company. When I visited, there was a small exhibition of old newspaper articles and other memorabilia, mostly concerned with Firestone's fiftieth-anniversary celebrations. To my surprise, there was a copy of the local newspaper, the *Akron Beacon Journal,* for August 2, 1950, the very same day as my visit in 1991. The next day, August 3, was the ninety-first anniversary of Firestone's foundation. But in 1991, there would be no celebratory articles in the *Akron Beacon Journal,* either on August 2 or 3.

For half a century Akron was the tire capital of the world. It is still the American headquarters of many big tiremakers: Goodyear, General, and Uniroyal Goodrich. But of those three only Goodyear remains in American hands, and tire manufacturing has already moved out of Akron. In the most poignant gesture of all, the old Firestone headquarters has also now gone. At the end of 1991, Bridgestone moved the firm's headquarters to Nashville, Tennessee, leaving just a research division, a synthetic rubber plant, and a computer center. The folks at the *Akron Beacon* are not at all pleased.

The aim is to give the firm a new start. That sounds like a positive thing, which it may well be, but it is also a sign of trouble, for it is the third new start the firm has had in the past four years. The first was when it was bought in 1988; the second, when Bridgestone's chairman moved to Akron to take charge of the former Firestone in January 1990. In that year, Bridgestone's American subsidiary suffered a net loss of $350 million. In 1991, losses reached $500 million. Thanks mainly to this American drain on its parent's profits, Bridgestone's consolidated net profits for 1991 were just Y5 billion ($40 million), following 1990 net profits of only $33 million—and in 1991, the firm only managed to make a consolidated profit by raising money with asset sales. In 1992, Firestone still lost $132 million, holding the parent company back. The three new starts do not even include the new starts that Firestone promised itself at several points during the 1980s, before it was sold to Bridgestone.

Admittedly, there are plenty of external reasons why, more than five years after the acquisition, Firestone is still in trouble. The American tire market has tumbled along with car sales; so has the European market; so, beginning in the autumn of 1991, did the Japanese market. These sluggish sales added to a structural problem in the car market: over-capacity caused by Michelin's development of radial tires in the 1960s and 1970s, superseding the old cross-ply or bias-ply tires. The new radial tires needed to be replaced less often than the old sort, thus reducing demand for replacement tires. All the other tire firms in America, bar a small independent firm called Cooper, are also losing money. And the foreign owners of big American tire firms—Michelin of France, the world's biggest, which owns Uniroyal Goodrich, and Continental of Germany, which owns General Tire—are bleeding billions in red ink.

Yet Bridgestone also accepts that many of Firestone's problems are homegrown, not just before the takeover but also since. It had known that it was buying a firm that had lost its way in the early 1970s, had been hit by fraud in 1978 and by a massive recall of defective tires in the same year. Thus battered, Firestone halved its workforce over the next ten years and struggled back to profit, but hardly invested at all.

By 1991, the Japanese firm had expected to have raised the productivity and quality of Firestone's factories almost to Japanese levels and to be expanding output as well as market share. Most of all, Bridgestone did not expect Firestone still to be experiencing losses or to be requiring huge injections of capital. The Japanese owner has not yet succeeded in tackling the problem of merging the Japanese business culture with that in the United States. In particular, it has not managed to change the attitudes of workers and shop floor managers in Firestone's plants. All of these problems are proving painful for Bridgestone's Japanese managers, back at its headquarters in Kyobashi, near Tokyo's main railway station. Japanese firms are renowned for taking a long view. But that does not mean that short-term pains are expected, or easily absorbed.

Those pains frame essential questions. Did Bridgestone leap too far, too fast? Did it have another option? Given that it chose the American-style strategy of expansion through acquisition, was it too slow to take control, or should it have left locals fully in charge?

———

American commentators on the takeover of Firestone saw Bridgestone as a rather alien company, with a different heritage and different ways of operating from those of their own historic company. There is truth in that, but what is also striking is how similar Bridgestone is in some ways to the other giants of the tire industry.

Like Michelin, Pirelli, and Firestone itself, Bridgestone began as a family firm (in 1931). Members of the founding Ishibashi family still hold a controlling stake, just as family members continue to play an important role at Michelin and Pirelli, and did until recently at Firestone. Bridgestone was founded by an enterprising individual, Shojiro Ishibashi, who also became a patron of the arts. The Bridgestone Museum of Art in Kyobashi, Tokyo, is now famous especially for its collection of European impressionist art.

One thing Bridgestone was not, however, was international. By contrast Firestone became a multinational as early as 1919, when it opened a plant in Singapore for the preparation and shipping of rubber. In 1928, still before the Bridgestone tire company had even been formed, Firestone opened its first tire factory outside North America, in England. The site was in Brentford, which was then a few miles to the west of London and is now a suburb. By coincidence, the Firestone factory was only a few hundred yards from the house where I grew up. Its building, right by a big main road and with a canal running behind it, was a beautiful white, art deco construction.

As recently as 1980, Bridgestone had only a small presence overseas, chiefly exporting replacement tires from Japan to follow Japanese car exports. It had just 2 percent of the American market for car tires. But Honda and Nissan then began a trend that was followed by other Japanese car firms: building factories in America and, later, in Europe. These factories were likely to require locally made tires, delivered "just in time"; and the market for replacement tires is heavily influenced by those originally fitted. So Bridgestone felt it had to move factories abroad if it was to keep the Japanese carmakers' business.

The question was: how? It could have done so in one of two ways: by building its own factories and gradually establishing an international network; or by buying a foreign tiremaker, and so gaining a network quickly.

Some precedents in the industry favored organic growth, for when France's Michelin invented the steel-belted radial tire, it expanded in North America by building eight new factories. Japanese precedents certainly favored the organic method of building an international network factory by factory. With a few exceptions, Japanese firms venturing abroad prefer to build their own factories, for fear that a takeover would involve a culture clash. In buying a firm, the Japanese would also buy its history of labor disputes, outdated working practices, and us-versus-them form of adversarial management. Far safer to build a new firm from scratch. That was what all the Japanese carmakers were choosing to do.

Yet Bridgestone's then chief executive, Akira Yeiri, decided to be a pioneer. He now says that organic growth would have taken too long, as tire factories have to be big to be viable; to justify new plants, Bridgestone needed 10 percent of the American car-tire market. So Yeiri opted to buy in order to turn Bridgestone into a multinational.

In the initial stages, however, Yeiri nevertheless obeyed the first rule of acquisition: do not rush. Firestone's then boss, John Nevin, first approached Bridgestone with ideas of partnership or sale in December 1984. He was turned down then, and again in July 1986. Bridgestone did not feel ready for such a big step. Firestone was a troubled company, which meant that buying it would have been painful. From 1900 until the mid-1970s, the firm had been a great success, with revenues and profits growing virtually without interruption. But it was hit hard by the advent of the radial tire, competition from which exposed the fact that the firm's management had become asleep at the wheel.

In 1976, Firestone was hit by the first of several scandals: an investigation by the Securities and Exchange Commission found it had been making unlawful political contributions in the United States and overseas. In 1978, the firm's chief financial officer was sent to a federal prison after pleading guilty to five counts of criminal fraud, and the following year, the firm itself pleaded guilty to criminal charges in a federal tax case. Worse still for Firestone's tire business was the fact that in 1978 the firm had to recall more than 13 million defective "Firestone 500" radial tires, and suffered a big liability suit from accident victims. At the end of the 1970s, all these problems combined meant that the firm was losing more than $250 million a year.

It was after these troubles, in late 1979, that John Nevin was brought into Firestone's top management. The appointment was almost a classic of American industrial history. The Firestone family had been close friends of the Ford family since early in the century. Worried about their firm, they asked Lee Iacocca, who was then in Ford's top management, to help. He declined to join, but suggested Nevin. And in August 1980, Nevin became the firm's chief executive, with a mandate to take drastic action.

That is exactly what he did, closing seven bias-ply tire plants in 1980 (out of its total of seventeen in North America), and selling a plastics business in 1981 and a radial-truck-tire plant in 1983. This latter plant was sold to—guess who?—Bridgestone. Nevin had been chairman of the Zenith television company in previous years, and had gotten to know Akio Morita of Sony. It was through Morita that he first approached Bridgestone's then chairman, Kanichiro Ishibashi, to sell him the truck-tire plant. That was the first contact between the two companies.

Later Nevin closed or sold five more tire plants and sold some of Firestone's peripheral businesses. This brought some temporary improvement to Firestone's finances, culminating in operating profits of $144 million in 1983. But by 1984, operating profits were again weak, falling to $8 million. Despite the fact that most of Firestone's main competitors (most notably Michelin) were also losing money, it appeared to Firestone's board that the firm could not survive as an independent firm. With hostile takeovers becoming increasingly common in the United States, it was clear that Firestone was ripe for attack: according to Nevin, in 1984 Firestone could have been profitably liquidated by a hostile raider. Its common stock was trading at just $16–18 per share, which was only about 55–65 percent of the firm's book value.

Yet Japanese firms have never been tempted by firms that are ripe for hostile takeovers. Purchase followed by breakup is not one of their standard strategies. Bridgestone wanted to expand overseas, but remained leery of buying a firm as troubled as Firestone. Such a purchase would have been revolutionary, and would also probably have involved immediate plant closures, the thought of which made Bridgestone shudder. So twice it declined Nevin's approaches. Officially, it was still working out its strategy for overseas expansion.

Then external events began to change Bridgestone's mind. In late 1987, Germany's Continental, which had just bought General Tire in America, announced a joint manufacturing and marketing deal with two Japanese firms, Toyo and Yokohama, which promised to help them get business with the new Japanese car plants in America. The thought of getting left behind prompted Bridgestone to act. It offered $1.25 billion for a 75 percent stake in Firestone's tire business, leaving Firestone with 25 percent, plus all of its tire-retailing outlets. In effect, the tire manufacturing business was to be set up as a joint venture, but with Bridgestone firmly in control. It sounded like a good deal. Unfortunately for Yeiri, he found himself in a bidding war with Italy's Pirelli.

At that point, Bridgestone disobeyed that first rule of acquisition: not to rush. Instead, it rushed to overtrump Pirelli's offer of $58 a share with its own far more generous $80 offer, at a total cost of $2.6 billion. At that time, this was attacked by American xenophobes as a case of national assets being sold too cheaply. Yet, as Bridgestone now knows, it paid far too much.

――――

Why did it do so? At the time, the decision to buy Firestone was not as extraordinary as it now appears. The reason is that Bridgestone had for several years been conducting a dress rehearsal for just such an acquisition. To the firm's managers, it may well have seemed that this rehearsal showed what a fine move a full acquisition would be.

Put another way, the point is that since 1983, Bridgestone had been conducting its own experiment in how to adapt a Firestone tire factory. And it was highly successful. Firestone first offered to sell its modern truck-tire plant in La Vergne, Tennessee, to Bridgestone in 1980, and eventually sold it in January 1983 for $52 million. The plant had employed six hundred workers, until two thirds of them were laid off in March 1982. Although the plant was modern, the tire it was making had not been well-received by customers. Despite that, when Bridgestone first talked about buying La Vergne, the United Rubber Workers union was hostile. Then Firestone threatened to close the plant unless it was sold. So the URW cooperated.

It was a wise decision. Within two years Bridgestone had restored the La Vergne plant to full-scale output and had rehired all the laid-off workers. It invested $68 million to modernize the equipment, raise productivity, and retrain workers. And in 1987, it added a car-tire line, hiring two hundred fifty more people. Expansion was a word that precious few tire-industry workers or managers heard anywhere in the 1980s.

Before buying the plant, Bridgestone studied its operations carefully, so that it knew exactly what it was buying. After it took over, the first changes Bridgestone made were to production methods;

changes in the more sensitive area of personnel were handled more slowly. All the Firestone production managers were kept on, while thirty-five Japanese arrived as "advisers." To the locals, one change stood out: under Firestone, the plant was tightly controlled by the Akron headquarters, with local managers just carrying out orders; under Bridgestone, control moved to the plant itself. This delighted the American managers and workers.

This management change is significant. At many Japanese plants the complaint is heard, whether from inside the firm or outside, that the Japanese owner exerts too much control. This is either because decisions are made in Tokyo or because Japanese expatriates occupy the most important posts. But at Bridgestone's La Vergne factory, this complaint was not heard, even though Japanese expatriates did move in to take many of the most important posts. The reason is that, compared with the previous owner, the local managers and workers still felt they had more control. They were not independent, but they felt a greater sense of ownership and responsibility. Against the difficulties of buying an existing plant, in other words, can be placed a potential benefit: that the new owner can gain from a favorable comparison with the old one.

By just about every measure the purchase was a success, as a 1988 study by Thomas Mahoney of Nashville's Vanderbilt University showed. By 1986, productivity, measured as tons per unit of labor, was 74.5 percent higher than in 1980, compared with an average rise of 44.6 percent among all American tire firms. The proportion of tires scrapped at La Vergne fell from 5.1 percent in 1983 to 1.3 percent in 1987. Output of tires with blemishes fell by 86 percent, from 2.8 percent of tires to 0.04 percent in 1986. The new owners had brought in new equipment and technology, but had also instituted their own Japanese-style "total quality control" system, inculcating it through a series of training courses for managers and supervisors.

Output rose from 16,400 tires a month in 1982 to 82,000 in 1987. Meanwhile the safety record improved: the number of accidents per 100 employees fell from 9.8 in 1983 to 2.2 in 1986, compared with an industry average of 13–14. This was achieved with virtually the same workforce as had been employed (or laid off) in 1983, and with the plant still organized by the URW. None of these measures is quite as good as in Japan: productivity at La Vergne is still only 80 percent of that in equivalent Japanese plants. But the rate of improvement shown in all these aspects made the La Vergne purchase virtually a perfect example of how to buy an existing factory, improve it, and make money out of the deal. The positive experience at La Vergne was enough to spur Yeiri on to the next step: buying the whole of Firestone.

––––––

It is easy to see why further acquisitions seemed to make sense. The Vanderbilt study of La Vergne concluded that Bridgestone's basic strength lay in its manufacturing methods. It had correctly concentrated on improving those at the truck-tire plant while leaving American managers to handle the workforce, a task at which it had no previous experience. So the conclusion seemed clear: the same trick could be applied throughout Firestone. Though no Japanese would ever say this, it probably looked like a license to print money.

This expectation was wrong. With the benefit of hindsight, the success at La Vergne ought to have suggested a third option, between organic growth and acquisition: buying lots of individual tire factories. The La Vergne experience also suggests that Yeiri was wrong when he said that 10 percent of the market would be needed to justify new factories. La Vergne had much less than 10 percent of the truck-tire market, yet Bridgestone still opened a new car-tire line at the site despite its small share. If Bridgestone had adopted a mixed strategy of opening new factories and buying old duds, by now it could have had a big share of the market.

Yet the lesson of Firestone runs even deeper. It was not simply that Bridgestone drew the wrong strategic conclusion. It was that once Bridgestone had decided to make a big acquisition, it implemented the acquisition badly.

The first problem came from Firestone's sheer size. To buy it, Bridgestone paid fifty times more than it paid for the La Vergne factory. For that price, it got twenty tire plants around the world, twenty other factories making synthetic rubber and fibers, and 53,000 employees. In 1988, Firestone's sales were only two thirds as large as Bridgestone's, but it had almost twice as many employees. It had a headquarters' staff of 3,000.

This transformed the task of bringing Firestone's factories up to Bridgestone's standards. Bridgestone could not simply repeat what it had done at La Vergne. For one thing, it did not have enough managers to send as teachers (or "technical advisers," as it called them) to Firestone. It had sent thirty-five Japanese to La Vergne. But taking only the tire plants into consideration, to repeat that exercise for the whole of Firestone would have required seven hundred Japanese managers, a huge drain on the parent. In the end, only two hundred were sent. So right from the start, one ingredient of the La Vergne success could not be duplicated.

The second problem arose from a classic issue for Japanese investing abroad: worries about local sensitivities, among workers, managers, and the communities. Bridgestone did not want to rush in to take control of Firestone, throwing out the top managers as it did so or changing the way in which they managed. It did not even merge its existing American operations with Firestone. Bizarrely, it moved its previous American headquarters from California to Nashville, rather than Akron, just a few months after taking over. And it tried to respect some of Firestone's traditions, moving corporate staff whom Firestone had shifted to Chicago in 1986 back to Akron.

This kid-glove approach was a mistake. When a takeover takes place, staff members expect dramatic changes and are prepared to accept them. It is rather like when a new government comes into office: at first, anything unpopular that it has to do can be blamed on the previous government. But as time passes, the staff becomes reluctant to accept radical change. By acting too slowly, Bridgestone lost the chance to make big changes and worsened the culture clash between American and Japanese methods.

––––

The difference between the methods used at Firestone and at Bridgestone could not have been larger. They were far larger than at La Vergne, because now they involved management styles right at the top of the company. Since he took over in 1980, Nevin had run the firm like an autocrat. While Japanese like to push decisions down into middle management, Firestone was run from the top. This was necessary because Nevin was making drastic changes to try to save the firm, and he carried out this task in what Yeiri describes as a "very American" manner: he had total power, worked day and night, and decided virtually everything himself. Nevin "acted like General MacArthur," Yeiri says.

Yeiri stresses that he is not trying to criticize Nevin's methods. But it meant that Bridgestone was faced with a completely different way of running things, and yet wanted to leave Nevin and his men in charge, at least for a while. The structure remained "top-down," yet that is precisely the style that makes it hardest to change the way in which a firm works on the shop floor.

If the operation of the shop floor is to be improved, information must be shared between the top management and those controlling production, and then decisions based on that information must also be made in a shared way. As Yeiri says, a top-down method makes it harder for factory managers to grasp the reality of what is going on. They will, for example, simply go on making tires according to the production schedule imposed on them, even if they are defective. They are just obeying orders. Since they are not given responsibility, they do not act responsibly.

The new Japanese owners felt unable to change this top-down way of doing things all at once. So they tried to graft their own methods onto it. The result was disastrous. The best (or worst) example came in Bridgestone's first efforts to improve quality control.

Wanting to leave management in American hands, the Japanese simply gave lectures about how to improve quality. They also sent rank-and-file workers to production workshops to give them firsthand experience of how to improve quality, and even sent some American workers over to the Japanese plants. The Japanese way is to absorb quality control into every worker's and manager's job. But in America job descriptions are strictly defined, producing resistance when management attempts to change the way in which jobs are performed. Quality control was not part of ordinary workers' or managers' job descriptions. So all that the Firestone managers did (grateful, of course, for their continued autonomy) was to hire five hundred quality-control experts without telling the parent, expanding the firm's bureaucracy by a sixth.

Another problem was that Bridgestone itself had no idea how to fit a big overseas subsidiary into its own management structure. Reporting lines became confused, with different, often contradictory, instructions coming from different levels in the parent company. Firestone managers in America, Europe, and elsewhere were left to deal with functional specialists in Japan rather than communicating through a single department.

What was needed was for Bridgestone to clarify its wishes and to show how Firestone fitted into its worldwide plans. One response Bridgestone made to this need was to move Teiji Eguchi, its chairman (a figurehead post in Japan), to Akron in early 1990. Akio Morita of Sony had made a similar step earlier in the decade, moving his office to New York, to much acclaim among management consultants like Kenichi Ohmae, who saw it as a clear demonstration to employees that they were now working for a global, borderless firm, not just a branch of a Japanese one. But Eguchi's move served only to lower morale rather than boosting it, since, confusingly, the move came only a few months after a new chairman, George Aucott, had been promoted from within to replace Nevin.

———

Eguchi's move suggested that Americans were no longer in charge, but neither were the Japanese. Japanese orders were still coming randomly and slowly from different parts of the parent. Eventually, in August 1990, a coordinator in Tokyo, Takashi Uchiyama, was appointed as the sole channel between the Americans and the Japanese parent. A separate channel was also set up for the European operations. Finally, in March 1991, Bridgestone sent a new Japanese chairman and chief executive to Akron, and Eguchi retired. Yoichiro Kaizaki, the new chairman, spoke little English and had spent much of his career in Bridgestone's nontire operations. But at last, the Japanese were taking full control. Two years later, Kaizaki got his reward for having taken on Firestone: Akira Yeri stepped aside and Kaizaki was appointed president of the parent company.

I interviewed Kaizaki just a few months after he had taken over at Akron. His office there was very American: wood-paneled, plush, with green leather sofas. Kaizaki clearly wanted to preserve the old American brand: at least, he used a Firestone cigarette lighter. But he looked uncomfortable in his new surroundings, and with reason. He was honest about how difficult his task was. Everything would be fine, he joked, if only he could speak English and the company was not in the red. The bad financial state of his firm was having a strong impact on his mind and his heart, he said.

Asked to assess how much progress had been made so far, Kaizaki answered that quality had improved a great deal, but efforts to increase productivity had achieved little so far, as had attempts to cut costs. The number of complaints about defective tires had fallen drastically, the firm has received quality awards from customers, and Ford had raised the share of its car output using the firm's tires from 40 percent to 42 percent, thanks to improved quality. In 1988, the levels of wasted tires and customers' complaints were ten times those in Bridgestone's Japanese plants; by 1991, the American plants were almost, but not quite, at Japanese levels.

Average productivity, however, was still only 60 percent of Japanese levels. It is often hard, Kaizaki pointed out, for Japanese firms with American affiliates to achieve two goals at once: quality and productivity. The first step must be quality. Kaizaki may well be right. Bridgestone attempted to achieve both goals simultaneously in 1988–91, but failed on productivity.

This was despite the fact that Bridgestone spent plenty of money. In addition to the $2.6 billion purchase price, it spent $1.5 billion upgrading equipment. In 1991, it injected a further $1.4 billion in new capital. But the message had not gotten through about how methods and attitudes must change.

Kaizaki blamed two factors. First, raising productivity requires trust between the top management and the plant workers, based on a joint view that high productivity is required if profits are to improve. But this view was not well-accepted, according to Kaizaki. The second problem is ignorance: staff in the plants do not know how to increase productivity, and seem to be resistant to learning new methods. Bridgestone has tried to train workers in their new, better methods, but has been less successful than Toyota has been, for instance, in its newly built car factory in Kentucky.

How much could Bridgestone achieve? Kaizaki admits that, because much of the Firestone plant is old, the best result on average will be 80 percent of the Japanese level. The La Vergne truck-tire and car-tire plants are at around 80 percent; a new plant at Warren has hit even better levels than that because its equipment is new and its newly hired workers have been more willing to accept different training methods.

All this is made no easier by hard times: all seven North American plants had temporary shutdowns in 1991, and two hundred workers were laid off. This is a better state of affairs than in rival American factories, but it is still hurting morale. Part of Bridgestone's trouble, in fact, is that while Goodyear and Michelin were both starting to cut their capacity and hence workforces as early as 1989, Bridgestone/Firestone was actually hiring new people and expanding, full of enthusiasm for the new company. After all, expansion worked at La Vergne, so why not at the whole firm, the new owners presumably thought.

One reason Bridgestone was loath to buy Firestone in the early 1980s, remember, was that it did not want to have to handle plant closures and layoffs at its new American purchase. Yet, thanks to its initial expansion, that is just what it was faced with in the early 1990s. In 1991, the number of salaried staff was cut by five hundred, half of them in Akron.

This retrenchment is not being done in a paternalistic Japanese way. In Japan, if the firm was forced to shut down temporarily because of poor sales and excessive inventory, it would still pay the workforce, allowing them to come to the plant to do painting, and maintenance work and to sit through quality-control courses. But it is not doing this in America. The reason is not just a difference of philosophy, although that plays a part. The main reason is that the American firm cannot afford to keep the workforce on, even though to do so would help morale, industrial relations, and probably eventually productivity. The losses are simply too big to do this. And Bridgestone Japan has no intention of subsidizing Firestone to give its workers the full Japanese treatment.

Yet failure to do this is making Bridgestone's task harder. Firestone's relationship with the union had been a troubled one, and the new owner cannot escape from that history. At Japanese affiliates that are not in such financial trouble, however, the new owner has been able to win support from the union by treating it in a sharply different way from the old management. Bridgestone has not been able to do this: it had to lay off workers and shut down plants, just as Firestone had to do. As far as the workers are concerned, therefore, Bridgestone still has not proved to them that it is any better than the old owner. Losses thus proved a vicious circle: they prevented Bridgestone from making some of the improvements in working practices and industrial relations that could themselves make the firm more profitable (or, at least, make it lose less money). Finally, in 1993, Bridgestone/Firestone broke back into the black, making a tiny profit. But even that owed more to a pick-up in the American tire market than to fundamental changes at the American subsidiary.

———

What, then, can be learned from Bridgestone's experiences? Basically, Bridgestone was too ambitious in one sense, and not ambitious enough in another. It bought a firm that was too big for it to absorb easily, with 53,000 employees and seventeen factories all around the world. Blessed with the cheap money of Japan's late-1980s booming economy and soaring stockmarket, it thought nothing of paying $2.6 billion, which was 30 percent above Pirelli's rival offer. It has since had to pay out even more money to its acquisition, bringing the latest total cost to at least $6 billion (Y750 billion). This is investment overstretch at its most extreme.

Bridgestone did not have the management resources to cope with this, but thought that money in modern, successful Japan grew on trees—or, rather, the stockmarket. It is now finding that even raising money is a strain. With hindsight, acquisition, at least of a firm as big as Firestone, was not the right strategy. Bridgestone could have had more success by a mixture of building its own factories and buying smaller units. Yet having been so ambitious in its purchase of Firestone, Bridgestone was far too meek in the way in which it took over management of the firm. It was too worried about local sensitivities to alien Japanese ways, and about the danger of annoying incumbent American managers. Thus, by waiting too long to take control, Bridgestone lost the initiative.

Bridgestone also had no idea how to integrate its new multinational toy into the parent company: in other words, it had no plan for how to handle the purchase, despite having been thinking for years about international strategy. It is crucial with any acquisition to have a plan beforehand about how to deal with the purchase, and then to stick to the plan. Bridgestone did not do either.

Perhaps because it was buying as long ago as 1988, when the takeover tactic was still a novelty for Japanese firms, Bridgestone lacked confidence in its ability to instill Japanese methods into a foreign firm. But that prevented it from reaping what were precisely the potential benefits of a merger: the chance to get more out of Firestone's assets by imposing superior Japanese management upon them. Nor did Bridgestone give itself the other frequent benefit from a takeover: the opportunity to shock incumbent managers and workers. By its meekness, Bridgestone did its best to prevent any shock at all. Firestone was left to feel as if nothing had changed—except of course that it now had a superrich parent, thousands of miles away.

All those missed opportunities explain the move of the American headquarters to Nashville at the end of 1991, and the talk of giving the firm a new start. A new start was exactly what was needed. By sticking to Firestone's traditions, Bridgestone simply stuck to its bad old ways. It also retained the defeatism that had set in during the 1970s.

The sorry experience of Bridgestone and Firestone shows that Japanese investors make just the same sort of screwups as American or European ones. None of the mistakes made were special to the Japanese. They were all classic acquisition stories: the management textbooks are full of Western firms doing the same sorts of things. So Bridgestone cannot be said to have been a better acquirer of Firestone than a typical American firm, nor a worse one. The question that pundits posed at the time—is it best for America to have Firestone in American hands or Japanese hands?—is irrelevant. The right question would have been: which potential owner is least likely to screw up?

6

<hr/>

THE MONEY BAZAAR

Tarnished is the gold—
with young leaves round us, we look back
to days of old.

CHORA

O F all the world's businesses, the one to which globalization
has come most rapidly and profoundly is finance. Money
is like water: it will always find its own level, flowing to the
places and at the speeds that are dictated by gravity and its sur-
rounding obstacles. And of all Japan's overseas adventurers, some
of the most global, powerful, and, to foreign observers, frightening have been the financial firms—especially Nomura Securities,
by far the world's biggest securities house or investment bank.

It was the combination in the 1980s of tumbling barriers to the
international movement of capital and rapid improvements in
communications and computer technology that turned finance
into a worldwide business. The disappearance of barriers released
the financial waters, and the improvements in technology ensured
that the water could move more swiftly than ever before. And, to
extend the metaphor still further, on the crest of those waves surfed
the world's securities houses and commercial banks.

Multinational finance houses are far from a novelty. In the
nineteenth century, Barings of London was financing overseas
investment in Argentina and India, and J. P. Morgan was straddling
the Atlantic Ocean, first channeling British money to America,

then later the other way around. Big commercial banks, too, have long had worldwide networks of offices, lending wherever customers could be found. In the 1950s, '60s, and '70s, chief among these commercial banks were the big American "moneycenter" banks such as Bank of America, Citicorp, and Chase Manhattan.

The 1980s brought several genuine innovations, however. Cheaper, more powerful technology was an important enabling force, but it did not signify a qualitative change. One such change, however, was the opening up of several major domestic capital markets to competition from outsiders, which meant both domestic newcomers and foreigners. In London, the "Big Bang" regulatory reforms of 1986 permitted banks and foreign firms to join the London Stock Exchange for the first time. The new-issue market for British government bonds, or "gilts," was also reformed, allowing foreign firms to apply to become market-makers. In New York, membership on the stock exchange was opened to foreigners, and so too was the privileged club of "primary dealers," firms allowed to bid for new issues of Treasury bonds directly with the issuer, the Federal Reserve Bank of New York. Later, market authorities in Paris, Frankfurt, Madrid, and Brussels also followed similar reforms.

The opening of domestic capital markets permitted securities houses to set up shop in foreign financial centers and to seek business in domestic securities. The second innovation actually gave them some business. This was the abolition of exchange and capital controls, notably in Britain in 1979 and Japan in 1980. Although there had always been ways for capital to flow across borders, this made it easier. So did an associated change in Japan: the finance ministry relaxed its rules governing the proportion of their assets that Japanese pension funds and life insurance companies could hold in foreign securities, raising the limit gradually from 10 percent to 30 percent. All this meant that the big institutional investors from Japan, Europe, and America were seeking to buy and sell foreign securities. Their old servants, their domestic securities houses, could thus have a head start in getting that business: after all, they had been building personal and corporate relationships with these investors for years.

The third innovation was more by way of coincidence, though

not entirely so. It was that in the mid-1980s the world's biggest economies developed huge imbalances on the current accounts of their balances of payments; notably, America ran a huge deficit while Japan built up its infamous surpluses, reaching $100 billion in 1987. Imbalances on current accounts cause capital to swirl about across borders; one way or another, current-account deficits have to be financed through an inflow of capital and current-account surpluses must prompt an outflow. Such flows can take a number of different forms, including bank lending, portfolio investment in stocks and bonds, increases or decreases in the reserves held by central banks, and foreign direct investment. Whichever form the flows take, they will be intermediated by financial firms of one sort or another. Again, business arrived with a spectacular explosion on the doorsteps of multinational financial firms.

The reason this innovation was not entirely coincidental is that many economists believe there was a chicken-and-egg connection between the large current-account imbalances and the new freedoms for the international movement of capital. In other words, freer movement may have made the imbalances possible and allowed them to last much longer than they otherwise would have; without it, America's deficit could not have been financed so easily and for so long without prompting a recession in the United States, a collapse in imports, and thus an end to the imbalance.

Along with those imbalances, however, came the fourth innovation, and the one that is most relevant to the present analysis. It was that, for the first time, Japanese securities houses and commercial banks became multinationals. And not just any old multinationals: almost from nowhere, they became the biggest of them all. When the 1980s began, scarcely anyone on Wall Street or in the City of London rated Nomura Securities as worth a second glance, just as scarcely anyone thought of the Sumitomo Bank or the Industrial Bank of Japan as major international forces. By the end of the 1980s, however, all these firms were of the very top rank. Scarcely anyone could be found who dared to ignore them.

———

Almost as fast as the Japanese multinational finance houses rose, so they have declined, stung by scandal at home and the ups and downs of Japan's own financial markets. Yet it is safe to predict, at least as far as any prediction can be safe, that they are far from finished. Japanese banks and brokers will again be important, competitive international businesses, and in some ways have anyway remained competitive. They are now prominent, but no longer preeminent, and will remain prominent for the foreseeable future.

Such long-term prominence is not the only reason for studying them, however. The causes of their rise and then their relative decline are also useful indicators of the nature of the financial business itself and the likely shape of its future globalization. And, finally, Japan's financial multinationals are a microcosm of the international ebb and flow of Japan itself, and of its global reach. Because money is like water, it transmits pressures perfectly; financial firms move with those pressures in faster and more extreme ways than do manufacturers. But that also makes the financiers a proxy for the way in which those same pressures will eventually affect the manufacturers, albeit in their slower and more lumbering ways.

As stated earlier, in 1980 few observers in London or on Wall Street considered the then small offices of Japan's four top securities houses—Nomura, Daiwa, Nikko, and Yamaichi—as of anything more than marginal interest. Nomura had been in New York as early as 1928, and was then the first Japanese broker to reopen there after the war in 1953, but nobody really cared about its presence. It was not a hot topic, nor a smart place to work. A good indicator of such things is the cocktail party: does it attract a big crowd of the great and the good? Is it a lavish affair? A Japanese party in 1980 was not a fashionable financial affair; it was relatively small and attended only by the cognoscenti.

Yet by 1984 and 1985, things were changing radically. Japan's "Big Four" were expanding their London and New York offices to handle a rapidly rising volume of business. They were hiring prominent local figures as executive and nonexecutive chairmen and top directors: Sir Douglas Wass, a former permanent secretary at Britain's Treasury, was hired to head Nomura in London; in New York, Stephen Axilrod, former staff director of the Federal Reserve's Open Market Committee, America's main monetary policymaker, went to Nikko Securities.

Sure enough, the parties became more lavish: a ballroom in a big hotel, an ice statue in the center of the room, often a dozen or more small stalls around the room serving up different Japanese dishes. And what was most noticeable was the guests: by the mid-1980s, if you wanted to meet London's or New York's top bankers, merchant bankers, and even civil servants, the simplest way was to go to a Nomura Securities cocktail party.

Although financial people might superficially appear to be snobbish, in fact, even in London, they adhere to a simple rule: they go to where the money is, regardless of who is holding it. By 1985, that meant Nomura Securities and its Japanese rivals.

Japanese firms were holding the money because Japan's current-account surplus was by now ballooning, and with it the country's exports of long-term capital, principally for portfolio investment. At the same time, Japanese and American negotiators had agreed on improved access for American securities firms to the Tokyo stock and money markets, in return for which Nomura, Daiwa, Nikko, and Yamaichi all eventually received primary dealerships for Treasury bonds. The T-bond business was a godsend to the Japanese houses: a straightforward commodity business that required fairly little local expertise. Their Tokyo offices could take the now vast orders from Japanese life insurers and pass them to New York for implementation.

If this first flood of Japanese investment had headed for equities and other instruments, the Japanese houses would not have dominated it; even a Japanese institution might reckon that a local, American house was a better channel for such investments, since it would have more research expertise concerning American companies or the futures market, say. But T-bonds are what financial folk call plain vanilla: simple and straightforward. Anyone can handle them.

So although American houses also picked up some business, the Japanese took the bulk of it thanks to their contacts back home. In 1986–88, the Japanese Big Four often bought up to 40 percent of a new American T-bond issue. In 1986–87, Nomura's New York office expanded from two hundred staff to five hundred, and plans were laid to reach as much as two thousand by the end of the decade. The vast majority of those were Americans: since they were dealing in the American markets, they had to be locals, even though locals were typically more expensive to hire than the relatively poorly paid Japanese expatriates.

This T–bond business provided a strong platform from which to expand into other areas, with two aims in mind. One was to build sufficient research expertise and local contacts to capture Japanese orders for American equities, derivatives (e.g., futures and options), and other sorts of bonds, such as junk and municipals. The other aim was to gain sufficient clout to capture domestic American business from the other Wall Street houses—to trade Treasury bonds, equities, and junk for American institutions and not just Japanese ones. This would make the Big Four less reliant on Japanese capital flows, would lead them toward more profitable businesses, and could eventually allow them to challenge American investment banks for the leadership of their own market.

It was a similar story in London, but with an important twist. Again, the Big Four expanded rapidly in London in the mid-1980s on the back of Japanese capital flows. This time the money was flowing into Eurobonds, the offshore corporate securities market that London dominates. Pushed offshore by Japan's domestic regulations, vast numbers of Japanese companies came to London to issue Eurobonds, which were then mostly sold to Japanese institutional investors. Their close contacts with the companies enabled Nomura, Daiwa, Nikko, and Yamaichi to underwrite the bonds, and then to sell them to their Japanese institutional clients. That gave them juicy profits from two deals in one: the underwriting and the sale.

The twist, however, was this: the Eurobond market is an international market with no connection to London's domestic capital markets. Issues are denominated in foreign currencies, and only rarely in sterling. This separation turned out to be a virtue. For it meant that the Big Four were not tempted to expand rapidly in search of local business. Unlike in New York, they stuck to their golden goose.

The result is that the Big Four have been far more successful—and profitable—in London than in New York. So have Japanese commercial banks, since they are allowed by Japan's finance ministry to underwrite some Eurobonds in London. In New York, the

Japanese firms have lost money year after year trying to buy their way into local businesses. Any time they were asked, in the late 1980s, who their customers were, the Big Four would boast that they were doing a third or more of their trades with domestic American institutions. But, if it was true, it was profitless prosperity.

Building the research and trading capability needed for large equities, derivatives, and corporate bond departments sent fixed costs soaring. A series of culture clashes between the team-oriented, suppress-your-ego, consult-Tokyo-first Japanese and the hotshot individual egotists the firms had to hire on Wall Street turned their staffing policy into a costly revolving door.

The Big Four have so far failed to break into Wall Street's two most profitable businesses: mergers and acquisitions advice, and the underwriting of new shares and bonds for American corporations. Both require far too much local knowledge. They also require a customer to open up the intimate details of its finances and strategic plans to its investment bank, something American corporations have not been willing to do with the Japanese firms.

The Japanese firms' closeness to Japanese corporations, and their, well, Japaneseness, mean that American clients simply will not trust them. Scandals in Japan in 1990–92 and a long-standing association of the Japanese houses with shady dealing have not helped: the loss of reputation is not fatal, since most customers assume that all financial firms are shysters, but still, it has been a disadvantage. American companies have used the Japanese investment banks to underwrite Eurobonds, especially those denominated in yen, because they assume this will make it easier to sell the bonds to Japanese investors. But they have not used them to underwrite domestic American issues.

Life in the United States has been a long series of blind alleys for the Big Four. Efforts to break into full-service broking of equities have come and gone: teams of forty or more equity analysts were hired, and later fired. Yamaichi, the smallest of the four, made the meekest attempt by forming a team of just four analysts to explain American stocks to Japanese investors, but even that has now been disbanded.

Another apparently juicy business was encouraging American

companies to list their shares on the Tokyo stock market, which many did in 1986–88. The Big Four were paraded in virtual "beauty contests" for the honor of handling the listing, but soon American companies became disillusioned with the idea. Tokyo listings cost at least $150,000 to maintain, yet brought little benefit in terms of broadening the shareholder base. This was especially disappointing to the New York offices of the Big Four, as they had hoped that out of Tokyo listings would develop "friendships" with American companies that might bring other business in the United States. This has not happened.

A further area of interest to the Japanese brokers was the market for state and local government bonds. The Big Four trooped around all fifty states, but to little avail. The tax exemption on municipal bonds is only available to resident American investors, few of whom numbered among the Japanese client base; unable to enjoy the tax advantage, Japanese clients showed scant interest. Efforts were made to persuade states to issue bonds denominated in yen to be sold to Japanese investors; Nomura managed to persuade the state of Kentucky to do so. The state had to change its laws to be able to do this, and really only made the issue to help encourage Japanese multinationals to invest in Kentucky. This was at about the time when Toyota was deciding on where to locate its American car plant. The notion did not catch on, however, since none of the states actually wanted their money raised in yen; they would need to use it in dollars, and so would incur a currency risk by borrowing yen.

One of the best money-making efforts was a trick called the "dividend roll." Japanese life insurance companies can only pay yields to their policyholders out of dividends, not capital gains. So brokers devised a way for these investors to get hold of the high dividends paid on American stocks without having to hold the share for long. They bought big blocks of shares, generally of utility companies that pay high dividends, on the eve of a dividend pay-out, and sold them to Japanese life insurers who contracted to sell them back a day later at more or less the same price. The insurer would just own the share for a day but would collect the dividend.

On August 3, 1987, some 27 million shares in American Electric Power changed hands on a single day, chiefly in the form of dividend rolls. But this practice was controversial, and caused complaints in Congress. So Japan's finance ministry called in the country's life insurers and told them to stop—which they did. The business was not hugely lucrative for the brokers, since it typically earned them three cents a share or less, but it came in very handy as well as gaining them a name for handling huge trades. Yet it was gone as quickly as it arrived.

Other tricks popped up, such as "country funds" that pooled investments in small stockmarkets. But all depended on a single point: the brokers' Japanese client base. Daiwa Securities did secure a lead-management role in one American corporate-bond issue, but it lost so much money on it that none of the houses has sought to repeat it in a big way. In 1991, Nomura took sixteenth place in domestic American lead underwriting, while Daiwa took nineteenth. That means that they were hovering between the second tier of Wall Street houses and the third. They were nowhere near the top.

The final path, trodden in 1988 and 1989, led toward mergers and acquisitions. Unable to gather this business in their own right, the big Japanese houses chased it through joint ventures or equity partnerships with small American M&A specialists. Nomura led the way with a $100 million investment in Wasserstein Perella in July 1988. This firm had only been formed the previous February, albeit by New York's two preeminent takeover advisers, Bruce Wasserstein and Joe Perella, who had quit First Boston to start up on their own. Yet Nomura's money bought just 20 percent of the firm, valuing this fledgling employer of just forty executives at $500 million. When Nomura leads, the others generally follow, and so they did: Nikko tied itself up with the Blackstone Group, run by Peter G. Petersen, a former Commerce secretary; and Yamaichi took a 25 percent stake in Lodestar Partners, a firm set up by two defectors from Merrill Lynch.

Even these deals, however, were essentially made in search of business linked with the Japanese brokers' domestic client base. Japanese multinationals were shopping all over America for companies to buy, yet all the advisory fees were going to Americans. Nomura wanted a chunk of that action. Yet the investment in Wasserstein Perella has not paid off. The relationship has cooled considerably, as has the enthusiasm of Japanese companies for acquisitions in America. The firms' joint venture in Tokyo, Nomura Wasserstein Perella, is virtually defunct.

So where does this leave the Japanese investment banks in New York? Certainly not nowhere, but also far from the global power-houses they, and many pundits, predicted they would be by now.

Nomura employs about six hundred people in New York, little more than it did in 1987. Intellectually, its strongest area is its subsidiary, Nomura Research Institute, which conducts research on some American equities as well as American industries and the economy in general. It has established a good name for itself, and is frequently quoted in the press. After all, publicity is the main function of analysts and economists on Wall Street, regardless of who employs them.

Nomura's clearest strategy has been to build a capability in computerized trading of big baskets of stocks, futures, and op-tions—so-called program trading—for two reasons. One is simply that this is a profitable and growing business. But the other is that increasingly Nomura has been losing out to American houses that are more adept at this. And, horror of horrors, not just in New York but also in Tokyo. Salomon Brothers and Morgan Stanley have earned millions on program trading between Japan's stock and futures markets. With such computerized trading technology, they have secured far more Japanese domestic clients than Nomura has been able to secure American clients.

Nomura's American boss since late 1989 has been Max Chap-man, hired from Kidder Peabody to bring in precisely this sort of trading expertise. Beyond that, Nomura still has its primary dealer-ship in Treasury bonds, and is active in the mortgage-backed securities market and in junk bonds. But its huge size—in mid-1988, its market capitalization was more than $50 billion, which was twenty times bigger than that of America's biggest broker, Merrill Lynch—has not enabled it to gobble up Wall Street. In principle, it could have bought Merrill Lynch and dozens of smaller firms. But what would be the point? In finance, both the staff and the business can disappear in a flash. Buying up Wall Street would have been as wise a strategy as lighting a huge bonfire of Y10,000 notes in front of Trinity Church.

The other houses are in a similar position: well-established, respected, but no longer feared. Daiwa has been successful in the mortgage-backed securities market, making pots of money there in 1991. Nikko has fared well in futures and options, and its Blackstone venture in M&A has developed more successfully than has Nomura's with Wasserstein Perella. Yamaichi has opted for a handful of separate deals in fund management and a joint venture in computerized trading with a professor of mathematics from New York University. All are bumbling along. But none of the Big Four have been really successful.

————

The difference in London is that Nomura, Daiwa, Nikko, and Yamaichi set their sights far lower. Basically, they devoted their attention to the Euromarkets and to the task of raising money there for Japanese companies. They did not attempt aggressively and expensively to build a strong position in Britain's small domestic securities markets. All have burrowed their way in, however, more in the cautious manner of Japanese carmakers than in the reckless manner adopted in New York, and have been pretty successful in doing so.

Japan's takeover of the Euromarkets was spectacularly fast, as well as devastating for many of the incumbent non-Japanese investment banks. In 1985, Credit Suisse First Boston (CSFB), an entrepreneurial joint venture between a Swiss bank and a Wall Street securities house, dominated the rankings of lead managers of new Eurobond issues. It had a 14.4 percent share of new issues in that year, with a combined value of $19.2 billion. Its nearest rival was Deutsche Bank, with $8.7 billion and a 6.5 percent share. The best-placed Japanese firm was Nomura, in eighth place, with just $5 billion worth and a 3.8 percent share.

Two years later, however, Nomura toppled CSFB from the top slot. As it did so, it went on a hiring spree: for a time, Nomura was the biggest single private recruiter of new graduates from Oxford and Cambridge universities. For in 1989, Japanese houses absolutely swamped the Euromarket. Nomura was top, with a 15 percent share, and issues totaling $32 billion; the next three places were taken by Daiwa, Yamaichi, and Nikko, with 7–8 percent each. The once mighty CSFB had disappeared into sixth place, with $9 billion worth of issues and a share of only 4.3 percent. That decline was mitigated to an extent by the rise of a new market, a market for offshore equity issues, or Euro-equities, in which CSFB established a strong position. Yet this much smaller market could not fully compensate for the loss of the huge Eurobond market.

The spectacular rise in the Japanese Euromarket position was entirely caused by what was happening in Japan's domestic capital markets. On the one hand, Japanese institutional investors were looking for places to put their cash offshore, and were interested in diversifying away from American Treasury bonds. On the other hand, Japanese companies wanted to raise cash, and saw that they could exploit their compatriot investors' desire for foreign securities by issuing their own securities offshore.

Then came yet another powerful force, which made raising cash overseas a low-cost bonanza for Japanese corporations and which made buying offshore securities look like a one-way street to profit: the boom on Tokyo's own stock market. In 1986–89, Japanese shares rose more rapidly than ever before. Smart Japanese brokers saw how to link this rise to the Euromarkets: companies issued Eurobonds with warrants attached that entitled the holder to buy the firm's equities back in Tokyo at a prefixed price. Since buyers expected Japanese share prices to go on rising, they were willing to accept tiny interest rates on the Eurobonds, for once the share price overtook that prefixed exercise price, there would be a fat profit on the warrant.

Every Japanese company worth its salt—and many that were not—rushed to issue these warrant bonds. The finance ministry relaxed its rules to allow almost any public company to do so. In the early 1980s, only around 200–300 Japanese firms had issued bonds abroad. By the end of the decade, more than 1,200 had put their snouts in this extremely tempting trough.

That is what gave Nomura its $32 billion worth of Eurobond underwritings in 1989 alone. But in early January 1990, things suddenly began to change. The Tokyo stock market's Nikkei average had peaked at 39,000 in late December, shortly after the Bank of Japan had begun a program of interest-rate rises. Thanks to this tighter monetary policy, the stock market slumped, falling by 30 percent in three months. Warrant bonds are creatures of rising share prices; when share prices fall, warrants are killed stone dead. That is what happened in 1990–92; warrant issues by Japanese firms virtually ceased.

Now, those warrant-bond issuers had to think about what happened when the bonds reach maturity. At that time, the borrower has to repay the bonds, which previously Japanese firms had counted on doing by using the money received from warrant-holders when they bought the equities. Now that share prices had crashed, however, warrant-holders looked unlikely ever to buy the equities, since the prefixed exercise price now exceeded the share price. The biggest bulge of these bonds came due in 1992 ($20.4 billion worth) and in 1993 ($64.1 billion worth). To the issuers, this meant that the funds had not been so ultra-cheap after all, since on maturity, or in anticipation of it, they would have to raise higher-cost funds to repay the bonds. When the Nikkei slumped below 17,000 in April 1992, more than 50 percent below its peak, it left about $100 billion worth of warrant bonds in need of such refinancing.

To the big Japanese brokers, this huge refinancing requirement meant new business. Financial history is full of such occasions when investment banks take fees for getting their clients into a mess and then take a further set of fees for getting them out of it. That is what American investment banks were doing in 1991–93 for American corporations that had over-indebted themselves with junk bonds. So, beginning as early as 1990–91, it is what the Japanese brokers began to do. Yet this new spate of Eurobond issues was not enough to replace the warrant market that had died with the Tokyo stock market.

In 1990, Nomura hung on to its top slot in the league table for Eurobond underwritings, but with an issue total of $16.1 billion, almost half its 1989 record, and a share of the market of 9.2 percent. Daiwa fell to fourth place, Nikko to seventh, and Yamaichi to tenth. CSFB was back in business, climbing to second place with $11.6 billion worth of issues and a 6.6 percent share. The following year, refinancings helped Nomura hold its lead, with $21.5 billion worth of issues and an 8.7 percent share of a growing market. CSFB was a close second, however, and in the first quarter of 1992 it overtook Nomura to regain the lead.

That still leaves the Japanese investment banks with a strong position in London's international capital market. In New York, their hold on the T-bond market depended only on Japanese investors; in Eurobonds, remember, they had the advantage of business coming not just from Japanese investors but also from issuers. The investors have waxed and waned with Japan's capital outflows. But since Japanese companies remain large and credit-worthy and need to refinance themselves, these corporate issuers are likely to leave the Japanese houses among the top dozen or so underwriters for the foreseeable future. It is a feast that has turned into merely a steady and satisfying diet.

Beyond the Eurobond market, the Japanese firms have built themselves a reasonable position as distinguished outsiders in the equity and gilts markets: never vying for leadership, but a signifi-cant presence nevertheless. There have been staff cutbacks— Nomura set the trend by cutting fifty equity market-makers and analysts in London in late 1992—but so far nothing drastic. As in New York, research analysts at all four houses (all locals) have done a good job in getting their names known and their companies quoted in the press and on television, and by no means solely about Japanese matters. The brokers are building a little domestic British business, while principally selling British and European shares and government bonds to their Japanese clients.

Accordingly, their analysts in London typically cover a whole European sector, rather than, say, merely the British bank shares, since that keeps costs down and is better suited to the interests of Japanese investors. Life insurance firms and pension funds in Tokyo want to allocate a slice of their money to European stocks in general, and leave it to the analysts and salesmen to tell them which country's shares look best. The brokers also have smaller branch offices in Paris, Frankfurt, Madrid, and Milan, but these are generally controlled from London. All have been built up cau-tiously. But all are there for one true purpose: to serve Japanese clients.

———

What of the banks, whose huge size has given them a prominent position in all scare books about Japanese power overseas? They rose on the back of Japan's huge capital flows and fell back when those flows subsided in 1989–93. That is as true of Japanese commercial banks as it has been of the Big Four securities houses. Like the securities houses, the banks are simply intermediaries for Japanese capital: they are as strong as that capital permits or as weak as it demands.

The strength of that intermediary role took a different form for commercial banks than for the brokers, however. The capital strength brought two distinct advantages: one was that Japanese commercial banks became the low-cost producers of the banking industry; the other arose because part of their own capital base is linked to the Tokyo stock market.

Until 1988, the finance ministry allowed them to count 70 percent of unrealized gains on shares in their own portfolios as capital. After 1988, when a new international deal was struck on capital ratios for banks, that figure was lowered to 45 percent. Still, it meant that Japanese banks' capital remained closely tied to the fate of the Tokyo stock market. Just as the stock market boom of 1986–89 produced the brokers' warrant-bond business, so it inflated the commercial banks' capital. And capital is what any bank lends against: the larger the capital, the more loans a bank can make. Hence the higher the Tokyo stock market, the more the Japanese banks were able and willing to expand their lending, at home and abroad.

The table on page 146 shows how they expanded their lending in one of their main international spheres of operation: London. The City is one of the main homes of cross-border lending, whether by individual banks or syndicated among many banks, and in a variety of different currencies. It was natural, therefore, for Japanese banks to expand their own international operations through a hefty base in London.

———

JAPANESE BANKS IN LONDON

	Percent of All UK Sterling Loans	*Percent of All UK Nonsterling Loans*
1980	1.1	21.5
1981	1.7	23.8
1982	1.5	26.3
1983	1.7	28.0
1984	0.3	30.9
1985	2.6	31.6
1986	2.9	37.1
1987	3.2	36.5
1988	3.8	37.2
1989	4.6	36.5
1990	4.7	33.4
1991	4.5	32.1

Source: Bank of England

As the table indicates, Japanese banks' presence in London looms much larger in the market for nonsterling lending than in that denominated in sterling and thus destined for the British market. Between 1980 and 1990, Japanese banks did more than quadruple their share of all sterling lending in Britain, yet that still meant only that their share rose from 1.1 percent to 4.7 percent of the market. Japanese banks opened branches outside London to chase the business of Japanese multinationals investing in Wales, the northeast of England, the Midlands, and Scotland; and they expanded their lending especially aggressively to commercial-property developers in Britain. Sumitomo Bank even entered the market for residential mortgages. Yet it still did not amount to much. Japanese banks are visible in the domestic British banking market, but only just.

In the international, nonsterling market, by contrast, they are much more prominent. They already accounted for a sizeable 21.5 percent of all nonsterling loans booked in London in 1980, but then expanded that share dramatically to reach a peak of 37.2 percent of the market in 1988. As a group, that gave the Japanese the largest combined share of any nationality.

The Bank for International Settlements (BIS), in effect the central bankers' central bank, monitors cross-border lending more broadly.

The BIS reports a similar figure for Japanese banks' share of total outstanding cross-border loans in 1988 of 38 percent, which declined to 35.5 percent at the end of 1990. Both these figures, from the BIS and from the Bank of England, exaggerate the Japanese presence somewhat, since a large chunk of these cross-border, nonsterling loans are interbank loans: in other words, one Japanese bank lending to another.

Such interbank lending typically accounts for half of all cross-border assets, according to BIS figures: at the end of 1990, interbank lending was thought to account for $3.9 trillion worth of the $7.2 trillion of total gross international bank assets outstanding. Nevertheless, if you assume that Japanese banks are no more prone to interbank lending than any other, it could be said that they still accounted for 35.5 percent of the $3.3 trillion worth of non-interbank international loans. In other words, they held a little over $1 trillion worth of international loans. That is equivalent to roughly a fifth of the American GDP.

The actual Japanese presence in the United States, both at its peak and now, is smaller than those international shares but much larger than their presence in Britain. By mid-1990, Japanese banks held 12.4 percent of all American banking assets (i.e., loans). They were heavily concentrated in California, where many of the biggest Japanese banks bought local banks during the 1980s or established their American headquarters. By 1990, Japanese banks accounted for almost a quarter of all bank loans outstanding in California. Their share of commercial and industrial loans in the state is much higher even than that, reaching almost 35 percent in 1991. Late in the decade, they expanded most aggressively in lending to Californian property, doubling their share of such loans in the state from 10 percent to 20 percent.

Enough of these numbers. Suffice it to say that the Japanese banks are big, and certainly big enough to have made many people start worrying in the late 1980s about Japanese banks' hold on the financial arteries not just of the United States but also of the world. In particular niche markets, competition from these rapidly expanding Japanese lenders drove down profit margins painfully; the Japanese banks' low cost of funds meant that a loan or a letter of credit guarantee could be profitable to them where it would not make sense to a local bank. The inevitable cry went out, in Britain and America: this was financial dumping.

That cry can no longer be heard. The reason is that Japanese banks are in the midst of a painful withdrawal from international markets. The slump in the Tokyo stock market means that they now have much less capital to support their loans, both at home and abroad. Their withdrawal has fattened profit margins for local banks. It has left the Japanese with severely burned fingers, however. As with all newcomers to a banking market, despite their low-cost funds they tended to end up chasing the riskiest loan. Pick a leveraged buy-out in late 1980s America and you will find a horde of Japanese lenders. Pick a defaulted property loan in Britain or America and you will often find a Japanese bank holding the bad debts.

The picture has been clearest in California. In 1991, Bank of California, which is owned by Mitsubishi Bank, had to ask its parent for $250 million to cover loan-loss provisions and reported a net loss for 1991 of $188 million. It cut its staff by 15 percent, the first Japanese bank in California to resort to firings. Union Bank, owned by Bank of Tokyo, has also had to make a big provision. Mitsui Manufacturers Bank, owned by what is now called Sakura Bank, made a net loss of $57 million in 1991. Now that the Californian property market is sliding, lagging well behind other major American property markets, those provisions are bound to rise in 1993 and beyond.

In all, a report in the *Nihon Keizai Shimbun,* Japan's top financial daily, in February 1992, estimated that Japanese commercial banks' bad overseas loans then totaled more than Y5 trillion, which is $37 billion or £22 billion. Of that, the newspaper reckoned Y2 trillion were loans to private entities in Europe and the United States. These are colossal sums, by any standards—especially since the Japanese banks' domestic nonperforming loans are even larger.

Go back to the Japanese shares of international bank lending in London. As the table showed, the share peaked in 1988 at 37.2 percent and by 1991 had fallen back to 32.1 percent. That probably understates the retreat, because banks cannot withdraw credit lines easily, once granted, nor even refuse to renew them. All they can do is to cease making new loans, which is what the Japanese have been doing. Most likely, the Japanese share will tumble further in the next few years, perhaps back to as low as 25–28 percent. Japanese banks are in severe pain, strangled by the fallen stock market and weighed down by a pile of bad debts. Something has to go, both at home and abroad. One thing that is going for the time being is the Japanese commercial banks' multinational ambitions.

———

The Japanese securities houses and commercial banks were swept around the world by Japan's capital exports and its soaring financial markets; but they were swept back again equally rapidly when the exports disappeared and the financial markets crashed. They were not alone, however, in failing to achieve their global ambitions in the 1980s. For all nationalities, those ambitions proved to be based on a false notion of the source of success in finance.

This is not just a Japanese phenomenon. Regardless of nationality, the number of banks or securities houses that have succeeded in establishing a strong presence in a foreign financial market can be counted on the fingers of one hand. Salomon Brothers and Morgan Stanley have managed it in Tokyo. Goldman Sachs has had a fair bit of success in London. Citicorp runs successful local banks in Germany and Brazil. But that is about it.

Why? Because although money now flows freely across frontiers, the users of it do not. Borrowers, investors, lenders, all are nationals of one particular market, with their principal interest not in finance but in some other business that generally has a more parochial character: manufacturing, building, pension-fund management. As in any business, the customers are king: and their needs and instincts favor the domestic banks and investment banks. Money may swirl around, but relationships with customers do not. Banks and investment banks are intermediaries for the flow of money but they are not merely random pipelines, for they intermediate between one set of customers and another. So closeness to those customers matters a great deal.

This is what has hindered Nomura, Nikko, Daiwa, and Yamaichi from building genuinely domestic businesses in America: their

149

remoteness from the customer. It has also hindered the commercial banks, despite the supposed fact that borrowers these days are only interested in price. That tendency pushes the newcomer banks to the riskiest business, which in turn exposes them to greater pain during a recession. But the tendency is not as widespread as it is commonly thought. Big American corporations still favor close relationships with their banks; increased global competition in finance has merely meant that big companies have now narrowed down the number of banks they talk to regularly to half a dozen or so. They know that global competition means that those half a dozen will offer keen rates. Breaking into those small circles is tough.

Finance no longer respects geography, but it still respects nationality and personality. This has meant that, regardless of their size and capital strength, Japan's financial multinationals could attain international prominence only for as long as their Japanese customers had pots of money. Once the pots of money disappeared, so did the prominence of the Japanese financiers. Only if the pots return will they return.

7

A QUESTION OF CONTROL

In my old home,
which I forsook, the cherries
are in bloom.

ISSA

THE four industries—cars, entertainment, tires, and finance—I have so far examined reveal a great deal about
the operations and experiences of Japanese multinationals in the
United States and Europe. They cover easily the biggest and
most visible cases of Japanese foreign investment. But it would
not be right to draw general conclusions from just four case
studies. In particular, it would be wrong to infer that these four
cases offer a fair picture of the balance between success and failure for the Japanese firms. The car industry is a pretty clear success story; the other three are failures, or at least highly prob-
lematic. Yet this does not mean that only one in four Japanese
investments is a success. Far from it. There are plenty of dia-
monds, plenty of duds. I make no pretense of drawing up a balance sheet for that investment, whether from the firms' point of
view, from Japan's point of view, or from the host countries'
point of view.

Nevertheless, there are legitimate general issues to be raised about the Japanese multinationals. Four case studies, even of quite broad subject matter, are insufficient to address those issues. It would be misleading to use such anecdotal evidence to reach general conclusions, even though to do so is a common fault among commentators of every stripe. The Fallacy of the Aggregated Anecdote is one of the most common of all errors.

In the effort to avoid that fallacy and yet to gather some generally applicable data about the behavior and organizational methods of Japanese multinationals, I conducted a questionnaire survey. It was sent to roughly 500 affiliates of Japanese manufacturing firms in the United States and Western Europe. Exactly 150 firms returned usable replies, in late 1991 and early 1992. Of these, 92 were in the United States, 41 in Britain, and 17 in the remainder of the European Community. Only manufacturers were included in the survey because directing questions at that sort of business offered the greatest chance of producing data that was comparable across very different sectors and industries. If you compare a travel agency and a machine tool maker there are few issues in common between them; but if you compare a computer firm, a machine tool maker, and a car factory there is plenty of common ground.

The survey was made confidential, in the hope that this might lead respondents, whether of Japanese or Western nationality, to be more candid. By and large, it worked, with the result that the survey yielded not just raw, impersonal data but also a variety of personal comments and observations, of value because they come from such a wide variety of firms.

Finally, the survey promised to be useful in another important respect. In the late 1950s, a British industrial economist, John Dunning, conducted a survey of American manufacturing subsidiaries in Britain. His purpose was to map how these American multinationals were organizing themselves in Britain, what they thought of their alien surroundings, and, to a lesser extent, what their alien surroundings thought of them. Though Dunning's research was far more rigorous and academic than the present work (and he is now one of the world's leading authorities on multinational investment), this nevertheless opened up an opportunity: if some of the same questions could be posed now of Japanese multinationals as were posed in the 1950s of American ones, we would get some indication of whether and how Japanese multinationals were really different.

For those who love to pore over numbers, the full results of the survey, as well as a list of respondents and of questions, are in the three appendices at the back of the book. As these show, the survey covered firms employing a total of 107,167 workers, including 2,345 expatriate Japanese managers. But for the benefit of those who do not love to study statistics, let us for the present purpose concentrate on the main questions. These can be grouped into five major areas:

> How productive are overseas factories compared with those back home? What explains the differences?
>
> Who controls these subsidiaries: Japanese or foreigners?
>
> Is research and development conducted overseas? Or is the best work kept back home?
>
> Do these subsidiaries prefer to import from Japan rather than buying locally?
>
> How different are they from their American forebears in Professor Dunning's survey? Is there something special about being Japanese?

Start with productivity. Hypothesis: Japanese manufacturers invest abroad because they believe their management methods are superior. They ought therefore to be achieving high levels of productivity in their foreign factories, helping to bring local productivity up toward Japanese levels. To many enthusiasts, that is a prime reason for encouraging Japanese investors. Are they proving productive?

The answer appears to be: no. Or, at least, the results are not exactly world-beating. Making a success of overseas investment is proving quite a grind, at least if the relevant benchmark is productivity back in Japan. Asked to compare their foreign factories' productivity with that in their Japanese parents' factories, the result was that average output per man-hour in the foreign factories was thought to be only 84 percent of the level at the Japanese parents. The three regions differed little.

Why the underperformance? A first clue lies in whether the

firms had built their own factories or had bought them or had formed a joint venture. Most of the firms replying to the question-naire had made "greenfield" investments, building their factories from the ground up. But 34 (or 23 percent) were formed by acquisition and 27 (18 percent) were joint ventures rather than wholly owned firms. The acquired firms reported lower produc-tivity figures (78 percent, on average) relative to their Japanese parents than did greenfield firms; but joint ventures reported iden-tical figures (84 percent, on average) to those reported by the whole sample.

So acquisition holds performance back; the acquirer is saddled by past practices. Yet there must be other, more important, expla-nations, too. The clearest and simplest answers are the overseas factories' small scale and relative youth. Most of the factories built by Japanese firms abroad are smaller than those at home and are consequently less automated and less able to exploit economies of scale in production. They are also newer, with workforces that are less experienced and who have spent less of their careers working with Japanese methods. The questionnaire asked firms to say why they thought that there was a productivity difference between Japan and abroad. Answers citing the small scale of production and lack of experience among workers appeared more than any other.

The survey does show that productivity has been improving, suggesting that experience is an important factor. Asked what the comparable figure for output per man-hour as a percentage of Japanese levels was at the time when production (or ownership) commenced, the average reply was that it had only been 63.6 percent. The figure was higher (66 percent) in America than in Britain or Europe (59.6 percent and 59 percent, respectively), which is not surprising given that, generally, American productiv-ity is higher than in Europe and that most of the American plants were likelier to have been larger right from the start than those in Europe. Cheeringly, a joint venture firm in Britain said that "Our workers work much harder than before when we started produc-tion."

Quality is much less of a problem than productivity, it seems. Many respondents thought their product quality was as good if not better than their Japanese parents', and felt quality had improved greatly since their operations were set up. Techniques for quality control do depend on fairly transferrable factors, such as the machinery and process adopted, as well as the quality of the workforce, though the workforce must also be an important factor.

This discrepancy between quality and productivity may also explain the results of a question about costs: asked whether overall costs of production were higher, about the same, or lower than in Japan, 47 percent replied that they were higher and only 22 percent thought they were lower. This may partly be caused by scale and by infancy; but the need to devote more resources to quality control overseas than in Japan may also be a factor. Unlike low productivity, poor quality control would otherwise be punished directly in the marketplace by choosy consumers.

One explanation for poor productivity that many Japanese find tempting is industrial relations. Heading abroad, most Japanese expect to find their workers organized by an uncooperative trade union, interested more in pursuing some form of class struggle than in working together with managers for the overall prosperity and growth of the firm. Yet this is not born out by the survey. Around 70 percent of the firms polled do not have any of their workers organized by a trade union. In the United States, a union at a Japanese plant is as rare as frost in Florida: it only existed in 9 out of the 92 replies, or less than 10 percent.

So Japanese firms repel all unions? No: in Britain roughly half of all the firms polled were unionized. Trade unions are far more common in British industry, so the Japanese investors are reflecting that local practice. They are showing their flexibility by adopting American personnel habits in America, British ones in Britain. Sensibly, they are not being rigidly Japanese; they are seeking to blend in with their local surroundings.

Still, in general, unions cannot be the answer. Rather, the explanation of poor productivity performance may well lie in other differences in operating methods used abroad compared with those common in Japanese factories. In other words, Japanese firms and their managers are forced to compromise between the Japanese methods they consider to be superior and those to which the local workforce and managers are accustomed. Some of that adaptation is unavoidable: education standards differ, and local labor laws often dictate how workers can be used or organized.

Many firms identified such qualitative, legal, or subjective reasons for the deficiency in productivity. Some in America, for instance, blamed the fact that American workers tend to have tighter, more specified job descriptions than Japanese workers do and are unwilling to take on tasks outside their job description. Japanese workers are likelier to have rather vague, overlapping responsibilities, with all workers encouraged to feel a collective commitment and a collective responsibility. Others blamed absenteeism and a high rate of staff turnover, which meant that their firm was forever having to train new people.

In Europe, labor laws came in for some blame; in many European countries these circumscribe the use of workers (with overtime limits, compulsory break times, and so on) far more than would be the case in Japan. Replies did not, however, all fall into the stereotypical pattern of British workers being considered as lazy while Germans are harder working: one firm in Germany described its workers as "very poor" (this was a German firm that had been acquired by a Japanese one). Another said there was high absenteeism and poor motivation in Germany.

Nevertheless a German subsidiary gave one of the most detailed and informative answers on the difference in methods and attitudes between Germany and Japan, showing many common traits with American equivalents:

> The European way of management (or I should say "German way") is that there exists a rather clear job description for every level, even for each individual job. It is comparable to the organization of an army: an order always comes from the top; a manager should give an order, a member should obey; a member should not help another unit which is under the control of another manager; if a unit suffers from difficulties, it is its manager who should manage them.
>
> The Japanese way, if anything, is that there are relatively vague job descriptions, and sometimes even none. The responsibility is not clear: if a problem exists, everybody feels (or should

feel) responsible for it and try to solve it together. A typical manager is not a decisionmaker or *Befehlgeber* [a person who gives an order] but rather an able coordinator who can harmonize the different interests of several departments.

We basically operate the German method because 95 percent of our employees are German. However we sometimes apply the Japanese way, in case the typical German way could not help to solve a problem.

Not everyone was as careful and pro-Japanese as this. A manager at a joint-venture plant in Britain said that, where a productivity difference exists "it is due largely to the Japanese military approach to industry, i.e., management by fear." And at a Japanese firm in the United States, an American respondent explained the low quality of management by observing that "it is probably because good quality managers do not want to work at a Japanese company." Others were just as condemnatory of Japanese methods. An American respondent (for a computer software firm) said:

Their perceptions differ radically from ours in terms of social, ethical, business and market dynamics. The product which we market is based upon one which has had great success in Japan. They tried to sell it in the United States and failed. Our firm modified the product and has had a remarkable success. Now they question whether we should proceed as in the past, adding functionality.

Their business practices are reminiscent of the seventeenth-century shogunate.

However, as individuals outside of work they are nice people.

Nice of him to add that. Still, two can play at stereotypes. This was a Japanese manager at a firm operating either side of the Mexican border: "Productivity in Mexico is generally about 60–70 percent of Japan due to the special character of Hispanic people. Their philosophy is 'much money with less labor.' "

Whether or not this is true in this specific case, it is not true that Japanese firms generally think their workers are lazy. Asked whether their local labor works harder, equally as hard, or less hard than their Japanese workforce at home, exactly half answered that they work equally as hard. Very few thought local labor actually worked harder than labor in Japan; 42 percent thought the answer was "less hard." Even higher percentages thought their local managers were as effective as in Japan: 67 percent overall, of which Britain's 75 percent stood out as surprising in a country that generally bemoans the quality of its own managers. To an extent, respondents might have wished to be polite about their colleagues, but in a confidential survey this ought not to have been a major distortion.

A Japanese president of an acquired American subsidiary who says his firm's productivity is only 80 percent of his parent's (a rise from 60 percent at the time of acquisition) gave the following list of explanations for the gap in the United States:

1. There are so many kinds, races, and levels of people.
2. There is a basic antagonism toward management.
3. If productivity improves, people are laid off.
4. Cost of labor is "expenses" in the United States, i.e., a variable cost. The attitude toward people differs.

Getting down to specifics, a Japanese in America echoed a common theme when he wrote:

> Japanese high-school graduates have much higher math, physics and science knowledge than Americans. These knowledges are key to operate today's state-of-the-art operation, including statistical process control and statistical quality control. The education system needs to be improved greatly for the future of the United States. The United States has resources to do it, much better than other developing countries, but they are not yet used in the way they should be.

His American colleagues might not enjoy their homeland being described as a developing country, but that is indeed what he wrote.

Although most Japanese firms do not think their foreign workers are idle layabouts, many clearly do think there are differences in how effectively people work, related in particular to how flexibly they can be organized in a factory overseas. Flexibility is one of the key factors in the best firms in Japan: workers are willing to learn and move, and employers are willing to train them to do so.

To illustrate this point, one respondent in America said:

> As for salaried workers, it is difficult to train them by rotating them through different departments like we do in Japan since the working policy here is "same profession, same salary scheme." As for hourly workers, it is difficult to select a person for a higher position due to the idea of "equal treatment." So we have to give promotions to the workers with longer time in the company.

Yet there may also be faults on the Japanese side. Managers have to be flexible, too, adapting to their local surroundings in more than merely the superficial arrangements between management and unions. Stressing the importance of clashing managerial cultures, a Japanese respondent in America said:

> Japanese expatriates are making sincere efforts to assimilate themselves to a different business culture in the United States by listening to Americans attentively. (Japanese are good at listening, but not too good at expressing!) Behind their confidence, I think they do maintain a good tradition of modesty and humbleness, patience, etc., which attribute partly to the success of their business, although as a nation Japan sometimes behaves in a different way.

Anecdotes are all very well, but are the methods used in Japanese firms abroad generally different from those tried and tested at home? To find out whether firms really felt that operating methods differed substantially at home from the overseas factory, the survey included the following question: "Are your operating methods a) markedly different, b) marginally different, or c) the same in this country as in Japan?"

The result did not support the view that things are markedly different abroad compared with factories in Japan. Only 18 percent of firms replying thought so, with roughly the same percentages in each of the three areas, America, Continental Europe, and Britain.

More than half thought their methods were only marginally different, while only 25 percent thought they were markedly different.

Put all this together, and what do you get? Japanese manufacturing multinationals have so far failed to achieve the same levels of productivity as they do in Japan, even though they claim to be applying similar management and operating methods abroad as they do at home. Industrial relations is not the problem, though Japanese firms do have to adopt many of the local ways of handling personnel, restricting their flexibility in deploying their labor. Their costs are often higher than in Japan.

Yet the Japanese are still new kids on their respective blocks and have often invested cautiously, with output remaining at a small scale compared with their plants in Japan. From the Japanese point of view, life abroad is not as difficult or dangerous as many would have assumed as recently as a decade or so ago. From the American or European point of view, the average Japanese subsidiary is not the industrial paragon or powerhouse that Japanese firms are so often reputed to be.

——

As we have seen, Sony and Matsushita have both delegated control over their entertainment software divisions to foreigners, based well away from the head office. But this is worth repeating again only to stress the key fact: the move is interesting precisely because it is so unusual. Most Japanese multinationals do not cede control in this way. Indeed, neither Sony nor Matsushita does so in the rest of its overseas operations.

Japanese car companies, tire makers, semiconductor manufacturers, investment banks, advertising agencies, even travel firms, do not typically hand over control to local managers. If local managers hold senior positions, they are nevertheless "shadowed" by Japanese expatriates and have to report often and in detail to their Japanese seniors in the head office. The big strategic decisions take place at home; only tactical ones are devolved to the overseas subsidiaries. Japanese multinationals prefer to keep control. It is clear from the survey, as well as from the case studies, that this is the normal way in which Japanese firms operate across borders.

But what is less clear is whether, compared with other multinationals, the Japanese are unusual in this desire to retain control.

American and European multinationals have also, now and in the past, been prone to dispatching expatriates to occupy the top positions in overseas affiliates and still have very few foreigners in top management at home, let alone on the main board of directors. Shell, the Anglo-Dutch oil company, is one of the world's most international companies, yet the vast bulk of its top managers come from one of its two home countries: Britain or Holland. Philips is also an extremely international firm since its home market in Holland is small, yet it is tightly controlled by the central bureaucracy in Eindhoven and has never yet had anyone as chairman or chief executive who is not Dutch.

These and other Western firms exercise control through their expatriates, through reporting lines back to the head office, and through their close and careful monitoring of financial flows in subsidiary companies. They may not use methods identical to those used by the Japanese, but the intent is similar. If there is any difference it can only be one of degree, not kind.

There is a strong perception inside Japanese affiliates that they are controlled quite tightly by the head office. This was also true of American firms in Britain in the 1950s. In his 1958 survey, Professor Dunning asked his 150 American firms in Britain whether they thought that their firms were strongly, partly, or negligibly controlled by their American associates. Many of his firms had been in Britain for years, often as long as half a century. Still, 32.7 percent thought they were strongly controlled and 39.3 percent felt they were partly controlled. That adds up to 72 percent feeling that they were by no means independent of the head office.

My questionnaire posed an identical question. The bulk of respondents (53 percent) said that their firm was partly controlled from Japan, while only 12 percent said it was strongly controlled. That low score for "strong control" probably needs to be interpreted cautiously. It would be understandable given today's climate of resentment at foreign ownership in America and Europe if some subsidiaries were oversensitive about the accusation of strong Japanese control and were therefore keen to play the issue down. Nevertheless, this can be controlled for by comparing the total of "strongly" and "partly," rather than putting too much store in each category.

Adding the two together produces 65 percent who accepted that their firms were subject to Japanese parental control, compared with the slightly higher total of 72 percent in Dunning's 1958 survey. These are close enough, given today's political sensitivities, to be considered as more or less the same result.

As to the method by which control is exerted, the most direct method is clearly the expatriate manager. Firms vary considerably in the number of expatriates they send to affiliates abroad, partly because of different strategies but also because some lack the managerial resources at home to be able to dispatch dozens overseas. The average firm in my Japanese survey had fifteen to sixteen expatriate Japanese employees, with slightly more at firms in the United States (perhaps because it is a more important market and because the affiliates are a little bigger) than in Britain or Europe.

Almost 60 percent of those polled gave the central post of chief financial officer to a Japanese expatriate, ensuring that an agent of the parent firm was able to monitor the flows of funds. This tendency was again slightly more marked for firms in America than in Britain or Continental Europe. It reflects a natural desire of all businesses: to keep a keen eye on the lifeblood of the company, in other words, the money.

Such a keen eye can act as an early warning signal, it makes fraud less likely and also, in today's globally integrated financial markets, it makes it easier for a multinational to exploit its scale and creditworthiness in raising and deploying its funds. Asked whether they had a separate treasury function or one centralized in the parent firm, the vast majority of Japanese subsidiaries—77 percent—answered that they had a separate treasury. Since many are now large firms generating sizable flows of cash, it is not surprising that the subsidiaries have separate treasuries. But put that result together with the 60 percent of firms that had a Japanese CFO, and the picture changes somewhat: these treasuries may be separate from the parent, but as they are under the supervision of an expatriate they are capable of a high degree of central control and coordination.

In addition to this direct question about the number of expatriates, the survey also asked Japanese-owned firms to name the top slots occupied by a Japanese and a non-Japanese, and to say what proportion of the twenty "most senior" positions were held by non-Japanese. Such is the propensity in all companies to inflate job titles or to render them meaningless that the top slots occupied by Japanese or non-Japanese provided little real information.

It was common to have a Japanese chairman and a non-Japanese chief executive; or a Japanese chief executive and a non-Japanese "chief operating officer"; or the equivalent titles in Europe to these essentially American ones. But the reverse was also true, with a non-Japanese in nominally the most senior position and the top Japanese in a somewhat less fancy slot. Without detailed study of each company, however, it is impossible to tell whether the titles mean what they suggest or not: many will certainly have powerless non-Japanese chairmen, while others will have powerless Japanese figureheads who spend all day reading the newspaper or playing golf.

A more informative answer was provided by the question asking what proportion of the ten most senior jobs are held by non-Japanese. Most firms replied that the bulk of their twenty most senior jobs were occupied by non-Japanese; an average of 67 percent were taken by such locals, with the proportion higher in the United States than elsewhere.

This may still be misleading: the judgment as to which are the "senior" jobs can be ambiguous, especially given the common Japanese habit of sending expatriates as "advisers" or "shadows" with no formal place in the management hierarchy but nevertheless a crucial monitoring and teaching role. It will also be the case that certain jobs are virtually always held by locals—personnel manager, for instance, and probably also purchasing manager—while some tend to be filled by "experts" from Japan, such as chief engineer.

Perhaps that gap between the formal reply and the reality of the Japanese presence explains the following statement from an American:

> Our company is considered small to medium-sized globally. We have a reputation for being very "Japanese" among the other

U.S. Japanese-owned subsidiaries. My personal opinion is that the larger Japanese companies are more adept at "localizing" than the smaller companies. I expect this operation to be profitable soon. However, the morale of the U.S. management is poor and I expect it to worsen since top management is slow or unwilling to allow for any difference in culture such as work hours, holidays, vacations. Surprisingly, management turnover has been virtually zero so far—perhaps because most of the management was recruited directly out of college.

Many Japanese expatriates identify their role as essentially one of acting as a communication channel between the head office and the local managers. Hideaki Hirano, the most senior Japanese at Nissan's British car factory, is called a "senior adviser." His background sounds pretty suitable for this channeling role: before moving to Britain he worked in the international public relations department at Nissan in Tokyo, before which he had a spell in the Japanese diplomatic service on a temporary transfer from Nissan's trade union. He said in an interview that his role is very vague, even conceding, "In a sense, I am useless."

What he meant by that is that he does not take a direct part in management, but rather acts as an intermediary between Nissan's British boss, Ian Gibson, and the parent company. When Gibson makes a decision, or needs to make one, he seeks comments and information from Hirano and, through him, from Tokyo.

Japanese control does not necessarily mean control from Japan. Gradually, Nissan has been building up its European headquarters in Amsterdam, transferring Japanese staff there from Tokyo. Once that headquarters is fully established, the advisory and intermediary role played by Hirano will be more or less redundant. The man who was Hirano's counterpart in Tokyo will be in Amsterdam, and Gibson can deal with him directly. Control will be no less Japanese, but it will be operated from Amsterdam, not from Japan. In turn, the Amsterdam headquarters will be controlled by Tokyo.

In this respect, Nissan will be adopting a structure pretty similar to that used by General Motors. GM has its European headquarters in Zurich, with the top slots occupied by expatriate Americans. Zurich controls the main operating subsidiaries, Vauxhall in Britain and Opel in Germany.

The Nissan case promises to be typical of the larger manufacturing firms, as they become more and more established overseas. They will remain heavily Japanese, but the locus of Japanese control is likely also to be shifted offshore. For the time being, many overseas manufacturing operations report straight back to headquarters, and do so not through a special international division but rather through the various functional equivalents in the parent company: in other words, a manager of a compact-disk factory will link up with the Japanese compact-disk division, not simply through a general international chief.

But firms do vary widely. A little over 53 percent of the subsidiaries polled said that reporting lines lead to such functional equivalents, against almost 35 percent for whom reporting takes place through a single contact point. Such variety reflects a tension, common to all multinationals, between reporting lines that have the virtue of clarity and neatness—i.e., those to a single contact point—and the messier sort that nevertheless allow specialists to genuinely share and coordinate their expertise.

———

This tension between generalists and specialists looms especially large in research and development. Scientists and developers of new products are the ultimate specialists, dedicated by their training, experience, and interests to one set of tasks: inventing new technologies and implementing them in order to bring new products to market. As such, R&D poses a particular problem for the multinational, as well as prompting particular worries in the host country. The problem for the multinational is how to keep R&D under control, both in terms of its cost and its direction, while at the same time ensuring that it is constantly adaptable to differing market conditions around the world and that the firm is able to seek out the most advanced technology wherever it may be found.

The worries for the host country are twofold. The first is that all R&D will be conducted at the head office, thus leaving only relatively poorly paid and unsophisticated tasks for the overseas subsidiary. The second, related, worry is that a multinational will direct its investment to "capture" the host country's technology through acquisitions, joint ventures, and scientific recruitment.

The benefits of that technology are then "lost" by being shifted to the multinational's head office and will thus provide fewer spin-off benefits to the local economy. Either it will keep its own brainy bits at home, or it will steal ours.

The general notion that R&D takes place chiefly at a multinational's headquarters is born out by anecdotal evidence, both for American and European multinationals and for Japanese ones. As mentioned earlier, Raymond Vernon of Harvard cited this as a concern in the early 1970s about American firms.

Yet this notion, that multinationals are stingy with R&D, is not born out by aggregate data. Here the best comparative data is not my own humble survey but rather one by Edward Graham and Paul Krugman, presented in their 1991 book, *Foreign Direct Investment in the United States*. Graham is a fellow of the Institute for International Economics, a Washington think tank; Krugman is an economics professor at MIT.

Graham and Krugman analyzed data on the performance of American affiliates of foreign firms and compared it to data on American-owned firms. They found that, taking the economy as a whole, foreign-affiliated firms actually perform more R&D per worker than American-owned companies. As Graham and Krugman concede, this may be principally because of a compositional effect: foreign ownership is concentrated in manufacturing, which has quite a high R&D content, but the American economy as a whole consists of a lot of other types of companies as well, many of which do not require much research. So Graham and Krugman also studied figures simply for manufacturing, which showed R&D per worker of $3,630 in 1988 for foreign affiliates compared with company-funded R&D of just $3,110 for American firms. The American figure is higher if all R&D is included, but that would be misleading since it would consist largely of government-funded defense programs.

When Graham and Krugman divided their data up to show the different nationalities of foreign affiliates, they found that there was considerable variation. At the bottom of the pack came British multinationals, which spent $1,720 per worker on R&D in America. At the top came Germany, with $5,230. Japanese firms came a bit below average, spending $2,880 per worker, even though they were at the top of the pack in terms of the value-added per worker. Graham and Krugman concluded that it was not true that Japanese firms kept the most sophisticated, high value-added activities at home, but it nevertheless did seem to be true that they spent relatively little on research and development abroad.

The data comes with a health warning, however: statistics on foreign-owned firms are always poor since those who collect data for a national economy do not classify it initially by nationality. The result is that the data can be unreliably incomplete: Graham and Krugman point out, for instance, that their data for value-added per worker and R&D per worker for Japanese firms does not include the Japanese carmakers' operations in the United States. Since these are among the biggest and most prominent Japanese investors, that is quite a gap. Almost certainly, inclusion of the carmakers would raise the value-added per worker but might depress R&D per worker a bit, since the car firms' American-based research operations are fairly rudimentary.

By contrast, my survey bears out the notion that Japanese firms conduct relatively little research overseas. But I asked a different question: whether subsidiaries do research, rather than whether subsidiaries are more, or less, research-intensive than local firms.

Of the 150 subsidiaries polled, only 35.3 percent said that they did conduct research locally, while 62 percent said that they did not. The astute reader will, however, have noticed that an ampersand and a word have been missing: & development. For this question merely asked firms whether they conducted research locally. A separate question asked whether they conducted development work locally, and the result was almost the reverse: 58.6 percent said that yes, they did, while only 38.6 percent said that they did not. The difference is crucial: broadly, research involves dreaming up new ideas and products; development involves bringing them off the lab bench or the drawing board and into a salable condition.

This result confirms what common sense would dictate: that a Japanese multinational investing abroad would prefer to keep research at home where it can be done on a larger scale, under head-office supervision, and closer to the marketing divisions for the company's principal market: Japan. Ideas tried and tested at home can then be transferred to factories and markets abroad. But that same multinational might well want to do design and development work at the local factory, and thus in the local market, in order to ensure that its products were correctly tailored to local requirements.

This would be true both of new products and of old ones: new ones might be developed with local needs especially in mind, but old ones would also need adaptation, for instance to meet local electrical standards. The survey also asked respondents to explain why they did, or did not, do R&D work locally, and the answers were extremely consistent. If the firm had answered yes to either question, its explanation generally touched upon the needs of local customers; if no, then mention was often made of the high costs of local research, the small scale of production, and a lack of manpower.

The only exceptions were firms that were not technological leaders in their industries and were located in a country or region where the technology was more advanced than their own. Firms in computer software and hardware and telecommunications in America, for instance, said that they were conducting research locally, generally because American technology was superior. They were not, in other words, grabbing it and taking it back to the head office, but they were trying to improve their own technical abilities by employing local scientists and participating in local consortia. So it is the technologically weak who do research locally, not the technologically strong.

———

Those who keep their research at home may often also be those who import the most. They are often importing technology embedded in parts and capital goods, rather than obtaining it locally.

This propensity to import is one of the stickiest stories of all about Japanese multinationals. Graham and Krugman found in their (admittedly flawed) data on foreign-owned affiliates in the United States that in 1988, Japanese-owned firms imported an average of $48,270 worth per worker, far more than affiliates of any other nationality. The nearest rivals were German firms with imports of $22,240 per worker or French ones with $16,100. These figures, remember, did not include the big carmakers, although those firms are also widely criticized for their imports.

Graham and Krugman also point out that the Japanese figures might have been further distorted because American data frequently classifies marketing and sales companies as manufacturers. Since many Japanese firms in America are merely operating sales networks, this causes a large distortion; such networks are by definition importers if they are not associated with a manufacturing plant. Nevertheless, it may still be true that Japanese multinationals have a high propensity to import, so let us assume that is correct for the present purpose.

The first response to this, and the most appealing to a free trader, is: so what? There is nothing wrong with importing, and it should not make a firm any less desirable as an investor since, by definition, it is not going to be importing 100 percent of its output (otherwise it would not be bothering to invest). The second response, however, is that the propensity to import is intriguing. It begs an explanation, which may in turn shed some light on the way in which Japanese multinationals are operating.

Two obviously plausible explanations immediately spring to mind. One is related to the fact that a common Japanese motivation for investment in America and Europe is the avoidance of barriers to trade. In other words, if voluntary or compulsory restraints had not been put on Japanese cars or compact disk players or computer printers entering the American and European markets, then many of the firms would have chosen to continue to serve those markets through exports rather than local production. Exporting is what was dictated by their technological and managerial advantages, and by relative prices. Once the barriers were erected, however, it made sense to invest in local production.

In many cases, though, such barriers apply only to finished products, not to their component parts. Local manufacturers prefer it that way, since a barrier to parts imports will raise their costs as well, while a barrier to finished products will only affect their foreign rivals. When there is such a barrier to finished products, the economics of the components business is unchanged: suppliers retain whatever technological, managerial, and cost advantages they had before. It is not altogether surprising, therefore, to find that Japanese barrier-hopping investors choose to import many of their parts from their old suppliers back home and merely assemble them inside the new trade barrier. The old suppliers now have to suffer higher transport costs, but their other advantages might still give them a lead over local rivals, if local rivals even exist, at least at first.

The first hypothesis is therefore that a high import content for Japanese multinational investors occurs because these investors are barrier-hoppers, and the barriers apply to the finished product, not the imported parts. This is the local-content issue that was addressed in the case of cars earlier in this book.

Plausible explanation number two also has echoes of the local-content rumpus. It is that the very structure of Japanese companies inclines them to import. Many of the biggest and most well-known Japanese firms are members of what the Japanese call *keiretsu:* industrial groups that are bound together by cross-shareholdings and that commonly do business with one another.

The keiretsu come in two varieties. One is the "horizontal" keiretsu, groups of firms in unrelated industries, akin to Western conglomerates. Examples include Mitsubishi, Mitsui, Sumitomo, and the Fuyo group, all of which were founded in the nineteenth century and which before the Second World War were closely held *zaibatsu* conglomerates but were then broken up by General Douglas MacArthur. Although these firms are in unrelated businesses, the groups are so large that inevitably they will do some business with one another, an insurance firm providing cover for a manufacturer, for example. The other variety is the "vertical" keiretsu, connecting firms that are in the same business. Generally, that means firms at different points on the supply-and-assembly chain for a product. So there is the Toyota group of parts suppliers and car manufacturers or the Matsushita group of similar firms in the electronics business.

Whether the keiretsu is horizontal or vertical, it nevertheless shares some common characteristics. Its members are tied together by small shareholdings, and they have been doing business with one another for many years. When the core member of a vertical keiretsu or simply any member of a horizontal keiretsu opts to invest abroad, suppliers to those firms begin with an advantage when it comes to negotiating contracts for parts supply to a foreign factory. They have worked together before, there is a great deal of mutual trust (presumably), there may well be economies of scale available in linking production for domestic factories to production for the new overseas one, and there is a financial incentive provided by the shareholding.

Therefore, the second hypothesis is that when a firm establishes multinational production it remains likely to buy a significant proportion of its supplies from old keiretsu partners. Initially, a large proportion of those keiretsu supplies will be imports, since the suppliers will either be disinclined to shift their own factories abroad or will take time to do so.

This keiretsu inclination is, however, eventually capable of being reproduced locally. In other words, keiretsu suppliers will follow their customer by investing in factories overseas, and the customer will then be inclined to buy from them rather than from local suppliers. Is that true? It is hard to establish statistically whether or not this tendency is on the increase, which is what you might expect given that Japanese multinationals are a relatively recent development. But what my questionnaire did was to find out whether or not, as of now, Japanese manufacturers claim a high local content or admit to a low one, and whether they principally buy from Japanese-owned suppliers or from local ones.

The answer is that they claim to rely heavily on local suppliers rather than imports, and they say that the local suppliers are not principally Japanese-owned. On average, the respondents claimed a local content of 68.6 percent, with a slightly higher figure in the United States. The lowest was in Europe, where "screwdriver" plants (i.e., plants merely assembling imported parts) are likelier as a higher proportion of Japanese manufacturing investment there has arrived to circumvent trade barriers. This local-content claim will certainly be exaggerated, since it is a sensitive question, and is anyway a measure open to wide interpretation. The actual figure cannot be relied upon; but the trend over time should be more dependable.

Local content typically rises over time as the factory builds up its production volume and builds closer relationships with local suppliers; the average local content for the 150 firms surveyed was 54 percent when they commenced production, and on average they expected it to rise to almost 80 percent in five years' time.

A Japanese electronics firm in Britain illustrated the way in which this develops:

> Because of this [recent opening] and the fact that the plant was built and equipped using fast-track methods, we in some cases opted to use equipment and materials with which we were familiar rather than to take time to investigate alternatives. However, as the plant generates its own routine, we will take the opportunity to consider alternative suppliers both in terms of equipment and consumables. In addition, we shall be approaching the development of further phases of our project with the benefit of UK experience available and with time to consider in advance questions relevant to the selection of equipment. Future progress with phase 1 of the project will also see a dilution of the Japanese content of the work force in accordance with the intention to "Europeanize" the operation as quickly as possible.

As you might expect, firms replying to the survey varied greatly in how many suppliers they use depending on the sort of industry they were in. In all, 128 firms replied to the survey's questions about suppliers; together, they had a total of 17,500 suppliers, or an average of more than 135 per firm. The firms were asked to say how many, out of all their suppliers, were wholly or partly Japanese-owned.

The answer was surprisingly few: only 1,500 suppliers, or an average of a little over 12 for each firm replying. The average was slightly higher in the United States (13.6) and lowest in Continental Europe (5.6) where the scale of Japanese investment is far lower and so where fewer Japanese suppliers may yet have taken the trouble to invest. As a proportion of all suppliers, however, the share that is Japanese-owned is pretty low: 9 percent across the whole survey, ranging from 5.1 percent in Europe to 9.7 percent in America.

This does not mean that keiretsu do not exist, nor that they are not having an impact on Japanese foreign direct investment. But it does suggest that they are not a dominant factor in the supply decisions of Japanese-owned manufacturers, taken as a whole. They may be more common in certain industries, such as cars and electronics. And the raw data from the survey is not weighted by value, but is merely sheer numbers of suppliers. So in some cases, a single Japanese-owned keiretsu supplier might be providing some hugely valuable parts, while 100 non-Japanese firms are providing all the dross. Such an outcome is entirely possible, and indeed consistent with the way in which Japanese firms go about their business. But it is unlikely to have greatly distorted the aggregate outcome.

Nevertheless, keiretsu will continue to arouse concern, especially in the United States, because of suspicions that they may break American antitrust laws. The Sherman Antitrust Act of 1890 makes it illegal (and punishable through fines or jail sentences) for companies to conspire to restrain trade or to establish monopolies; the Clayton Antitrust Act of 1914 also banned exclusive dealing arrangements, interlocking directorates between competitors, and the buying of shares in competitors. But do keiretsu do any of these things?

Vertical keiretsu, such as the Toyota group, cannot be accused of establishing monopolies, or of interlocking directorships, or of shareholdings between competitors. The firms in the group are not competitors, so their cross-shareholdings cannot be said to restrain trade. They are exactly analogous to a large vertically integrated firm that produces its own parts, which Ford and General Motors, for example, are more inclined to do than Toyota is.

Choosing to buy from related subcontractors rather than producing in-house is not a crime, in and of itself. The vertical groups' only vulnerability, therefore, is to provisions that ban a customer from refusing to do business with outsiders even though they meet its terms on price and quality. In other words, it is illegal in the United States to make membership in a keiretsu group a requirement for a supplier to be able to gain business. In 1991–92, America's Federal Trade Commission (FTC) began an investigation to see if this might have been occurring in the car-parts business. The truth is that it might well have been, but it will be difficult to prove. The difficulty arises from the need to define exactly what is meant by a customers' terms on price and quality.

The horizontal keiretsu may be more vulnerable to attack. These do sometimes group together firms that compete in certain parts of their business, so it may be possible for the FTC to establish a charge of conspiracy. One difficulty will be, however, that these groups are diffuse and that each individual firm will not, typically, account for a large share of the American market for its products. That will make it harder to find damage to local rivals, or anything approaching a monopoly position. It is the vertical keiretsu such as Toyota or Matsushita that typically account for large shares of the American market, not the horizontal ones.

For these reasons, any effort to attack Japanese multinationals in America through antitrust laws is unlikely to meet with much success. It may cause a pinprick or two, but is not going to play a large part in determining the success or failure of Japanese firms abroad. There is more justice in Western claims that antitrust violations take place in Japan itself, which then serve to help Japanese firms' competiveness in export markets. But that is a separate issue.

There is probably justice in Western grievances about feeble antitrust enforcement in Japan for the big Japanese firms. But attempting to extend United States jurisdiction to cover such behavior is unlikely to be fruitful. Sovereign countries tend not to take kindly to other countries' efforts to interfere in their legal affairs. To attempt that is to risk retaliation, not just by Japan but also by the European Community, which will fear similar treatment being meted out to its own, far larger, multinational investors in America.

———

Retaliation? Surely not, if everyone agreed that Japanese multinationals were a special case. But are they? That is the final big question that my survey seeks to answer.

One way in which Japanese multinationals seem different is that they are widely lionized as being in some way superior to Western companies. Their management philosophies, their concern for quality, their just-in-time stock control, their emphasis on continuous improvement, their concern for employees as assets rather than as wage slaves: all of these and more are frequently cited as ways in which the Japanese are special.

Yet I find it hard to avoid a sneaking suspicion that today's Japanese superiority is pretty similar to yesterday's American one. In 1958, when John Dunning was studying American manufacturing firms investing in Britain, he did so in the same sort of way in which people nowadays view the Japanese; in other words, with a considerable amount of admiration. He noted many ways in which American firms were different from their British counterparts: "Another common criticism levelled against British suppliers by American firms relates to their failure to adhere to the delivery dates stipulated, thus dislocating production time-tables and the general desire to keep inventories down to a minimum." Sound familiar? So just-in-time stock control was not dreamed up in Nagoya. Throughout Dunning's book the same sort of issues crop up. My survey of 150 Japanese-owned firms in Europe and America used several questions identical to Dunning's 1958 survey, in order to facilitate comparisons.

When Dunning surveyed 150 American firms in Britain, he asked his respondents the following question: "Is the quality of your labor (i.e., its power to be effective) a) better, b) as good as, or c) not as good as in your parent's plants?" His finding was that 28 percent replied that the labor quality was better, 42 percent thought it about the same, and 30 percent thought it not as good as in the parent plants. Among the Japanese firms replying to the same question in my survey, the result was that only 6 percent thought that foreign labor was better, but 56 percent thought it was as good as that in Japan. About the same percentage as in Dunning's survey—31 percent—thought that foreign labor was less effective, and there were 6 percent "don't knows."

Similarly, the Japanese respondents were asked a question about whether foreign labor had the will to work: did it work harder, as hard, or less hard, than in the parent company? Dunning's American firms divided thus: 12 percent thought British labor worked harder than at home, 35 percent as hard, and 53 percent less hard. As stated earlier, few Japanese firms reckoned their foreign workers were more hardworking than Japanese workers: just 4 percent. But

50.6 percent thought foreigners worked just as hard as Japanese, and only 42 percent thought they worked less hard. There were 3 percent "don't knows."

It is in the more subjective judgments that the greatest and most convincing similarities can be found between the American investors of the 1950s and the Japanese ones of the 1980s. Dunning's survey reported gripes among American firms about labor in Britain similar to those common at Japanese overseas plants, such as low skill levels and poor education. He also found that American firms devoted far more of their resources to research and development than British ones. Just as with Japanese companies today, especially in America, he found that few American firms in Britain were fully unionized: just 15 percent. He explained this in a way that could just as well be used in a commentary about a Japanese carmaker in Britain today. The high wage offered by many branch plants, he wrote, had enabled an open-shop policy to be successfully maintained, and ensured that work relationships could be exceptionally congenial.

He found "a marked paternalistic attitude" in the way American-affiliated firms viewed their personnel responsibilities. Labor suggestion schemes were common, with rewards for useful ideas; that is a policy now in widespread use by Japanese companies, inside Japan and out. Many companies apparently stressed the importance of frequent management/labor production meetings, as a result of which one firm claimed that labor relationships and productivity had improved "out of all recognition." Suffice it to note, Dunning wrote, that "many American-financed firms are recognized as being amongst the most progressive and enlightened of employers, both for their willingness to adopt the latest wage and incentive systems, and for their belief that labor well-paid and properly trained pays dividends in the long run through improved personnel efficiency and reduced labor turnover." Finally, in comparing the British attitude with that of American workers, Dunning reported that in Britain "There was less appreciation of the function of time and motion study, less interest and enthusiasm shown in the actual job at hand, and less willingness of the worker to identify his interests with those of the company."

All this makes today's Japanese "superiority" mighty similar to the sorts of superiority identified among American multinationals in the past. Admittedly, this claim may be a bit too superficial: methods have varied over time, as that mention of "time and motion study" suggests, and it would not be fair to suggest that American firms investing in the 1950s were identical to Japanese ones investing in the 1980s.

What can be said, however, is that such international relocation of production tends to happen when a firm or group of firms considers itself to have managerial advantages over local firms engaged in the same business. Those advantages tend to be identified in essentially similar ways: the firms' ability to manage inventories, their ability to motivate workers, the resources they devote to research and development, the constructive and cooperative nature of their relationships to suppliers. Such things are all answers to the question: what is the best practice in the business of manufacturing? They are not answers to the question: what is the Japanese (or American) secret? There is no such secret, bar current overall superiority.

———

So, guilty or not guilty? That is the way the question is usually posed. But if my survey shows anything it is that this question is irrelevant. The Japanese multinational is a multifaceted creature. It is a creature that is evolving all the time. As such it is something to be observed, not praised or condemned.

For the most part, Japanese multinationals remain fairly small and immature. This helps explain why their productivity performance is disappointing. It may also explain why they have a high import propensity, though whether this will disappear in time must be a matter for speculation. In principle, it looks likely to. But practice could be different.

The principle is chiefly one of control balanced against efficiency. As was shown in the case of the car industry, it appears to be wise for Japanese multinational manufacturers to stay Japanese-controlled and managed at first. Yet, as they mature, they need gradually to become more localized. If Japanese firms are fully to implement their superior manufacturing skills they must do so locally, to eliminate the waste and risk of long-distance supply lines and to ensure that their output is sensitive to local tastes. Yet to get from here to there requires strict control from Japan: it is crucial not to allow competitive advantages to be eroded by copying the failed methods of local competitors.

Japanese firms abroad are only partway along that road. Many are recent arrivals, still with a relatively small scale of production. The average firm in this survey employed just 714 workers, and only 24 of the 150 firms employed more than 1,001 workers. Few therefore can afford to carry out research or development locally, unless local technology is in fact more advanced than at the parent company. More than half of the firms polled are either suffering a loss in their overseas factories or did not answer the question (which in most cases implies a loss). All these are telltale signs of immaturity.

Indeed, more than 80 percent of the firms polled said they planned to raise output, even though the questionnaire arrived in the midst of a recession in America and Britain, and during an economic slowdown in most of Europe. They are still in an early stage of what, to them, is a gigantic experiment. Some of the experimenters will succeed; others will fail painfully.

PART THREE

THE
AWKWARD
FUTURE

8

THE SHADOW OF JAPAN'S SUNSET

The first cold showers pour.
Even the monkey seems to want
a little coat of straw.

BASHŌ

JAPAN has established global reach, with investments and business empires stretching all around the world. Yet this new Japan, this brave, far more international entity, is undergoing changes of its own at home, changes that are having, and will have, a big impact on Japanese multinationals. Such a juxtaposition of worldwide strength with domestic economic turmoil is apt to confuse. Yet it can also reveal. The future of Japan's economy will play a large part in determining the future of Japan's global reach. And, in the short term at least, that future is poor.

The confusion arises from the fact that many Japanese feel confidently superior to Americans and Europeans: they think the Japanese economy is stronger, Japanese technology is superior, management is better, the work ethic is stronger, and society is safer and less prone to conflict. To an extent they are right. Accordingly, Americans and Europeans return the compliment by feeling unconfidently inferior.

Regardless of events at home, surely the big Japanese multinationals are so strong, so well-managed, so full of advanced technology that they will be unaffected? The answer is that although these points are relevant, especially to the performance of individual companies, they will not prevent change from taking place in the aggregate. Japan's superconfidence sits uncomfortably alongside events in Japanese financial markets and even in the real world of business. All is not well in the Japanese economy. The sun has slipped temporarily below the horizon.

The country entered an economic slowdown in 1992, its first real recession in more than fifteen years. This slowdown followed, and resulted directly from, the bursting in 1990–92 of what was a highly speculative financial bubble in Japan's stock and property markets. That bubble had been inflated in 1986–89 by a powerful mixture of low interest rates, financial deregulation, and a crowd mentality among investors, borrowers, and lenders. At the time in Japan, this period of financial frenzy was thought to herald the start of a golden age of power and prosperity for the country and its formidable new multinationals. Now, it is known derogatorily as "the bubble economy."

In any country, financial turmoil is transmitted to the real, underlying economy chiefly through the banking system, and that is what is happening in Japan. Recession has brought with it a rich diet of scandals, bankruptcies, and controversies. For the country's multinationals, what it principally means is that their own diet has changed: it no longer includes the wonder drugs of ultracheap capital and booming domestic demand that so helped them in the late 1980s. But those multinationals do remain strong. In a sense, they are similar to Ben Johnson, the Canadian sprinter who won the 100-meter gold medal in the 1988 Olympics only to forfeit it when he was found to have been taking anabolic steroids. Like Johnson, Japan's multinationals are no longer being helped by steroids, in their case the cheap capital provided by a financial boom. But also like him, they remain extremely impressive athletes: still fast, but no longer artificially fast.

That enduring competitive strength of Japanese industry is why the cold showers of 1992 will not last long: Japan will again be growing strongly and steadily by 1994–95. Even so, this period is an important one for Japan: it has revealed some of the limits to

Japan's economic power, as well as confirming how some of the supposed strengths were in fact illusions.

In part, this is also why the recession is a necessary and salutary setback for Japan, since the excesses and distortions of the late 1980s had to be removed. The bubble economy made a setback inevitable. It produced that sense of hubris and overconfidence already referred to many times in this book; behind that hubris stalked Nemesis, or retribution. It also disguised longer-term trends in consumption, in savings, and in work behavior that are ensuring that the Japanese economy will take a different shape in the 1990s.

———

The end of the bubble economy first revealed itself in January 1990, when the Tokyo stock market began its long slide. But the real Japanese economy continued to grow rapidly and healthily for the next eighteen months or more, with GDP growth hitting levels not seen since the 1960s. That gap between the financial world and the world of industry and ordinary people made it seem as if the two are, or were, not connected. This was and is wrong. The bubble economy helped the real economy to grow rapidly in the late 1980s. In late 1991 and 1992, its collapse sent the economy into recession. The gap between the bubble's bursting and the onset of recession was merely a time-lag.

It is important to understand this time-lag, and the connections between the bubble and the real economy, in order to get a better idea of what the prospects are for Japan. There are three main links between the bubble economy and the real economy of industry and commerce. Both of the first two begin with the fact that the financial world supplies the capital that the real economy needs for investment and to pay its daily bills.

The first link is that rapidly rising stock prices in 1986–89 made new equity capital very cheap for Japanese companies. They could issue new equity easily, either directly or through the sale of bonds convertible into equity, because their share prices were rising so rapidly. The rise in property prices also helped, because companies owned a lot of property and could use it as collateral for bank loans; as property assets are very important to the value of a firm, rising property prices also pushed share prices even higher. But hence the opposite is also true: falling share and property prices make it harder for companies to raise new capital. At the end of 1989, the Bank of Japan raised its interest rates sharply, thus making it more expensive to borrow. At the same time, the falling Tokyo stock market made it much harder, and thus more expensive, to raise capital through equity issues.

Why did this not have an immediate impact on the real economy? Because companies do not always need external capital instantly. To a large extent, they finance themselves through retaining their profits, rather than passing them on to shareholders as dividends: in 1989–90, Japanese firms were making record profits, so they had plenty of cash. Also, they had raised far more capital in 1987–89 than they needed immediately. They repaid old bank debts and simply put the cash in the bank. Many of them were financially far stronger than the banks themselves.

So for the first two years or so after the bubble began to burst, Japanese companies as a whole could carry on operating, and investing, using the capital they had already raised in the previous few years. Put in technical terms, corporate liquidity was at record levels. It was only in the last few months of 1991 that this liquidity began to dry up quickly. That is why corporate investment had to be cut drastically for 1992 and beyond: the capital either was not there, or was too expensive.

That brings in link number two: the state of Japan's banks. This was dealt with in some detail in an earlier chapter on Japanese finance overseas. But it bears repeating here, for in banking there is no real distinction between home and abroad. Money is money, wherever it is raised, spent, and lent. And for banks, trouble is trouble, wherever it occurs, and will affect the whole institution. Until 1984 or so, banks provided most of the external finance required by industry in Japan. Then, big business switched to the equity markets and the overseas bond markets because capital was cheaper there. But banks remained important, especially for smaller companies. They found new sectors to lend to, especially property, construction and leasing companies, and foreign borrowers. But what was their ability to lend based on? The bubble economy.

Banks can only lend if they have a firm capital base; regulators everywhere stipulate a minimum ratio for banks between their capital and their total value of loans outstanding. As stated earlier, until the Bank for International Settlements (BIS) presided over an international agreement to harmonize rules about banks' capital, Japan's finance ministry allowed Japanese banks to count as capital 70 percent of the unrealized gains on the banks' huge shareholdings. The BIS deal reduced that proportion to 45 percent, but the basic principle remained: a large chunk of Japanese banks' capital depended on the level of share prices on the Tokyo stock market.

It was a political compromise of the worst sort. Intellectually, it is an absurdity: capital is meant to be a cushion in case times go bad. But shares are a lousy cushion: they are affected directly themselves when things go wrong. So at exactly the time when the capital is needed, it will disappear. It is fine in the good times, which is why the rule was tolerated for so long: when share prices went up, the banks had more capital and so could lend more. But if share prices go down, so does banks' capital and thus their ability to lend. That is why in late 1991 the growth of bank lending fell to its lowest level since records began in 1965.

This second link between the real economy and the bubble economy has been the most dangerous of all. In 1991, the Bank of Japan's high interest-rate policy achieved its desired effect, namely to slow Japanese economic growth and to puncture the bubble, but without causing a crash. That is what central bankers call a "soft landing"; it is something they dream of. That soft landing ought, in principle, to have been a cause for celebration, both in the central bank and outside. But it was not. The reason is that underneath this soft cushion on which the Japanese economy was landing there was something else: a trapdoor. That trapdoor was formed by the role of share prices in sustaining bank capital. A sustained fall below around 21,000 on the Nikkei index was enough to pull Japanese banks' capital below the 8 percent minimum that was required by 1993, forcing them to raise more capital (which is difficult) or to cut lending. In other words, it opens the trapdoor. Sure enough, that trapdoor was opened in March and April of 1992, when the Nikkei slumped well below the 20,000 mark, and stayed there for several months.

The presence of that trapdoor brings us to link number three between the bubble economy and the real economy: confidence, both of consumers and of businessmen. When economies slow down, confidence is crucial, since the spending and borrowing behavior of consumers and businesses makes all the difference to economic growth. Are they willing to buy goods and to invest, or do they prefer to keep their cash in the bank for a rainy day, or might they repay debts? If it is the former, growth will continue; if the latter, it will slow. In Japan's case, the bursting of the bubble gradually weakened confidence. The presence of the trapdoor further damaged that confidence, especially given the lack of information available from banks and the finance ministry about how big the banks' pile of bad debts really was.

———

These links—capital costs, bank lending, and confidence—are what has made the bursting of the bubble at last affect the real Japanese economy. Yet, in three senses, the bubble had still not really burst properly as Japan entered 1992, which is why economic life in the short-term, 1993 and 1994, looks quite difficult.

One of the delayed punctures was in the property market: unlike stock market prices, which began their descent at the beginning of 1990, real estate prices failed to drop in 1990 despite high interest rates. Why? Because the demand for office space in the cities remained quite strong in 1990–91, thanks to continued economic growth. And the rise in supply due to redevelopment of parts of Tokyo and elsewhere took time to arrive. But in the end even this had to change. Slower growth reduced the demand for office space. New supply arrived. Prices had to fall. And so they did, beginning in the second half of 1991.

That helped bring on the second delayed puncture: again it involves Japanese banks, since they had 20–30 percent of their loans outstanding directly and indirectly to property. The official figure in 1991 was only 11 percent, but that only included direct loans; it excluded the large quantity of loans made via leasing subsidiaries and other finance companies. Until property prices began to fall sharply, Japanese banks did not have to be honest about their bad debts, i.e., those loans that the borrowers were never going to pay back. This was despite the fact that 1991 was full of banking scandals, and despite a record level of bankruptcies among Japanese companies.

Slowdown in the real economy, combined with the real property slump made this pretense unsustainable. Japanese banks now simply have to be honest about their bad debts, have to write them off against capital, and have to change the way in which they manage themselves. A big scandal involving Industrial Bank of Japan (IBJ) in 1991 gave the clue: Japan's most prestigious bank had exposed itself to major lending risks and had failed to control collateral properly, all because of a friendship with a restaurateur, Nui Onoue, who turned out to be a massive speculator in stocks. Her debts (not all to the IBJ) totalled $2 billion. And this was merely the most public proof of a widely hidden fact: banks have lent poorly and managed themselves dismally.

The third delayed puncture for the bubble economy is a much more general one. It is directly connected to the confidence factor mentioned earlier, however: not so much a delayed puncture, perhaps, as an acceleration of a previous one. In 1992 and 1993, it is becoming one of the most crucial factors of all in determining the severity of the downturn. Before going into the details, however, try this quiz: Which country—Japan or the United States—has the highest level of household debt as a proportion of households' annual disposable income?

As almost all comparisons of the Japanese and American economies conclude that one of the main differences between the nations is that Japanese like to save but Americans love to borrow and spend as if there is no tomorrow, you can be forgiven for having answered that America has the higher household debts. But you would be wrong.

You would have been correct in 1980, when household debt in America was 80 percent of annual disposable income compared with 77 percent in Japan, which is still surprisingly high given the common stereotype about Japan. But the trend of the 1980s was exactly the opposite of what everybody thinks it was: Japanese household debts grew more rapidly than did those in America, measured against household incomes. In 1990, household debt in America was 103 percent of annual income; in Japan it was 117 percent. The real nation of profligate debtors is not America but Japan.

The reason these figures did not make economists in Japan panic during the 1980s was that, on their own, they are misleading. It makes no sense to look at household debts on their own if you are interested in the general health of the economy and the stability of consumer spending. Instead, you must compare the trend of households' debts with what is happening to their assets: stocks, bonds, bank deposits, houses, or wherever else households were storing up their wealth. As long as households' assets are still growing as fast as debts or, better still, faster, there is no need to worry. The statistic to watch is "net household wealth"—assets minus debts. As long as this is still growing, there should be no cause for concern.

Household assets grew spectacularly in Japan during the 1980s, which is why the level of debt did not look like a problem. Overall, net household wealth was also still growing in 1990 and for some of 1991. Although stock prices fell by almost 50 percent in 1990, shares make up only a small proportion of aggregate household assets, so the stock market collapse made only a small difference to the wealth of most ordinary Japanese. But property is a different matter.

Just over 60 percent of Japanese households own their own homes, a level of home-ownership that is very high by international standards. The statistic is a little misleading compared to those in other countries: the reason is that a Japanese household contains, on average, more generations than does, say, a British household. Taking the average, the Japanese level of home ownership would perhaps have to be lowered to 50 percent or so to compare it with those in Europe. It would then be a lot lower than in Britain—an Englishman's home is his castle, remember—but above that in France and Germany.

Regardless of the international comparison, a level of 60 percent still means that to virtually all of those owning homes, the value of their property is far and away their biggest financial asset. To many, it has also become the biggest source of their debts; huge sums were borrowed to buy houses during the 1980s (including, amazingly, intergenerational mortgages), and huge sums were also borrowed using houses as collateral even if the ownership was not changing hands. This applies to ordinary people as well as to speculators; ordinary people could take out home equity loans, borrowing against their house or apartment in order to consume some of their wealth now rather than waiting to sell or to pass on the wealth to children or the taxman.

While the value of those assets was going up, then, there seemed to be no need for households, or economists, to worry about the levels of debts that were being piled up. Japanese households' debts, it is worth repeating, are the largest in proportion to income of any of the seven richest industrial economies. But when house prices fall, it is time to worry. For then the asset values are sliding, while the debts remain the same. Typically, in any country, it takes households some time to realize the importance of what this is doing to their finances. It also does not affect them very much when the economy is growing, as so are their incomes, and their jobs feel secure.

But sooner or later, households start to realize that their debts are out of line with what their assets can, or ideally should, support. In economies where unemployment is high, individuals start to default on their debts; that happened in Britain during 1991. In an economy like Japan where unemployment is low, the reaction takes a different form: households simply cut their spending in order to make money available to reduce or to service their debts.

Such rapid debt reduction is a powerful delayed puncture for the bubble economy. It means that consumer spending falls drastically instead of merely gently, and it makes consumers reluctant to take on new debts for quite some time. This is what was happening in Japan in 1992–93, following the big fall in property prices: an attempt to repay record levels of debt, alongside a growing aversion to taking on new debts. In the end, this reduction in debt will make the economy healthy again. But while it is happening, the results are distinctly uncomfortable.

———

All that explains how Japan arrived at its present state in mid 1993. The bubble economy began to burst in January 1990. There was a long time-lag before capital costs, shrinking bank lending, and fading confidence affected the real, industrial, economy, but eventually it did. Then there were three delayed punctures of the bubble: the property market, further problems at Japanese banks, and households' efforts to reduce their debts.

What next? In the short term, the prospects remain gloomy. Companies' capital investment, which collapsed in late 1991 and 1992, is unlikely to recover rapidly. The cheap-money, bubble era encouraged excessive growth in investment by Japanese companies, at home and overseas. Business investment rose to 20 percent of GNP, a level not seen since the country's high-growth era of the 1960s. That level of investment in 1990–91 was gloated about in Japan and worried about in the United States because it seemed to represent Japan's rise to power relative to America. But it was not all that it seemed.

The high level of capital investment was an aberration, caused by the bubble economy and the illusion that capital was cheap. In the future, it will be looked at as a costly mistake. At best, this excess will hamper corporate Japan; at worst it will injure it quite severely. Put more mildly, it means that now that capital is short, new investment plans cannot be as ambitious as before.

At home and abroad, companies built too much new capacity in businesses such as semiconductors and automobiles. Japanese companies were expanding to satisfy markets that simply no longer exist, or at least they will not exist for a year or two. Although laborsaving investment and research-and-development spending will remain high, such investment to expand capacity will not now be repeated for a long time. Capital investment sounds like just a technical matter. But it is not, for capital investment means the purchase of goods and services from all sorts of sectors around Japan, and in the rest of Asia too. Its collapse is hurting all those other suppliers, and so is in turn depressing demand in other areas.

In principle, Japanese consumers could save the day, by drawing upon their savings and spending more. If consumers thus increase their spending faster than their incomes rise, this can revive economic growth. But this is unlikely in Japan for the coming few years. The personal savings rate already fell to record lows in fiscal 1990 of 13.7 percent of disposable income, lower than the 1980s' average of 17–18 percent and well below the peak level of 23 percent in 1975.

This rundown of savings was accelerated by the cheap-money era, since, as with the example of household debts, this induced Japanese consumers to spend and borrow rather than to put their extra income into bank deposits. Although in the long term personal savings are likely to fall gradually in Japan, in the short term they are likelier to rise than to fall because of households' worries about their debts. So, on its own, consumer spending cannot be the engine that drives the Japanese economy.

———

Might trade come to the rescue? In the mid-1980s, Japan's rapid economic growth produced rapidly rising surpluses on the country's balance of payments. Exports were the main engine of economic growth. Could they be strong again?

Many people, in Japan and abroad, saw these surpluses as proof of Japan's success, its fundamental strength. To an economist, such an idea is at best naive, at worst misleading. A surplus is not a proof of anything. In fact, it meant that Japan was not consuming (i.e., enjoying) as much as it could at home, and was instead sending the money abroad to be invested in other countries (i.e., enjoyed by non-Japanese).

Too many Japanese have been taught to consider imports as bad and exports as good, but this idea conveniently forgets a basic fact: the only reason why a country has to export is in order to pay for its imports. So exports are a necessary sacrifice in order to buy the things you want, whether those are raw materials or luxury sports cars. Imports are what you want; exports are what you have to sell in order to pay for them. This is true for a whole country; it is not true simply for a company, which aims to sell its products in as large a market as possible. That difference, between the country and the company, partly explains this common popular confusion.

Fortunately, 1991 and 1992 offered a neat illustration of why this popular misunderstanding is wrong. In the mid-1980s, the country's current-account and trade surpluses expanded alongside rapid Japanese growth. They then halved in size in 1987–90 as export growth was choked off by a strengthening yen and imports grew speedily, thanks to booming consumer spending (people were borrowing against the collateral of their houses to buy BMW cars) and, again, the strong yen.

But then the picture changed once again. In 1991 and 1992, the surpluses rose sharply to levels even higher than those seen in 1985–87. This time, however, the context was different: Japanese economic growth was slowing. The rising surpluses were thus a sign of weakness rather than one of strength or success. Exports stayed high, but demand for imports fell sharply, as consumer demand fell after the bubble economy's collapse. The booming current-account surplus was a sign of trouble in the economy.

Such surpluses are, in effect, a reflection of the excess of savings over investment in an economy. Personal savings fell in Japan. So why has the excess risen in 1991 and 1992 at the same time as those savings were sliding? One answer is that investment has itself fallen. But another, bigger answer is that there are other forms of savings beyond the Japanese household: companies, and the government.

Companies built up huge savings in 1989–90, though they began to spend them in 1991 and 1992 as profits were falling fast. But the government is the biggest saver of them all. Add together the central government, local government, and social security funds, and the overall Japanese public sector had a budget surplus in 1991 equivalent to 2.7 percent of GDP. The central government still has a small deficit. But local government's deficit has fallen virtually to zero, and the social security funds have a massive surplus.

In effect, the finance ministry is building up savings and, instead of spending the money in Japan, is sending it abroad, via the current-account surplus. It is doing so for a good reason: Japan's population will be aging rapidly early in the twenty-first century, and thus will be using up lots of money in pensions and health care. But that sensible long-term reason is causing short-term problems: it is restricting Japanese economic growth; and it is forcing the current-account surplus to widen. As long as the finance ministry's policy remains as it is, Japanese recovery from the recession will be slower, and tensions over trade surpluses with foreign countries will be much nastier.

There has long been a strange, even bewildering gap in perceptions of the Japanese government's financial position between insiders and outsiders, especially foreign ones. To outsiders, it looks terrifically strong. With the United States struggling to cope with a budget deficit of as much as 6 percent of GDP in the 1980s and early 1990s, Japan's surplus looks like paradise. Not to the folk in the Japanese finance ministry, however.

Talk to anyone in the finance ministry's budget bureau, or anyone in the Economic Planning Agency, about the Japanese government's budget, and you will be told that it is in a state of crisis. The nation is deeply in debt. Japan needs desperately to repay old bonds, to cut its debt. In the finance ministry's budget for fiscal 1991, the ministry said that "Japan's fiscal situation remains grim in comparison with that of other countries," illustrating this by saying that debt service will eat up more than 20 percent of the total budget.

This last fact is true, and is of course regrettable. No one likes to devote such a large chunk of their tax revenue and public spending simply to paying interest and principal on debt. Even so, it is ridiculous to pretend that Japan's fiscal situation is grim compared with that of other countries. The finance ministry always makes it seem grim by quoting figures for Japan's gross government debt. In 1990, this debt equalled 66.5 percent of GDP, compared with 52 percent in 1980 and just 12.1 percent in 1970. It sounds terrible, especially compared with Britain's gross government debt of 35.6 percent of GDP, Germany's of 43.8 percent, and France's of 46.9 percent. Even the United States, famous for its federal budget deficit, has a gross government debt equal to only 54.6 percent of GDP.

So Japan is in a terrible state? Well, no, actually. This gross figure is grossly misleading. Who does the Japanese government owe all this money to? The answer is revealing: most of it is owed to the social security funds, as these are the biggest buyers of government bonds. In other words, the government owes the money to itself, and pays interest to itself. Look not at the gross figure but rather the net one.

The Japanese government's net debt—i.e., its gross debt minus the assets of the social security system—was only 10.9 percent of

GDP in 1990, one of the lowest ratios of any of the world's rich, industrialized countries. Britain's net figure is 28.9 percent; Germany's is 22.6 percent; that for the United States is 31.2 percent. So the picture changes: far from being "grim in comparison with that of other countries," in fact Japan's government finances are among the healthiest in the world.

That is not a reason to criticize the finance ministry; in fact it is a reason to praise it, lavishly. For the ministry has planned well ahead of the time early next century when those social security assets will be matched by high and rising liabilities, namely the costs of Japan's aging population. A prudent individual would also want to take account of such future liabilities in his present financial affairs, so it would be wrong to blame the ministry for doing so. But what the ministry has been reluctant to accept is that it has also achieved a big short-term benefit: fiscal flexibility. Its low net debts, and its overall budget surplus give it more room to maneuver in times of economic difficulty than virtually any other finance ministry in the world. Japan's finance ministry is the envy of the world.

The short-term, credit crunch recession of 1992–93 made it high time that this flexibility should be exploited. To do so requires an awkward choice. But economic policy must always involve choices between conflicting aims. In the past decade, the priority was fiscal reconstruction and saving for the aging population; and that priority can return later in the 1990s.

For the time being that is not a wise priority. It conflicts with immediate needs in the domestic economy and in the international economy. In other words, revival from the recession of 1992 requires a kick-start from the finance ministry. In late August 1992, and again in April 1993, the ministry provided that kick with two huge public spending packages, including (hard to measure) extra spending worth around $60–80 billion in each of those packages. Even so, further measures will likely be needed, probably tax cuts. Despite the tax reforms of the late 1980s, marginal rates of tax on personal incomes in Japan remain high by international standards. There is plenty of room to cut them.

By increasing demand for imports, tax cuts will also help to reduce the trade surplus. But that is only a secondary reason. The main target must be to revive domestic demand. Monetary policy cannot work to revive lending when banks are in a state of collapse and confidence is low: as John Maynard Keynes said, lowering interest rates, at such a time, is like pushing on a string. That is why interest rate cuts in 1991 and 1992 have not been enough. What needs to happen now is that monetary policy should be left alone; it is time to rely on fiscal policy.

If it remains unconvinced, Japan's finance ministry needs to look into history books about the 1930s to see why it must drop its previously sensible policy of fiscal consolidation. It would be wrong to be overdramatic about this, as a 1930s-style depression is not likely in Japan, so drastic action is unlikely to be required. But a parallel with the 1930s does help to understand the present situation, and the ministry's present choices. After the 1929 Wall Street crash in America, the Hoover government stuck to its principle that the best policy was to keep the budget balanced. This cautious, prudent policy must, it was thought, always be the right one: after all, the state of the economy did not look disastrous in 1930 and 1931. As in Japan, there was a time-lag between the bursting of Wall Street's bubble and the effect on the real economy.

Like the Japanese finance ministry's policy of fiscal consolidation, the Hoover policy was indeed sensible. But only in favorable circumstances. In the new conditions of 1930 and 1931, the result of this "sensible" policy was disastrous. Policies that are prudent in one set of economic conditions can become outrageously risky in another set of conditions, at another time. It is the same in Japan in 1993.

————

On February 19, 1992, Sony made a shocking announcement. It said that in the fiscal year ending on March 31, 1992, it expected the Japanese parent company to suffer an operating loss of Y20 billion ($154 million). The whole company's consolidated results were also poor, with a 45 percent fall in operating profits. For 1992–93, Sony planned to cut its capital spending by Y160 billion to just Y280 billion, a 36 percent cut.

There were many reasons for this announcement and for the

poor results. Consumer-electronics sales in Japan had been depressed, and the Japanese economy was slowing down. The entertainment business was a relatively bright spot, since Sony Pictures had increased its market share, and profits from Sony Music ensured that entertainment provided profits almost as big in the final quarter of 1991 as in the hardware business, worldwide.

Yet the announcement has a far wider significance than merely such quarterly or even yearly ups and downs. It was a harbinger of things to come for many of Japan's big overseas investors. Stretched beyond the limits of financial prudence, they were newly vulnerable to downturns in any of their main markets, especially Japan. The financing costs of their big overseas investments had yet to arrive, since many had been undertaken using ultracheap warrant bonds that would only have to be refinanced in 1993. But in that year the true costs would become apparent.

What this means is that, in the future, Japan's overseas investors will be divided into two groups: one group will have financed wisely, will not be overstretched, and will have built their overseas businesses slowly and cautiously for the long term. Typical of this group will be the biggest carmakers: Toyota, Nissan, Honda, and Mitsubishi Motors.

The other, larger group, will include Bridgestone and Sony: firms that did not finance their adventures wisely, that became carried away by their own wealth and success, and that sought to build global businesses through giant strides rather than small steps. There are plenty of small examples, too, including the speculator who bought the Pebble Beach golf course in California and promptly had to resell it. Other big culprits include banks that sought to build market shares aggressively in risky businesses such as real estate and leveraged buy-out lending, and many firms that invested directly in overpriced property.

It is the big firms that are most shocking, at least to outside observers. These firms will suffer from investment overstretch for most of the next four or five years. Struggling to cope with their overseas businesses, they will be short of new capital and will be hard-pressed to keep up their investment at home and thus to maintain their competitive positions.

This is, perhaps, the most surprising and yet most important consequence of the bubble economy of 1987–89: it has done severe damage to the competitiveness of many of Japan's biggest and most famous companies. Hubris followed by Nemesis: it is a familiar and inevitable story.

9

AFTER THE SUNSET

The short night is through:
on the hairy caterpillar,
little beads of dew.

BUSON

A STRANGE English saying holds that "the darkest hour comes just before the dawn." It is strange because it is generally untrue. But so be it: the saying remains appropriate for Japan and its global reach. The sunset of 1990–93, first in finance but then in the real economy, has made life appear dark. However, that darkness is likely to prove misleading. The long-term prospects for Japan are bright and warm. Those warm prospects will extend to the Japanese multinational corporations that are the concern of this book.

Why, you may ask, is so much space being devoted to Japan itself when it is Japanese firms abroad that we are really interested in? The reason is that, for all the hype about global companies, disconnected from their nation states and able to shift their centers of production at will, the truth is different. Multinational firms remain heavily dependent on conditions at home.

Japanese and American multinationals typically have more than half their sales in one country: their home. They recruit the bulk of their managers at home. They conduct most of the R&D at home. Their creditworthiness and thus ability to raise capital for expansion depends crucially on their performance in their biggest market. Ford and General Motors have vast worldwide sales. But they remain heavily influenced by events in the United States. It is the same for Japanese firms. The foundation of any judgment about the future strength and behavior of Japanese multinationals must lie in Japan.

For that reason, the biggest influence on Japanese multinationals will be the duration of Japan's dark night of recession. In turn, the length of that night will depend on many factors, inside and outside Japan. It will be made shorter, for instance, if the Japanese government opts for a powerful boost to the domestic economy through tax cuts or public-works spending. By thus stimulating domestic demand, it will revive growth and also help to reduce Japan's current-account and trade surpluses. Although these surpluses are not themselves an economic problem, they are a political one, especially in the United States and Europe.

So, by acting to boost the demand for imports, the finance ministry can achieve two targets at once: helping the domestic economy and gaining political credit for Japan abroad by helping world growth and lowering trade imbalances. Doing so will help avoid an external night-lengthening influence: protectionism tolerated (or even encouraged) by the Clinton administration and by a European Community struggling with the challenge of bringing Eastern Europe and the former Soviet Union not only into the market economy but also into Europe itself.

The length of Japan's night will certainly depend on the length of night elsewhere in the world economy, for the fate of demand in America, Europe, and even Asia will determine the strength of Japan's exports and thus the extent of corporate Japan's overinvestment in 1988–91. I believe that in the world economy night is likely to be followed by a brighter day than ever, that the world economy has the chance of a golden age for growth, capitalism, and prosperity.

The beginnings of that golden age, probably in the mid-1990s, will also cast warmth onto Japan at the same time as posing challenges for it. For Japan is well-placed to exploit this golden age: not in the apparently all-conquering spirit of the bubble economy period, but certainly in a spirit of confidence and strength.

Despite the overconfidence of the late 1980s and the overinvestment, Japan is strongly positioned in the key industries and technologies that will benefit from this age of growth. Even this claim needs to be moderated, however. Contrary to the beliefs of many ordinary Japanese, and certainly of an extraordinary, maverick Japanese politician, Shintaro Ishihara, in his book *The Japan That Can Say No,* Japanese industry is not a leader in all technologies, not even in those that promise the highest value-added.

Among manufactured goods, for example, the highest value-added products worldwide in the late 1980s were satellites, supercomputers, jet engines, and jet airplanes. Japan leads in none of these. Nor is it strong in the newest manufacturing industry to arrive on the economic scene in the 1990s: biotechnology. Weak already in areas such as chemical engineering and pharmaceuticals, Japanese industry is years behind its rivals in the United States in biotechnology in all its applications: drugs, medicine, seeds, and elsewhere in agriculture. In drugs and medicine, European industry also leaves the Japanese firms far behind.

Where Japan is very strong indeed is in medium value-added mass market technologies: video cameras, semiconductors, advanced color televisions and computer displays, semiconductor manufacturing equipment, computer-controlled machine tools, and, since the late 1980s, luxury cars. All those are very important areas of strength. But, in terms of competition between specific firms and industries, they should not be overrated.

In many of these areas, Japanese industry holds only second or third place, or is not anywhere near the leader in the higher value-added areas. Take semiconductors: Japanese companies clearly dominate the market for memory chips, the basic raw material of computers, consumer electronics, and many other goods. But these are low-priced, commodity products, even for memory chips at the frontier of the technology. The higher-priced, higher value-added products are in microprocessors or other specialty chips, where the chips are in fact a combination of hardware and software. American companies such as Intel and Motorola still dominate in these areas. There is no real sign of Japanese firms catching up.

It is the same with computers: although Japanese firms are often the manufacturers of all or part of desktop and notebook computers sold under American brand names, nevertheless the crucial design and engineering is done in America by firms such as Apple, Compaq, Dell, and IBM. Journalists have been wondering for at least a decade when Japanese companies would "invade" the world computer market and it has never happened, at least not to the degree that it happened in cars and consumer electronics. Japanese companies have found it too difficult to succeed in marketing such computers and in keeping pace with design and engineering changes. Most crucially, they have always been left a step or three behind by the developments in software. Toshiba, which led America's laptop computer market in 1990 before slipping back in 1991 and 1992, is a notable exception to the rule: Japanese have come second, at best.

Then there is a further point. Increasingly, in the industries in which Japan is strong, alternative sources of supply are springing up in Taiwan, South Korea, and elsewhere in Asia. This applies most strongly in semiconductors, advanced televisions, computer displays, and computer manufacture. In all these areas, Japanese firms have a lead over Asian rivals. But the lead is short: once many new products are released they can quickly be duplicated in Asia. This limits the profits Japanese firms can reap from their innovations: competition arrives too quickly, forcing prices down. It does not happen all the time, but it does happen often enough to limit Japan's industrial comfort.

This should put Ishihara's assertions in a better perspective: he claims that America's military effort "depends" on Japanese technology, because many American military systems contain Japanese chips, displays, and other components. He is right that many American military systems contain Japanese products. But he is wrong to say that this means that the systems are dependent on Japan, or that this somehow adds to Japanese power. Sensibly, the American military has bought goods from Japan (an ally) because they are low-priced and of good quality. But if Japan refused to supply memory chips or advanced displays, this would not cripple America's military effort: there are plenty of alternative suppliers. And if there were no alternatives today, there could easily be tomorrow. My car, for example, which was made in Germany, certainly contains some Japanese products: the audio system, for instance, and the chips in the computer that monitors the engine performance. But it is not "dependent" on Japan for them, any more than an American missile is dependent on Japan for its chips.

All this might appear like an attempt to denigrate Japanese industry, claiming that it is not as strong as it says it is. That would be unfair, and wrong. Rather, the intention is to explain where Japan's industrial strength does *not* lie, in order to be more convincing in showing where it does in fact lie. Japan's strength does not lie in an overall technological leadership, compared with the United States and the EC. It does not lie there because Japan is not an overall leader. Japan is strong in some technologies, including some that are vital in today's world economy. But it is weak in many others.

So where does Japan's industrial strength lie, if not in technological innovation? The answer begins with the high average level of technology in Japanese products and in Japanese processes. In other words, new and recent technologies have been understood and implemented in a very wide range of Japanese companies, driving productivity growth across a wide range of industries. It is similar to the importance of Japanese education. The best of Japanese education is not the best in the world: Japan has very good universities and schools, but cannot claim to have the world's leaders. But the *average* level of education is the world's highest.

Compare that to the United States, both in technology and education. The United States operates a dual economy and society in both these fields. America is the undoubted leader in most technologies. It also contains the world's best universities. But at the same time, America is home to technologically backward, low value-added industries and activities. It has many bad universities and its secondary education system is in deep crisis.

America's challenge is to narrow this gap between the excellent and the dismal in its economy and society. Japan's challenge is different. It has to continue the steady raising of its average technological level, spreading technical advances to parts of the economy that do not currently exploit them. It would be a mistake for Japan to try to leap to technological leadership; that might benefit the one or two firms or institutions at the forefront, but it would not benefit the whole economy. Instead, this task of steadily raising the average should be the main one. In companies, this will be the goal of research and development.

But in the Japanese economy as a whole, this task should be addressed in a different way. The obstacle to technical progress is chiefly inefficiency caused by regulations, cartels, and barriers that restrict competition and keep resources tied up in backward areas. The national goal must be to remove those inefficiencies in order to permit the spread of technical progress and productivity growth. Other areas will become apparent during the 1990s, for inefficiencies are not always obvious.

For the time being, it suffices to say that in the long term, Japan is well-placed to grow healthily and to increase its prosperity, thanks to its highly educated workforce, its high productivity growth, its rapid technological innovation, and its continued generation of capital for investment. The ease with which that process comes about will be affected importantly by whether the Japanese government deals with the inefficiencies described below, especially in finance, agriculture, and distribution. If it does deal with them, entry to the twenty-first century will be smooth and comfortable. If it does not, life could be harder.

To understand those future challenges, however, it is necessary first to understand some of the longer-term changes that Japanese society and its economy is passing through and which will continue in the 1990s. I wrote about many of these changes in my previous book, *The Sun Also Sets:* changing consumption patterns, attitudes toward savings, attitudes toward work, demographics, and corporate organization. Those who have read *The Sun Also Sets* will be familiar with these arguments, but I cannot expect everyone to have read my work, still less to recall it, so the arguments are well worth repeating, at least in briefer form. Some also require updating, since the bubble economy has either altered or distorted the picture.

Before these changes began, Japan could simply be characterized as a nation of producers rather than consumers, a nation of workers rather than pleasure seekers, a nation of savers rather than spenders, a nation of the young rather than of the old, and a nation of domestic and exporting businesses rather than of multinational companies.

Gradually, these descriptions are becoming obsolete. Although government policy and corporate behavior is still biased toward the interests of producers rather than consumers, the decisions of ordinary Japanese are altering the balance of the economy. Especially after 1986, they started to consume more, saving a smaller proportion of their incomes and borrowing more money than ever before. In 1980, Japanese households saved, on average, 18 percent of their disposable incomes. By March 31, 1990, that had fallen to 13.7 percent. During the recession, this savings rate may well rise again, as people become more worried about future prospects and as they try to rebuild financial assets depleted by falls in stock and property prices. But in the long term, it is likely that the gradual fall in the savings rate will resume.

There are several reasons for this prediction. One is that these days Japanese have fewer reasons to save than in the past. Jobs are more secure. Housing faded as a motive for saving in the 1980s when prices rose beyond the reach of ordinary Japanese (unless they were inheriting property or wealth, and even then taxes took a large bite), though it may revive if house prices fall sufficiently. Most important, there is less need to save for retirement. Pensions, whether public or private, have become more generous and reliable as pension funds have developed and matured. Some uncertainty does persist, particularly as many companies still pay pensions as a lump-sum payment on retirement rather than as a monthly income. But there is less uncertainty than before, and the provision of pensions continues to mature.

Another reason derives from generational change. The young people who entered the workforce in the 1980s were all born after the tough times of the war and the American occupation. They have grown up in relative affluence, their attitudes influenced by the most important new postwar phenomenon of all: television. This new breed of Japanese, termed *shin jinrui* by a weekly magazine called the *Asahi Journal,* has a different set of priorities from those of previous generations. The priorities are not 100 percent different; they represent a gradual evolution rather than an overnight revolution. But they are different: although willing to work hard, the new generation also wants to play hard, at weekends and during overseas vacations; although wanting to be part of groups, the new generation is forming into more diverse groups than before, each with a more evident search for individuality.

This new generation is less inclined to save than previous generations. Even more important, young people want to spend their money on different things, and are keener on more conspicuous forms of consumption—showing off, in other words. They do not pose much of a danger to the work ethic, except that they will form part of a gradual move toward longer holidays. But they do represent a slow but steady change in the structure of the economy, and the job market. The better educated members of this generation are less inclined to stay in the same job for the rest of their lives and more eager to work in smaller, more creative and more entrepreneurial companies.

These trends—away from saving, toward spending, borrowing, and pleasure-seeking—were exaggerated somewhat by the bubble economy. The boom years of 1987–90 created rapid growth in consumption, as well as creating a new class of superrich speculators in stocks and property who set new standards for conspicuous consumption.

Now that the bubble has burst, some of this conspicuous consumption has disappeared. Sales of luxury cars have fallen sharply, as have imports of high-priced Western art, for example. The consumer boom has faded, depressing imports at the same time. Ordinary consumers, as well as those who speculated or borrowed on the security of financial assets, now find themselves owing more in debts than they feel comfortable with. So they are retrenching again, cutting consumption relative to savings in order to reduce their debts.

Yet although the bubble period exaggerated these changes in behavior, it did not alter the fact that they existed, and exist still. Consumption, borrowing, and saving patterns are changing gradually in Japan. They do not make the economy as a whole either worse off or better off. They simply make it different. On the basis of developments in the 1980s, by the latter part of this decade the personal savings ratio may be as low as 10–12 percent, down from 15 percent in 1992–93. It is impossible to forecast any economic variable with anything approaching certainty, and savings rates are as unpredictable as any other statistic. One thing that is much more predictable, however, is demography.

––––––

It takes a very long time to alter a demographic trend, since changes in the birthrate take almost twenty years to produce changes in the labor force. One of the few things that can be said with certainty about Japan's next two decades is that during them the country will change from having an essentially youthful population to having a much older one. This is not at all disastrous—but it will affect savings, government spending, the labor market, and quite possibly the balance of payments.

The statistics are clear. In 1990, around 12 percent of the Japanese population was over the age of sixty-five, roughly the same proportion as in the United States. According to forecasts by the Economic Planning Agency, Japan's share of over-sixty-fives in its population will rise to 14 percent by 1995, 16.2 percent by 2000, 18 percent in 2005, and 23.5 percent by the time the figure peaks in 2020. Looking thirty years ahead is less certain than looking five years ahead, remember; if the birthrate were suddenly to rise now for some reason, then the balance could be altered substantially by 2020. Current trends, however, suggest that the birthrate is likelier to fall than to rise, suggesting that the figure for 2020 might even be an underestimate.

Look at those figures carefully. What they tell you first of all is that this is a very long-term phenomenon. It will have virtually no impact at all in the first half of the 1990s, and fairly little by the time the twenty-first century begins. But in 2000–2025, the aging population will become extremely important in shaping the way in which the Japanese economy behaves.

The most easily understood effect in the early part of the next century will be on government spending, broadly defined. The proportion of the population that is drawing a pension will rise, increasing the drain on social security funds. Healthcare costs will also rise substantially, placing a much more direct cost on the taxpayer. These two factors combined mean that, other things being equal, those who are working and are between twenty and sixty-five years old will be paying higher taxes and social security contributions in order to support those who are over sixty-five.

A more controversial and less predictable effect will be on the savings rate. Old people, including those drawing a pension, do continue to save part of their income. Some, indeed, save a higher proportion than when they were working. Japanese pensioners seem to be especially inclined to carry on saving. On average, however, researchers at the Bank of Japan tend to think that the existence of an older population will lower the personal savings rate a little. More important, though, is their impact on the overall savings position of Japan because of the higher social security spending already mentioned. Overall, they will depress the savings rate substantially.

Other things being equal (which they never really are in economics or in anything else, but it is a useful discipline for thinking through an issue), this lower overall savings rate makes it less likely that Japan will have a current-account surplus in the early twenty-first century, or that it will be exporting capital in large quantities. It does not make this absolutely certain. It just makes it less likely. Germany has recently been running a big current-account surplus (though it recently went away thanks to unification with East Germany) despite already having quite an elderly population.

The important point to keep in mind is that an aging population is not, in itself, a threat to prosperity. A strong economy such as Japan's can support an aging population quite comfortably. But to do so requires and produces change. It requires change in the balance of taxation and spending, as already described. It also produces change in the labor force and in the use of labor. As fewer new Japanese enter the labor force each year, the average age of Japanese workers will go up. This will have several effects: it will put pressure on employers to amend the seniority system for pay, as otherwise labor costs will rise inexorably; second, it will induce employers to carry on substituting capital (in other words, machines) for labor; finally, it will increase the power of those on the margins of labor supply. For the most part, that means women.

———

Japan already faces a labor shortage, with unemployment only around 2 percent of the labor force. Recession could ease this pressure for a time, but later there will be a force in the opposite direction: the gradual aging of the population. The labor shortage probably puts a limit on the annual economic growth that Japan can have in the long term, without causing price and wage inflation. Most people think Japan's maximum noninflationary growth rate in the medium term is now around 3.5–4 percent.

It is important to recognize, however, that for the Japanese people having a labor shortage is in fact an extremely good thing. It means, by definition, that unemployment is very low; it means that anyone seeking a job has a larger choice; and it means that real (inflation-adjusted) wages are likely to rise steadily through the decade. So standards of living of those in employment will improve markedly. That is something to celebrate, not to worry about. The time to worry is when you have a labor surplus, for it means unemployment and falling wages.

The labor shortage is more of a problem for Japanese companies than for Japanese people, since it is steadily raising the cost of production in Japan. That, in turn, has stimulated capital investment in laborsaving machines. Much of the investment boom of 1988–90 consisted of efforts to save labor, which is a big reason why in 1990 Japan invested more in absolute terms than the United States did, even though Japan's population is only half America's. Japanese companies have to invest to save labor; companies in America do not, because labor is abundant thanks to immigration and higher unemployment (more than 7 percent of the labor force).

In Japan, the labor shortage has also produced an increase in part-time working, as companies have sought to hire part-timers, especially married women, to fill jobs where they are unable to recruit full-timers at a viable wage. In 1970, part-time employees made up 7.1 percent of the labor force; by 1990, the proportion had doubled to 15.3 percent. The proportion of females in work in 1970 was 49.9 percent of those of working age; by 1980, that had fallen to 47.6 percent thanks largely to the fact that fewer women were working on farms; but by 1990, the figure had risen again, to 50.1 percent.

On balance, then, the labor shortage is not a very big problem; it is a side effect of prosperity, not a cause of impending economic difficulties. After all, the labor shortage would automatically be solved if the economy went into a slump and there was heavy unemployment. The shortage will restrain the economy's potential expansion: that is all. But it is a blessing for Japanese people, especially young ones and female ones, for it gives them much greater bargaining power over their lives and careers.

Currently, women are second-class citizens when they are in the Japanese labor force, but spend much of their lives out of it, as housewives and mothers. After graduation from high school or university, around 70 percent of Japanese women of that age go to work. But that proportion drops to around 50 percent by the age of thirty, as women leave their jobs to get married and start families. In addition to those who leave the labor force, many change jobs when they get married, either leaving their big firms to join smaller ones, or going part-time.

So, as Japan's labor shortage becomes increasingly important, there exists, conveniently, a spare supply of labor consisting of half of all women over thirty, waiting eagerly to walk back into jobs and help out the national effort. This notion appeals to the many complacent analysts and economists in Japanese ministries and research institutes: don't worry about the labor shortage, they say, for Japan's women will oblige.

In a sense, they are right: women do offer a solution. But that is not necessarily something for these male economists to be complacent about. Women over twenty-five or thirty are not simply waiting to step into the gap. They are a supply of labor, but only a potential one. Why? Because they have actually to want to work. And they will need some persuading, given that their experience at work in the past has been fairly bad: paid less than men, made to serve tea, rejected for promotion, and so on. So women will have to be lured back to work. That gives them a terrific opportunity. For the first time ever, young Japanese women are going to be in a strong bargaining position. In the 1990s, this is likely to mean that Japanese society passes through a revolution. It will be slow, so slow in fact that many will not notice that it is happening. But it will be a revolution nevertheless.

Companies are going to have to compete for women's work. Some of the first signs of this are already happening. In 1990, when I was filming a television program with NHK, Japan's state-run TV company, we visited an earthmoving site of Yamazaki Construction, used to supply earth for the Tokyo Bay bridge project. There, the firm had just begun to experiment with employing women to drive its bulldozers and dump trucks. To tempt them to work in such an unglamorous industry, Yamazaki was trying some ingenious methods. It had new working overalls designed by a fashion house, and had new truck cabs built with better air conditioning. The changes seem to be working: the women I spoke to there enjoyed their jobs, and the firm found that their productivity was high and that staff turnover among women was lower than that among men. And there are other examples in offices.

Little of this will be seen in big, traditional Japanese companies, for they will remain male bastions. In any case, they do not have a labor shortage. But in the increasing number of smaller, more innovative, more flexible firms, women are going to become increasingly important, and they will have more and more power to pick and choose how they want to build their new career portfolios of jobs and experiences.

Why should women want to work? Raising a family and playing tennis are both perfectly good ways to spend your time. That will stay true. But Japanese women have long lacked one thing that many, though certainly not all, increasingly want: independence. Only through working and earning your own money can you have independence, which means the independence to get a divorce if you want, or to travel, or to do whatever you want. Japan's divorce rate has been low chiefly because women do not have financial independence, either through their work or their legal rights. The labor shortage promises gradually to change that.

The next twenty years are going to be the era of the Japanese woman. At the end of it, they will still not feel on equal terms with men, and probably will not care much about that. But in the world of the labor shortage, employers are going to be competing for the chance to hire them. That will give them more of the basic resource of human life: choice. And, in the end, they will have more choice, in a way, than do the young men of their generation. They have to work. The women of Japan will have two choices: to work, or not to work. For them, that is truly revolutionary.

———

Now, let us return to the nuts and bolts of the economy. In the long term, the macroeconomic picture in Japan looks healthy, despite the short-term uncertainty posed by the bursting of the bubble economy and the associated financial turmoil of 1990–93. As was argued earlier, Japan's economy will emerge strongly from this period of turmoil. But the bubble will leave behind it some longer-term effects. It is worth dwelling on these for a while, for they, too, are part of a quiet revolution in Japan.

To an outside observer, one of the most puzzling things about the financial and business system in Japan has been that the difference between the credit terms given to weak companies and those given to strong ones has been remarkably narrow. This is part of what could be called "the socialization of credit risk"—the fact that credit risks in Japan have traditionally been shared, or socialized. This phenomenon of financial socialism is now dying in Japan; by the mid-1990s, it will be history.

To explain what is meant by financial socialism, it may be helpful to return to the bubble period when capital was cheap and abundant. The most striking thing about the boom in issues of convertible and warrant bonds in 1987–89 was how many firms were involved. As observed earlier, in the early 1980s only around 200–300 firms issued bonds abroad. By the end of the decade more than 1,200 were doing so. On an American basis, their credit ratings (i.e., their financial strengths, and thus the risks they posed to lenders) would have ranged from triple A to junk. But the yields on their bonds varied by far less than the ratings would suggest. Similarly, the range of interest rates charged on bank loans was much narrower than it would be in America or Britain.

This started to change in 1990–91, as bankruptcies grew in Japan. In 1989, the total liabilities of corporate failures in Japan fell to just Y1.2 trillion, the lowest for more than a decade. But in 1990, the total rose to Y2 trillion, thanks to bust share speculators; in 1991, the total more than doubled, and it had more than doubled again by the end of 1992. The immediate result is that lenders are having to discriminate between good risks and bad ones. In the past, Japanese banks might have protected the riskiest companies from higher interest rates. But no longer, since Japanese companies raise their money nowadays on international capital markets, not simply from domestic banks. Yields in the Swiss capital market for Japanese firms' bonds are already beginning to reflect the range of issuers' credit ratings.

This is going to spread throughout the economy, as a direct result of the banks' own weakness. Even those Japanese banks that still have strong capital bases (such as Mitsubishi) cannot afford to act as nursemaids to more than a few sick corporate clients, as they used to in the 1970s. Underneath them stand thousands of weaker regional banks, mutual banks, and credit unions, as well as nonbank banks such as leasing firms. These are the ones that will be hurt most directly by bankruptcies among property firms and smaller industrial companies, for those are their main clients. Like America's thrifts, Japan's mutual banks and credit unions rushed to lend to property developers in the hope of finding new sources of profit.

As those developers go bust and along with them the credit unions, larger banks will be goaded to take their weaker brethren over. In the end, the consolidation of Japan's banking industry will make it stronger. But while it happens, the big banks will be taking the strain of the smaller ones. They cannot at the same time absorb and spread the credit risks of their corporate clients as well. Something has to give.

Top companies are also changing of their own free will. Even among the biggest and most well-known firms, financial performance is becoming more important in separating the sheep from the goats, the strong from the weak. In the old days, it made precious little difference. Take one of the most prominent industries, cars. The gap between the operating incomes of Toyota, Honda, and Nissan or Toshiba, Hitachi, and Matsushita is not all that wide. But in 1990, Toyota made a big financial profit (it is popularly known as "Toyota Bank," so big are its financial resources), while Honda and Nissan both suffered financial losses. That gave Toyota a far bigger lead: its total income, as a percentage of its sales, was nearly four times as big as Nissan's, even though its operating income was only 50–60 percent bigger. In turn, that sort of advantage makes it easier for Toyota to finance its new investment and research and development projects. In the credit-crunched era of the 1990s, such financial strength is going to count for more and more.

———

The final long-term transformation is that a nation that had previously been chiefly a producer of goods for sale at home or for export is now becoming a nation of multinationals. Until the mid-1980s, few Japanese firms invested at all abroad, except to build distribution networks or, more expensively, to secure supplies of raw materials. But after 1985, that changed dramatically. Suddenly, Japanese firms became true multinationals, investing all over the world, producing all over the world, and employing all over the world.

In the immediate future, this overseas investment is unlikely to grow by very much. Indeed, in many countries Japanese investment is falling. It was artificially stimulated by the bubble economy; now that Japanese companies have less money to invest because of changes in the Japanese economy itself, they are less likely to build new factories abroad or to buy many more Rockefeller Centers. The stampede is over. But the internationalization of Japanese business is not. Later in the 1990s, possibly after a gap of as long as four or five years, investment abroad will revive, along with the recovery of foreign economies and the capital strength of corporate Japan.

One reason why the trend is here to stay is that there is no alternative to overseas expansion for many companies. The labor shortage in Japan means that, in time, the costs of employing Japanese will rise. There are three possible solutions: automation, women, and foreign labor. Automation will proceed, but at a slower pace thanks to higher capital costs. The employment of women will also grow in Japan. The use of foreign labor will remain tempting, however. Japan's aversion to immigration means that such labor will be sought more through foreign investment than through migration. So more and more low-tech production will be shipped offshore, leaving higher value-added processes in Japan.

Another reason is that the force of globalization increasingly demands a local presence from all businesses, whether Japanese or foreign. Think about it: transport and communication costs are falling, making it easier to sell all over the world. That increases the competition in most industries, since it lowers the costs of entry to new markets. You can be sitting in Arizona or in Australia and still be able to contemplate selling your goods in the German market, in competition with others.

That lowering of entry barriers is forcing businesses to try to find new competitive advantages that raise barriers to others, generating new sources of profit. Thus, companies are being forced to get closer and closer to the richest markets. They need to do so in order to gain competitive advantages through their knowledge of the market, the speed of their response to customers' demands, and the tailoring of the product to specific local tastes and needs. The result is that foreign direct investment is likely to be given a continuing push. Contrary to what one might imagine, this is not proof of the triumph of big business; it is a necessary defensive measure against other big businesses and against smaller newcomers.

Sadly, there will also be another source of barriers to entry in rich markets: protectionism is likely gradually to increase for industrial products, especially in Europe but also to some extent in the United States. This is conventional wisdom, but is also true. There is unlikely to be a sudden trade war similar to that of the 1930s. But there will be creeping protectionism. What that means is that Japanese companies will still need to build factories inside protective walls overseas if they are to increase their global market share.

Finally, Japan's global reach will continue to spread during the 1990s because it has built up a strong momentum. Japanese firms have overcome their old fear of employing foreigners and managing over long distances, and now have enough positive experiences to convince them that the task is achievable, the obstacles not insuperable.

As it revives and spreads, however, Japan's overseas investment will also change. It will no longer be rising in the leaps and bounds that were made possible by the cheap-money hubris of the late 1980s. More Japanese multinationals will follow the cautious model of the big carmakers; few will repeat the costly errors of Bridgestone and Sony. Beyond this, however, it will change not just because it wants to but also because it has to. All businesses, big and small, will have to adapt to a changing world economy. Japan's new multinational corporations will be no exception.

CONCLUSION

Night, and the moon!
My neighbor, playing on his flute—
out of tune!

KŌYŌ

T HREE questions were identified at the outset of this book as
being crucial for the consideration of Japanese multinational
investment. They were:

Is Japanese investment different from other people's?
Did American multinationals pose a threat to their host coun-
tries in their 1960s heyday?
Is there a case for adopting a special attitude to Japanese multina-
tionals as compared with all other businesses in the United
States?

These questions are crucial because they have been made so by the
Crichton School. Crichton's novel *Rising Sun* is not a seminal work
of analysis and argument concerning Japanese investment; nor does
it claim to be. But the novel's prominence and success as a mass
market bestseller make its premises, implications, and propositions
far more important in the debate than any learned tome or study by
a Washington think tank.

The explicit assertion in *Rising Sun* is that Japanese investment
in high technology industries in America ought not to be allowed

to continue without restraints and limitations. This is partly because such investment is deemed actually or potentially harmful regardless of the nationality of the investors. That is the reason for my question concerning the threat posed by American investors abroad; logically, if foreign investment poses a threat to America, then American investment must also, now and in the past, pose a similar threat to other countries.

The Crichton School singles out Japanese investment, however, for special attention. This is partly because of its different nature and behavior pattern: that it is ruthless ("Business is war," we are told, is a Japanese saying) and that it is founded on an apparently new kind of trade called "adversarial trade." This term (first used by Peter Drucker, the management guru) is defined by Crichton as "trade like war, trade intended to wipe out the competition," a form of trade the United States has apparently failed to understand for several decades. Hence my question concerning whether Japanese investment really is different, in this way or any other, from that made by companies of other nationalities.

Finally, the Crichton School draws a policy conclusion: that although it is absurd to blame Japan for its successful behavior, the United States should respond "realistically," taking a tough approach, part of which would consist of limitations on Japanese investment. Take their ideas, by all means, runs the argument, but do not let them swarm all over you in the vain hope that they will save you from yourself. Hence my third question: is there a case for thus singling out Japanese investors? Note that my question does not simply ask whether they deserve special treatment: the intent is also to inquire whether or not such singling out would in fact do more good than harm to the American economy. Would it have the effect that the well-meaning Crichton expects of it?

––––

The answers to my three questions are clear and unequivocal.

First, the experience and analysis charted in this book indicate that Japanese investment is not different from other people's, if by that is meant that, in the aggregate, it takes a notably different form or takes place for a markedly different motive. Japanese investment takes many forms and occurs for many motives. Some of it is successful, some unsuccessful. In some cases Japanese firms are lousy employers, in some cases they are exemplary; in some cases they break the law, in others they are as pure as the driven snow. That is as true of Japanese businesses as it is of any others. At least on this basis, of whether they are in the aggregate good or evil, there is no case for treating them any better than any other sort of business, or any worse.

One thing is certain, however: as Crichton himself argues, the Japanese are not saviors. That is neither their intent nor their likely effect. They do bring technology, and they do bring, in some cases, superior management methods. But their arrival can have only a marginal impact in an economy as large as America's. To be sure, Japanese competition has galvanized General Motors, Ford, and Chrysler into action to boost their efficiency and to produce cars that more people are likely to want to buy, but that competition would exist whether Japanese cars arrived as imports or as locally assembled vehicles. It is a consequence of increased worldwide interpenetration of markets, not simply of Japanese multinational investment. While that investment changes the competition's character, and may have increased it at the margin, it is not the sole cause.

So just as there is no case for objecting to them en masse, so there is no case for going out of your way to lure Japanese multinationals through the door. Handing out investment incentives to the Japanese will not succeed in raising either the overall level of investment in the American economy or its quality. It will make little difference either way. It is simply irrelevant.

———

Some host countries saw American multinationals in the 1950s as posing a pretty similar threat to the sort often perceived with Japanese investment today. American investments, it was thought, would imply eventual political control and loss of sovereignty. American businesses would operate in their own, or American, interests rather than in those of the host country. They would employ expatriates in the best jobs, not locals. They would import as much as they could, especially high-tech goods, making the host country's trade deficit larger rather than smaller. They would break the law with impunity, using their financial muscle to avoid facing any retribution.

Americans yesterday, Japanese today: it is pretty much the same. Except for an important difference. In the 1960s and 1970s, the countries that feared American multinationals the most were poor Third World countries. Europeans fussed a bit, but they did not turn American multinationals into such objects of fear and loathing as so many Third World nationalists did. Today, however, it is not these small, poor Third World countries that fear and loathe Japanese multinationals. It is the United States of America, the world's biggest economy.

Before coming to that, however, let us return to the question: were host countries correct to think that American multinationals posed a threat? The answer is only yes in a very special sort of circumstance: when the size and financial power of the company was large relative to that of the country. Yet this is rare, even in the Third World. Multinationals can be played off against one another; typically, their arrival in a country serves to increase competition rather than to diminish it or to provide scope for exploitation. When their behavior prompts calls for tighter regulation, as with the marketing tactics in the Third World of powdered milk firms in the 1970s, for instance, the need for controls is a general one: to restrain business malpractice regardless of the nationality of the firms involved.

American multinationals did cause a similar fuss in Europe in the 1960s to that caused by their Japanese counterparts in America today. Little was done about it, fortunately, since the fuss was unjustified. The arrival of American multinationals and their success may have been a symptom of European weakness but it was not a cause of it, and banning the Americans would not have made Europe any stronger.

The many extravagant forecasts and extrapolations made in the 1960s and early 1970s of an ever-increasing grip on world affairs by a handful of American multinationals has not proved correct. New multinationals have arrived on the scene to rival the Americans, not just from Japan but also from Western Europe and northeast Asia. Big companies have increasingly found themselves to be unwieldy relative to their smaller, more focused rivals. Many of today's multinational firms—such as Compaq, Reebok, TNT, Virgin, and Microsoft—either did not exist in 1970 or had barely been heard of. The world economy is more integrated than ever before. But competition is also fierce and fragmented. The multinational monster proved to be a mythical threat.

————

That multinationals are not all-devouring monsters is now widely accepted, at least for the time being. Countries in Latin America, South Asia, and Africa that for two decades sought to keep foreign investment at bay are now trying as hard as they can to attract it. They learned the hard way that borrowing billions from banks while closing their markets did not work. Better to stop borrowing and instead to open their markets to trade and investment—which is what most of the Third World is now doing.

There is one big exception to this pro-multinational tendency: the United States. It is in America where the most fractious and fierce debate goes on about foreign investment in general and the Japanese sort in particular. It is in America where serious people propose measures to single out Japanese multinationals for special treatment, in order to limit their penetration of the American market.

I have argued that there is no case for singling out Japanese businesses in this way. They do not pose a single threat, nor do they form a single phenomenon. And there is another reason for arguing this. It is that even if it seemed to be justified, to take measures against Japanese multinationals would not help achieve the intended goal: the revival of American industrial hegemony.

Admittedly, nobody seriously suggests that such measures could achieve this on their own. Clearly, they would merely be a small part of a broader policy aimed at boosting American competitiveness. But would they even make a positive contribution to that effort? Nobody can know for sure, since it is a hypothetical question. Such questions in economics do not have straightforward answers. All that can be done is to weigh the probabilities of different outcomes.

My own view is that the likeliest outcome is that measures to restrain Japanese investment would in fact have a negative effect on the strength of American business and the vitality of the American economy. Such measures would relieve local competitors from their stiffest international competition. Prices would rise. Managers could relax a little. Beleaguered firms would have a breathing space. The question is what they would do with that space: run faster, try harder? Or pour themselves a martini? To avoid the martini tendency, the government would have to enforce change.

Fine, say the interventionists: realism at last. For the denigrators of free trade and open markets generally use the following argument. Laissez-faire policies work well in the theoretical atmosphere of an economics textbook, but not in real life. In reality lots of governments intervene, shutting markets and limiting foreign investment. So why shouldn't America? The United States should get rid of its obsession with economic theory and get practical, like everyone else.

The trouble is that the reverse is true. There are plenty of wonderful theoretical cases for intervention of this sort. In the textbook, intervention can work. The problems come when you try to apply it in practice. Yes, in principle, the martini tendency could be countered by a strong, determined government. The Japanese way, after all, has long been to give industries help but only in return for strict programs of capacity cuts or other restructurings. With every carrot comes a stick. So in principle this could also happen in America. Keep out the Japanese competitor; at the same time force industry to spend its time in the gym, not the bar.

The important question is whether this benign theoretical outcome is in fact likely in the United States. Nobody can know in advance. So the reader should make up his own mind. Which do you think would be the most plausible reaction of those fine upstanding folk on Capitol Hill? Would they act with discipline, meting out strict conditions to the industries they choose to assist? Or would they collect the checks from their grateful industrial lobbyists and then head off to the next cocktail party?

The notion of a well-directed industrial policy requires politicians with discipline and expertise, who are willing to act farsightedly in the general interest rather than myopically in their own self-interest. Which of these descriptions best sums up the Washington political establishment? When push comes to shove, that is the real issue about whether or not to restrain Japanese investment in America. Would American policymakers take the necessary actions? They may, or they may not: nobody can know for sure in advance. That is why there can never be a final, definitive victor in the long debate about policy toward Japan, Japanese trade, and Japanese investment: determining such policy is not a simple, mechanical process in which one action is sure to lead to another. Unfortunately, economics is not like that.

So, in the end, the argument comes down to this: if you think your politicians are likely to carry out interventionist industrial policies effectively and in the general interest, then go ahead and vote for them. You are either very brave or very foolish. By now, you should know which of these I think you will be.

Acknowledgments

In preparing this book, I have received assistance from many quarters. Top of the list must come all the 150 firms who took the trouble to complete the questionnaire and the many employees of the companies in the case studies who gave up their time to see me. My agents, at first Dasha Shenkman and later Arthur Goodhart, acted with great efficiency and enthusiasm; my editor at Times Books, Steve Wasserman, used a fine blend of diplomacy and determination to help me improve the manuscript greatly. The incomparable Gordon Lee read the entire manuscript several times, making scores of helpful suggestions. All errors and opinions that remain are to be blamed, of course, entirely on me.

Appendix One:
Firms Replying to Survey

The following list of companies that sent usable replies to the questionnaire is arranged in alphabetical order by country.

BELGIUM
   NGK Ceramics Europe
   Pioneer Electronics Manufacturing

BRITAIN
   Aiwa (UK)
   Clarion Shoji (UK)
   Daiwa Sports
   Dia Plastics (UK)
   European Components Corporation
   Fujitsu Microelectronics
   IBC Vehicles
   Ikeda Hoover
   IK Precision Company
   JVC Manufacturing UK
   Lucas SEI
   Makita Manufacturing Europe
   Marusawa (Telford)
   Matsushita Communication Industrial UK
   Matsushita Electric (UK)
   Matsushita Electronic Magnetron Corp (UK)
   Mitsubishi Electric UK
   Murata Manufacturing (UK)

NEC Semiconductors UK
NEC Technologies (UK)
Nissan Motor Manufacturing UK
Nittan (UK)
NSK Bearings Europe
Oki (UK)
Phoenix Electric (UK)
Reydel
Ricoh UK Products
Sansetsu UK
Sanyo Electric Manufacturing (UK)
Sanyo Industries (UK)
Screen Engineering
Sharp Manufacturing Company of UK
Sony (UK)
SP Tyres UK
Tabuchi Electric UK
Tomatin Distillery
Toshiba Consumer Products (UK)
Toyota Motor Manufacturing (UK)
Tsuda (UK)
UK-NSI
Yamazaki Machinery (UK)

FRANCE
Honda France Industries
Mitsubishi Electric France
SOFICAR

GERMANY
Denon Consumer Electronics
Develop Dr Eisbein
Konica Business Machines Manufacturing
Shimadzu Europa
Toshiba Consumer Products Europe
Yoshida (Deutschland)

IRELAND
NEC Semiconductors Ireland

ITALY
Honda Italia Industriale

SPAIN
Nachi Industrial
Nissan Motor Iberica
Suzuki Motor España
Yamaha Motor España

UNITED STATES
Adaptive Information Systems
Ahresty Wilmington
Allen Bradley TDK Magnetics
Alpha Therapeutic
Alpine Electronics Manufacturing of America
Alps Electric (USA)
American Koyo
America Taisho Electric
Ari Industries
Arkansas Steel Associates
ASO
ATC
ATR Wire and Cable
Bando Manufacturing of America
Biokyowa
California Steel Industries
Clarion Manufacturing Corp of America
Contact International
Denon Digital Industries
DTR
Dunlop Tire
Fremont Beef Company
Fujirebio America
Gecom
Glico Foods USA
Heartland Lysine
Hiflo
Hitachi America
Hitachi Cable Indiana
Hitachi Seiki USA
Honda of America Manufacturing
Hosokawa Micron International
JAE Oregon
Judd Wire
Kaga (USA)
Kagome USA
Kasei Virginia

Kawasaki Loaders Manufacturing Corp USA
Kawasaki Thermal Systems
Kitz Corporation of America
Kobelco Compressors (America)
Kubota Manufacturing of America
Kyocera America
Matai (USA)
Mazak
MCI Optonix
Michigan Dynamics
Minolta Advanced Technology
Mitsubishi Pencil Corp of America
Munekata America
Nastech
NEC Electronics
NEC Technologies
New Hampshire Ball Bearing
NGT Controls
NHK-Associated Spring Suspension Components
Nichifu America
Nippondenso America
Nishikawa Standard Company
Nissan Motor Manufacturing
Nisshinbo California
NSK
Oiles America
Okamoto
Oki America
Omron Management Center of America
OTC Semiconductor
Oyo Geospace
Photonic Integration Research
Piolax
Polytribo
Q&B Foods
Rohm
Saki Magnetics
Sanoh Manufacturing
Shimadzu Scientific Instruments
Siltec Silicon
Silver Reed (USA)
SMK Electronics
Sony Corporation of America
Sumitomo Electric Fiber Optics

Sumitomo Machinery Corp of America
Sunbury Component Industries
Teijin Seiki America
Tokin Magnetics
Topy
Toyota Motor Manufacturing USA
TWN Fastener
Unytite
Wheeling-Nisshin
Yamakawa Manufacturing Corp of America
Yusa

Appendix Two:
The Questionnaire

The full text of the questionnaire sent out in 1991–92 follows. Some questions were too subjective for quantitative analysis and so are omitted from Appendix Three: Survey Results.

CONFIDENTIAL QUESTIONNAIRE
FOR BILL EMMOTT

A. OWNERSHIP

A.1 What is the name of your firm?

A.2 What is the name of your Japanese parent?

A.3 What is the form of ownership? (e.g., 100% Japanese owned, 51% owned, joint venture, etc.)

A.4 Was your firm set up by acquisition or as a "greenfield"?

A.5 Is today's structure the same as when you were established?

A.6 If no, what was the original structure?

A.7 Have you made additional investments since the original investment?

A.8 Were they financed from a) retained earnings, b) local borrowings, or c) capital provided by the parent?

B. EMPLOYMENT

B.1 How many employees do you have?

B.2 How many sites or factories?

B.3 Are any of the employees organized by a trade union?

B.4 If yes, what percentage of the workforce are union members?

B.5 How many unions represent workers at your firm?

B.6 If you have a union, is it the main vehicle for negotiation or consultation, or do you also have a company council or a similar body?

B.7 How many Japanese expatriate employees/managers do you have?

B.8 What is your most senior post occupied by a Japanese?

B.9 What is your most senior post occupied by a non-Japanese?

B.10 Is your chief financial officer Japanese?

B.11 Of the 20 most senior jobs, how many are occupied by non-Japanese?

C. PERFORMANCE MEASURES

C.1 Is the quality of your labor (i.e., its power to be effective) a) better, b) as good as, or c) not as good as in your parent's plants?

C.2 Do you consider that your local labor works a) harder, b) equally as hard, or c) less hard than your Japanese workers at home?

C.3 Is the quality of your local management (i.e., its power to be effective) a) better, b) as good as, or c) not as good as in your parent?

C.4 If your comparable Japanese factories were said to have a productivity (i.e., output per man-hour) of 100 percent, what percent have you achieved at your local plants?

C.5 What was the approximate figure when you commenced production?

C.6 What, briefly, explains the productivity difference between this country and Japan, if one exists?

C.7 If your comparable Japanese factories were said to achieve a product quality of 100 percent, what percent have you achieved at your local plants?

C.8 What was the approximate figure when you commenced production?

C.9 Are your overall costs of production (at the current rate of exchange) a) higher, b) about the same, or c) lower than in Japan?

C.10 Is your firm making a profit, before tax?

C.11 If no, how soon do you expect to make a profit?

C.12 Do your current plans include an increase in output?

C.13 If so, by how much over what period?

D. LOCAL CONTENT AND SUPPLIERS

D.1 What is the local content, in percent by value, of your finished output?

D.2 What was the content when you commenced production?

D.3 What do you expect it to be in five years' time?

D.4 How many suppliers do you use?

D.5 How many suppliers for each item purchased (on average)?

D.6 Out of your suppliers, how many are wholly or partly Japanese-owned?

D.7 Would you say that the quality and reliability of your suppliers in this country are a) better than, b) the same as, or c) worse than your suppliers in Japan?

E. RESEARCH AND DEVELOPMENT

E.1 Does your firm conduct research (as opposed to development) locally?

E.2 If so, why?

E.3 Does your firm conduct any development or design locally?

E.4 If so, why?

E.5 Do you consider that your local R&D contributes a) significantly, b) moderately, or c) marginally to your product and sales?

F. GENERAL MANAGEMENT

F.1 Are your operating methods a) markedly different, b) marginally different, or c) the same in this country as in Japan?

F.2 If a) or b), please briefly summarize the main difference.

F.3 Do you consider that the administration, operation, and overall management technique adopted by your plant in this country are a) strongly, b) partly, or c) negligibly controlled by your Japanese parent?

F.4 Do department or divisional heads at your company principally report or relate to the parent company a) through a single contact point, b) through functional equivalents in Japan, or c) other (please specify)?

F.5 What level or sort of expenditure needs to be referred to the Japanese parent for approval?

F.6 Do you have a separate treasury function, or is it centralized in the parent company?

F.7 Is your medium-term planning (3–5 years) handled by the parent, or by yourselves?

F.8 Who decides on top management (board level) appointments, you or the parent company?

F.9 Do you have a scheme to send non-Japanese managers to the parent firm for periods exceeding a few weeks?

F.10 If so, please give brief details.

G. EXPATRIATE JAPANESE LIFE

G.1 Do your expatriate Japanese employees typically bring their families with them?

G.2 What is the average length of a posting?

G.3 Is there a Japanese school near your company?

G.4 If yes, is it full-time or part-time?

G.5 Are there any local education courses available especially for your Japanese managers and their families?

G.6 Do you give English language training to Japanese managers or families?

G.7 How many Japanese restaurants are nearby? (if more than 10, just say "many").

G.8 Are there any local clubs or associations especially for Japanese?

H. ANY EXTRA COMMENTS?

Please attach extra pages if you wish.

Appendix Three:
Survey Results

A total of 150 firms worldwide responded to the survey: 41 firms in Britain, 17 in continental Europe, and 92 in the United States. The tables that follow summarize the results.

RESULTS OF SURVEY ON BEHAVIORAL AND ORGANIZATIONAL METHODS OF JAPANESE MULTINATIONALS

A. OWNERSHIP

A.3 What is the form of ownership?

	Total	United States	Britain	Europe
100 percent	122	76	33	13
Joint venture	28	16	8	4

A.4 Was your firm set up by acquisition or as a "greenfield"?

	Total	United States	Britain	Europe
Acquisition	34	21	9	4
Greenfield	114	70	31	13
Mixture	1		1	
No reply	1	1		

A.5 Is today's structure the same as when you were established?

	Total	United States	Britain	Europe
Yes	137	87	37	13
No	12	4	4	4
n/a	1	1		

NOTE: Throughout, *n/a* stands for "no answer" or "don't know."

A.6 If no, what was the original structure?

	Total	United States	Britain	Europe
Joint venture	9	2	3	4
Several firms	1	1		
100 percent owned	1		1	
Some assets later sold	1	1		

A.7 Have you made additional investments since the original investment?

	Total	United States	Britain	Europe
Yes	134	84	34	16
No	16	8	7	1

A.8 Were they financed from a) retained earnings, b) local borrowings, or c) capital provided by the parent?

	Total	United States	Britain	Europe
a	39	18	11	10
b	69	43	20	6
c	96	59	28	9
n/a	8	7		1

B. EMPLOYMENT

B.1 How many employees do you have?

	Total	United States	Britain	Europe
Total	107,167	67,148	28,868	11,151
Average	714	730	704	655
Sizes:				
1–100	49	40	8	1
101–1000	77	38	24	15
1001 +	24	14	9	1

B.2 How many sites or factories?

	Total	United States	Britain	Europe
Total	286	192	62	32
Average per firm	1.9	2.1	1.5	1.9

B.3 Are any of the employees organized by a trade union?

	Total	United States	Britain	Europe
Yes	43	9	21	13
No	105	82	20	3
n/a	2	1		1

B.4 If yes, what percentage of the workforce are union members?

	Total	United States	Britain	Europe
Average	61.8	45.2	66.7	73.6
Don't know	10		1	9

B.5 How many unions represent workers at your firm?

	Total	United States	Britain	Europe
Average	1.7	1.33	1.8	2

B.6 If you have a union, is it the main vehicle for negotiation or consultation, or do you also have a company council or a similar body?

	Total	United States	Britain	Europe
Union	26	6	12	8
Council	18	2	11	5
Mixture	5	1		4

B.7 How many Japanese expatriate employees/managers do you have?

	Total	United States	Britain	Europe
Total	2,345	1,643	529	173
Average per firm	15.6	17.9	12.9	10.2

B.10 Is your chief financial officer Japanese?

	Total	United States	Britain	Europe
Yes	88	59	21	8
No	62	33	20	9

B.11 Of the 20 most senior jobs, how many are occupied by non-Japanese?

	Total	United States	Britain	Europe
"Seniors"	2,751	1,670	761	320
Of which, non-Japanese	1,841	1,161	477	203
percent share	66.9	69.5	62.7	63.4

C. PERFORMANCE MEASURES

C.1 Is the quality of your labor (i.e., its power to be effective) a) better, b) as good as, or c) not as good as in your parent's plants?

	Total	United States	Britain	Europe
a	9	7	1	1
b	85	45	28	12
c	47	35	8	4
n/a	9	5	4	

C.2 Do you consider that your local labor works a) harder, b) equally as hard, or c) less hard than your Japanese workers at home?

	Total	United States	Britain	Europe
a	6	4	1	1
b	76	48	23	5
c	63	37	15	11
n/a	5	3	2	

C.3 Is the quality of your local management (i.e., its power to be effective) a) better, b) as good as, or c) not as good as in your parent?

	Total	United States	Britain	Europe
a	13	10	2	1
b	101	57	31	13
c	30	22	5	3
n/a	6	3	3	

C.4 If your comparable Japanese factories were said to have a productivity (i.e., output per man-hour) of 100 percent, what percent have you achieved at your local plants?

	Total	United States	Britain	Europe
Average percent	84.0	83.7	86.3	80.0

C.5 What was the approximate figure when you commenced production?

	Total	United States	Britain	Europe
Average, percent	63.6	66	59.6	59

C.7 If your comparable Japanese factories were said to achieve a product quality of 100 percent, what percent have you achieved at your local plants?

	Total	United States	Britain	Europe
Average, percent	91.0	90	94.0	89.3

C.8 What was the approximate figure when you commenced production?

	Total	United States	Britain	Europe
Average, percent	76.5	79.6	73.4	67.5

C.9 Are your overall costs of production (at the current rate of exchange) a) higher, b) about the same, or c) lower than in Japan?

	Total	United States	Britain	Europe
a	71	41	18	12
b	29	19	6	4
c	33	21	12	0
n/a	17	11	5	1

C.10 Is your firm making a profit, before tax?

	Total	United States	Britain	Europe
Yes	75	36	25	13
No	64	50	10	4
n/a	12	6	6	0

C.12 Do your current plans include an increase in output?

	Total	United States	Britain	Europe
Yes	122	78	32	12
No	23	11	7	5
n/a	5	3	2	0

D. LOCAL CONTENT AND SUPPLIERS

D.1 What is the local content, in percent by value, of your finished output?

	Total	United States	Britain	Europe
Average, percent	68.6	70.5	68.1	59.5

D.2 What was the content when you commenced production?

	Total	United States	Britain	Europe
Average, percent	54.0	60.4	51.8	26.4

D.3 What do you expect it to be in five years' time?

	Total	United States	Britain	Europe
Average, percent	79.8	80.1	80.6	76.0

D.4 How many suppliers do you use?

	Total	United States	Britain	Europe
Total	17,498	11,243	4,940	1,315
Average per firm	136.7	140.5	137	109.6
(replies:	128	80	36	12)

D.6 Out of your suppliers, how many are wholly or partly Japanese-owned?

	Total	United States	Britain	Europe
Total	1,502	1,060	381	61
Average, per firm replying	12.4	13.6	11.9	5.6
As percent of average no. of suppliers, per firm	9.0	9.7	8.7	5.1

D.7 Would you say that the quality and reliability of your suppliers in this country are a) better than, b) the same as, or c) worse than your suppliers in Japan?

	Total	United States	Britain	Europe
a	3	2	1	0
b	57	36	12	7
c	78	45	23	9
n/a	15	9	5	1

E. RESEARCH AND DEVELOPMENT

E.1 Does your firm conduct research (as opposed to development) locally?

	Total	United States	Britain	Europe
Yes	53	35	13	5
No	93	53	28	12
n/a	4	4		

E.3 Does your firm conduct any development or design locally?

	Total	United States	Britain	Europe
Yes	88	54	26	8
No	58	34	15	9
n/a	4	4		

E.5 Do you consider that your local R&D contributes a) significantly, b) moderately, or c) marginally to your product and sales?

	Total	United States	Britain	Europe
a	34	22	10	2
b	33	17	11	5
c	28	18	7	3
n/a	55	35	13	7

F. GENERAL MANAGEMENT

F.1 Are your operating methods a) markedly different, b) marginally different, or c) the same in this country as in Japan?

	Total	United States	Britain	Europe
a	27	17	7	3
b	78	48	19	11
c	40	24	13	3
n/a	5	3	2	

F.3 Do you consider that the administration, operation, and overall management technique adopted by your plant in this country are a) strongly, b) partly, or c) negligibly controlled by your Japanese parent?

	Total	United States	Britain	Europe
a	19	11	4	4
b	80	46	23	11
c	46	32	12	2
n/a	5	3	2	

F.4 Do department or divisional heads at your company principally
report or relate to the parent company a) through a single contact
point, b) through functional equivalents in Japan, or c) other
(please specify)?

	Total	United States	Britain	Europe
a	52	32	11	9
b	80	44	25	11
c	12	8	4	
n/a	10	10	1	

N.B.: Some respondents gave more than one answer, so colums may
add up to more than total number of firms polled.

F.6 Do you have a separate treasury function, or is it centralized in
the parent company?

	Total	United States	Britain	Europe
Separate	116	75	29	12
Central	27	13	10	4
n/a	7	4	2	1

F.7 Is your medium-term planning (3–5 years) handled by the parent,
or by yourselves?

	Total	United States	Britain	Europe
Ourselves	104	73	24	7
Parent	15	7	3	5
Both	29	10	14	5
n/a	2	2		

F.8 Who decides on top management (board level) appointments,
you or the parent company?

	Total	United States	Britain	Europe
Ourselves	29	13	11	5
Parent	92	61	21	10
Both	26	16	8	2
n/a	3	2	1	

F.9 Do you have a scheme to send non-Japanese managers to the
parent firm for periods exceeding a few weeks?

	Total	United States	Britain	Europe
Yes	73	46	21	6
No	74	44	19	11
n/a	3	2	1	

G. EXPATRIATE JAPANESE LIFE

G.1 Do your expatriate Japanese employees typically bring their families with them?

	Total	United States	Britain	Europe
Yes	134	84	34	16
No	5	2	3	
Some	6	2	3	1
n/a	5	4	1	

G.3 Is there a Japanese school near your company?

	Total	United States	Britain	Europe
Yes	98	65	21	12
No	48	24	19	5
n/a	4	3	1	

G.4 If yes, is it full-time or part-time?

	Total	United States	Britain	Europe
Full	27	11	6	10
Part	78	58	17	3

N.B.: some locations had both

G.5 Are there any local education courses available especially for your Japanese managers and their families?

	Total	United States	Britain	Europe
Yes	83	49	21	13
No	61	38	19	4
n/a	6	5	1	

G.6 Do you give language training to Japanese managers or families?

	Total	United States	Britain	Europe
Yes	81	46	27	8
No	64	43	13	8
n/a	5	3	1	1

G.7 How many Japanese restaurants are nearby? (if more than 10, just say "many")

	Total	United States	Britain	Europe
0	41	16	20	5
1	20	6	12	2
2–9	47	39	8	0
10+	42	31	1	10

G.8 Are there any local clubs or associations especially for Japanese?

	Total	United States	Britain	Europe
Yes	78	48	17	13
No	67	40	23	4
n/a	5	4	1	

Bibliography

Barnet, Richard J., and Ronald E. Mueller. *Global Reach: The Power of the Multinational Corporations.* New York: Simon & Schuster, 1974.

Bartlett, Christopher A., and Sumantra Ghoshal. *Managing Across Borders: The Transnational Solution.* Boston: Harvard Business School Press, 1989.

Bruck, Connie. "Leap of Faith." *The New Yorker,* September 9, 1991.

Chandler, Alfred D. *Scale and Scope: The Dynamics of Industrial Capitalism.* Cambridge, Mass.: Belknap Press of Harvard University Press, 1990.

Choate, Pat. *Agents of Influence: How Japan's Lobbyists in the United States Manipulate America's Political and Economic System.* New York: Alfred A. Knopf, 1990.

Crichton, Michael. *Rising Sun.* New York: Alfred A. Knopf, 1992.

Dore, Ronald. *Taking Japan Seriously: A Confucian Perspective on Leading Economic Issues.* London: The Athlone Press, 1987.

Dunning, J. H. *American Investment in British Manufacturing Industry.* London: Allen and Unwin, 1958.

———. *Explaining International Production.* London: Unwin Hyman, 1988.

Economic Strategy Institute. *The Future of the U.S. Auto Industry: Can It Compete, Can It Survive?* Final Report, Washington, D.C. June 1992.

Fucini, Joseph J., and Suzy Fucini. *Working for the Japanese: Inside Mazda's American Auto Plant.* New York: Free Press, 1990.

Graham, Edward, and Paul Krugman. *Foreign Direct Investment in the United States.* Second Edition. Washington, D.C.: Institute for International Economics, 1991.

Henderson, Harold G. *An Introduction to Haiku.* Garden City, N.Y.: Doubleday Anchor Books, 1958.

Imai, Masaaki. *Kaizen: The Key to Japan's Competitive Success.* New York: Random House, 1986.

Ishihara, Shintaro. *The Japan That Can Say No.* New York: Simon & Schuster, 1991.

Kearns, Robert L. *Zaibatsu America: How Japanese Firms Are Colonizing Vital U.S. Industries.* New York: Free Press, 1992.

Lewis, Michael. *Liar's Poker: Rising Through the Wreckage on Wall Street.* New York: W.W. Norton, 1989.

Lief, Alfred. *The Firestone Story.* New York: McGraw-Hill, 1951.

Mahoney, Thomas A. "From American to Japanese Management: The Conversion of a Tire Plant." Owen Graduate School of Management, Vanderbilt University. *Working Paper 88–14*, November 1988.

Munday, Max. *Japanese Manufacturing Investment in Wales.* Cardiff: University of Wales Press, 1990.

Nevin, John J. "The Bridgestone/Firestone Story." *California Management Review* 32 (Summer 1990).

Nora, Dominique. *L'Etreinte du Samourai: Le Défi Japonais.* Paris: Calmann-Lévy, 1991.

O'Brien, Richard. *Global Financial Integration: The End of Geography.* New York: Council on Foreign Relations, 1992.

Ohmae, Kenichi. *The Borderless World: Power and Strategy in the Interlinked Economy.* New York: Harper Business, 1990.

————. *Beyond National Borders: Reflections on Japan and the World.* Homewood, Ill.: Business 1 Irwin, 1987.

Parkinson, C. Northcote. *Big Business.* London: Weidenfeld & Nicolson, 1974.

Reich, Robert B. *The Work of Nations: Preparing Ourselves for 21st Century Capitalism.* New York: Alfred A. Knopf, 1991.

Servan-Schreiber, Jean-Jacques. *The American Challenge.* London: Hamish Hamilton, 1968.

Sloan, Alfred P. *My Years with General Motors.* Garden City, N.Y.: Anchor Books, 1972.

Thomsen, Stephen, and Phedon Nicolaides. *The Evolution of Japanese Direct Investment in Europe.* London: Harvester Wheatsheaf, 1991.

Trevor, Malcolm, and Ian Christie. *Manufacturers and Suppliers in Britain and Japan.* London: Policy Studies Institute, 1991.

Vernon, Raymond. *Sovereignty at Bay.* New York: Basic Books, 1971.

————. *Storm over the Multinationals: The Real Issues.* Cambridge, Mass.: Harvard University Press, 1977.

Womack, James P., Daniel T. Jones and Daniel Roos. *The Machine That Changed the World.* Greenwich, Conn.: Rawson Associates, 1990.

Index

ABOUT THE AUTHOR

BILL EMMOTT is editor of *The Economist,* one of the most respected journals on world affairs. He was for three years Tokyo bureau chief, and later became business affairs editor at the paper, responsible for all business, financial, and science reporting. He is the author of a previous book, *The Sun Also Sets: The Limits to Japan's Economic Power.* He lives in London and Wiltshire.